RECOMMENDATIONS

"The Congregationalist Joseph Hart played an especially important role in the rise of evangelicalism. He preached, engaged in social work, and wrote powerful hymns. Though little-known today, that says more about our own church historical amnesia than it says about him. He was one of our spiritual forefathers and Brian Najapfour has done us all a great service by connecting us again to his legacy."
—Douglas A. Sweeney, Dean, Beeson Divinity School,
Samford University

"Joseph Hart was, after Isaac Watts, the most appreciated hymn writer among the Independents of eighteenth-century England. His compositions share the emphasis on experienced religion that marks the hymnody of Charles Wesley, but in their theology they were much closer to the writings of Watts. Brian Najapfour shows how the teaching of Hart's hymns was not novel, but a powerful statement of Reformed orthodoxy."
—David W. Bebbington, Emeritus Professor of History,
University of Stirling

"This is the first major study of the hymns of Joseph Hart, and the first study of his life since 1910. It will make a valuable contribution to the study of dissenting hymnody in the eighteenth century."
—J. R. Watson, Emeritus Professor of English, University of Durham, UK,
and co-editor of the *Canterbury Dictionary of Hymnology*

"Joseph Hart and most of his hymns had almost gone into oblivion. However, Brian Najapfour has left all hymn singing saints in his debt for uncovering so much of Hart's life and work. New material has also been discovered. His book is assiduous in its scholarship with careful and detailed research, so that the Christian community is more able to appreciate Hart's worth."
—Peter C. Rae, author of "Joseph Hart and His Hymns"

"Brian Najapfour's book is an important contribution to our understanding of the eighteenth-century Evangelical Revival in England. Joseph Hart has been overlooked by many students of this period. After a very chequered life he exercised a powerful ministry in an Independent church in London. He was a supporter of George Whitefield. This is the most significant biography of Hart to date. Clearly his ministry in London was important during his lifetime, but his legacy of hymns has been cherished by all who value a ministry that speaks to the heart. There are similarities to the hymns of Charles Wesley, but Hart expresses a vibrant Calvinism in his hymns. They may not all be suitable for public worship, but for private meditation and prayer they are without equal. Hart was brought out of fearful backsliding by a profound work of the Holy Spirit and this experience comes to expression in his hymns. This excellent book deserves a wide circulation and at the same time is a reminder that a new edition of his hymn book is long over-due."
—Robert W. Oliver, author of *History of the English Calvinistic Baptists 1771–1892*

Joseph Hart (1712–1768),
Eighteenth-Century Hymnody,
and the British Evangelical Movement

Joseph Hart (1712–1768),
Eighteenth-Century Hymnody,
and the British Evangelical Movement

Brian G. Najapfour

PAIDEIA PRESS

 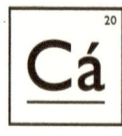

www.paideiapress.ca
www.cantaroinstitute.org

Joseph Hart (1712-1768), Eighteenth-Century Hymnody and the British Evangelical Movement

© 2024 by Brian G. Najapfour. All rights reserved. Published by Paideia Press, a publishing imprint of the Cántaro Institute, 3248 Twenty First St., Jordan Station, ON. L0R 1S0.

All rights reserved. Except for brief quotations in critical publications or reviews, no part of this book may be re-produced in any manner without prior written permission from Paideia Press at the address above.

ISBN 9781990771736

Printed in the United States of America

To my father
Hans Agdam

Table of Contents

Foreword xiii
Preface xv

1. Introduction 1
   1.1 Prologue and State of Literature 1
   1.2 Methodological Considerations 4
   1.3 Structure 8

2. The Life, Ministry, and Works of Joseph Hart 9
   2.1 Introduction 9
   2.2 A Biographical Sketch of Joseph Hart 11
      2.2.1 Hart as a Legalist 14
      2.2.2 Hart as an Antinomian 17
      2.2.3 Hart's English Translation of *Poiema nouthetikon* 21
      2.2.4 Hart's English Translation of Herodian's
            History of His Own Times 22
      2.2.5 Hart's *The Unreasonableness of Religion* 24
      2.2.6 Hart's Mere Outward Reform 32
      2.2.7 Hart's Deep Despondency 34
      2.2.8 Hart's Reconversion Experience 36
      2.2.9 Hart's Ministry 42
      2.2.10 Hart's Hymns 52
   2.3 Summary 57

3. Joseph Hart and Eighteenth-Century Evangelical Hymnody 59
   3.1 Introduction 59
   3.2 "The Golden Age of Hymns" 63
      3.2.1 Isaac Watts 64
      3.2.2 John and Charles Wesley 72

3.2.3 Anne Steele	83
3.2.4 William Cowper and John Newton	89
3.2.5 William Romaine	104
3.3 Summary	109
4. The Theology and Spirituality of Joseph Hart	**111**
4.1 Introduction	111
4.2 The Trinity	113
4.2.1 "God the Father"	121
4.2.2 "God the Son"	123
4.2.3 "God the Holy Ghost"	129
4.3 The Scriptures	136
4.4 Salvation	141
4.4.1 "So dead, so lost"	141
4.4.2 "Had not thy Choice prevented mine, / I ne'er had chosen *Thee*"	146
4.4.3 "The Lamb that died for *Me*"	151
4.4.4 "Salvation's of God, / Th' Effect of free grace"	153
4.4.5 "*God's Elect can never fail*"	156
4.5 Sanctification	160
4.6 Summary	168
5. Conclusion and Prospect	**171**
Afterword	**183**
Appendices	**185**
Appendix 1: Letter from Joseph Hart to William Shrubsole	187
Appendix 2: Letter from Joseph Hart to His Nephew	189
Appendix 3: Marriage Records of Joseph Hart to Mary Lamb	191
Appendix 4: Last Will and Testament of Joseph Hart	193
Appendix 5: Last Will and Testament of Mary Lamb	195
Appendix 6: Joseph Hart's Immediate Family	199
Bibliography	**203**
Primary Sources	203
Hart's *Hymns*	203
Other Editions	205
Other Works by Hart	206
Manuscript Materials	207

Secondary Sources 207
    Articles 207
    Books.. 212
    Electronic Sources.. 223
    Archival Sources 225

About the Author 227

Foreword

Even some individuals who know quite a bit about the evangelical awakenings of the eighteenth century think only about the leaders who have been the subject of so much scholarly and popular attention: John and Charles Wesley, George Whitefield, and Jonathan Edwards. Although these individuals certainly deserve the attention they have received, a proper grasp of where the revivals came from, what they meant at the time, and how they shaped the future require a much fuller roster of those who were responsible for the flourishing of evangelical faith. Works like Catherine Brekus's *Sarah Osborn's World: The Rise of Evangelical Christianity in Early America* (2013) have spotlighted the significant role godly women played in the expansion of awakened religion. The extensive two volumes of Donald Lewis's *Dictionary of Evangelical Biography, 1730–1860* (1995) made useful information readily available to show how modern evangelicalism enlisted a whole host of individuals from near and far throughout the English-speaking world.

Brian Najapfour's well-researched study of Joseph Hart once again underscores how much can be learned about eighteenth-century evangelicalism by extending attention from the Wesleys, Edwards, and Whitefield to those who, at the time, were almost as well known. This first full-scale account of an effective preacher, diligent guardian of orphans, and (most importantly) much-loved hymn-writer rescues Hart from undeserved obscurity. With full attention to Hart's published works, extensive employment of material about him from contemporaries, and manuscripts that Najapfour himself discovered, this book opens up the life, theology, and hymnody of an individual who truly made a difference.

The book's biographical treatment reveals Hart as typical in some of his responses to the gospel message, but untypical in the stresses and strains that accompanied his years-long process of conversion. Its examination of Hart's theology clearly outlines his moderate Calvinism and shows why his preaching as an Independent (or Congregational) minister was so highly valued by his contemporaries. Most of all, Najapfour skillfully positions Hart's efforts as a hymnwriter in the era after Isaac Watts when English hymnody came into its own.

Several modern collections contain Hart's best known hymn: "Come ye Sinners, poor and wretched, / Weak and wounded, sick and sore, / Jesus ready stands to save you, / Full of Pity, join'd with Pow'r. / He is able, he is willing, doubt no more." But Najapfour shows how several of Hart's other 222 known hymns enjoyed almost as much currency in his own day and at least shortly thereafter—and how they still serve as an effective rendering of first-order Christian realities. A strength of this part of the book is full attention to the context of eighteenth-century hymnody, within which Hart did his work.

As with the superficial attention often paid to the evangelical movement, stopping with the preeminent hymnwriters Isaac Watts and Charles Wesley stops too soon. Only by heeding the significant contributions of John Cennick, Anne Steele, Augustus M. Toplady, Philip Doddridge, William Cowper, John Newton, and other effective hymnists of the era can it be understood why the writing, singing, and private contemplation of hymns contributed so substantially to the evangelical movement. And among these others, Joseph Hart stood at the forefront.

For bringing Joseph Hart to the attention of modern readers, to scholars of the eighteenth century, as well as to all who value the evangelical message he proclaimed so well, we owe a significant debt to Brian Najapfour.

Mark A. Noll, author of *The Rise of Evangelicalism:*
The Age of Edwards, Whitefield, and the Wesleys (2003)

Preface

This book, first written as a doctoral dissertation, was conceived in 2010 when Dr. Michael A.G. Haykin introduced Joseph Hart to me. Until then I had not heard of Hart. As I studied Hart's life, I began to appreciate not only his hymnody but also his piety. This appreciation resulted in the publication of my article, "The Piety of Joseph Hart as Reflected in His Life, Ministry, and Hymns" in *Puritan Reformed Journal* (2012). Having discovered no one had written a dissertation on him, I became enthused to write one. In September 2020, with the encouragement of Dr. Adriaan C. Neele, who took a personal interest in this enterprise, I applied for the PhD program at the Theological University of Apeldoorn. With God's amazing providence and goodness, two months later I was able to start writing my dissertation under the supervision of Dr. Herman J. Selderhuis and Dr. Neele. I was blessed to have two humble and wise supervisors who patiently and lovingly guided me during my research. With their directions, suggestions, and corrections, they taught me how to think with meticulous attention to precision. And their quick and gracious responses to my numerous questions helped me to finish this research project in just a year.

Other people contributed as well to the process and completion of this work. I am grateful to my two friends who served *like* co-advisors— Chris Fenner and Rev. R. Sherman Isbell. Their editorial skills helped refine and clarify my thoughts to produce a readable work. In particular, with his wealth of knowledge about hymnology, Fenner provided me with valuable assistance, especially for chapter three. His scholarly website, hymnologyarchive.com, served as a repository for me of primary sources relevant to my research. As an archivist, he also transcribed some of Hart's manuscript artifacts. To encourage further research on Hart, these artifacts are appended to this volume. Likewise, I greatly profited from Rev. Isbell's impressive familiarity with the religious history of early modern Europe. His challenges to some of my suppositions proved to be invaluable, creating necessary nuances in my study.

I am blessed as well to benefit from the expertise of Dr. David W. Bebbington, who read my work and gave helpful feedback. He graciously took time to answer all my questions about early evangelicalism.

I also received invaluable insights from the intellectual generosity of the following individuals: Dr. JohnMark Beazley, Dr. Joel R. Beeke, Dr. D. Bruce Hindmarsh, Dr. Matthew Hyde, John Kingham, Dr. Karin Maag, Dr. Robert W. Oliver, Rev. Peter C. Rae, Marylynn Rouse, Rev. Paul M. Smalley, and Dr. J.R. Watson.

I wish to recognize the help of librarians, too, at Puritan Reformed Theological Seminary, Calvin Theological Seminary, the University of Manchester (for giving me a photo copy of *Letter from Joseph Hart to William Shrubsole*), and Duke University (for sending me a scanned copy of *An Elegy on the Death of the Rev. Mr. Joseph Hart*). Both these pieces are new discoveries, adding significant information to Hart research.

Furthermore, I would like to acknowledge Eastmanville United Reformed Church (where I served part-time as Pastor of Congregational Life while working on my doctoral thesis) and other generous churches and certain individuals, without whose financial support this dissertation would not have been possible.

I especially thank my wife, Sarah, for her love, encouragement, support, and prayer. Words cannot express how blessed I am by her unwavering commitment to me through this process. Her editorial skill also improved the readability of this work. I also want to thank my children, Anna, James, Abigail, Grace, and Jolia, who have been a source of joy throughout the strenuous process of completing this research. Thank you for your patience, flexibility, and prayer while this work was in progress.

Finally, and most importantly, I praise and thank God for his grace and mercy, without which this project would never have seen completion. *Soli Deo Gloria!*

—Brian G. Najapfour

CHAPTER 1

Introduction

1.1 Prologue and State of Literature

On June 5, 1768, Baptist minister John Hughes (d. 1773) preached a sermon during the funeral service for his brother-in-law, Joseph Hart.[1] In that sermon, which was based on 2 Timothy 4:7 and was published to help Hart's wife and children financially, Hughes appealed four times to his audience to remember their "dear departed friend" Hart: "O ye saints of God, he has a right to be remembered of you all" (Hughes: 1768, vi, 28-29). Unfortunately, today the Independent minister Hart is nearly forgotten,[2] even among evangelical Christians. Perhaps if not for his hymn "Come, Ye Sinners, Poor and Wretched,"[3] he may have been fully lost except to specialists. Yet, although Hart is not as well known today as other eighteenth-century hymn writers, in George Burder's *A Collection of Hymns from Various Authors, Intended as a Supplement to Dr. Watts's Hymns, and Imitation of the Psalms* (1784), Hart was given a place of equal prominence with the other great hymnists of his time. In the words of fellow Independent minister Burder (1752–1832), "Since the death of Dr. Watts, several eminent and pious authors, animated by his

---

1. According to Thomas Wright, "Mr. Hughes is styled Hart's brother-in-law, but whether Mrs. Hart was Hughes's sister or whether Hughes married Hart's sister is not disclosed" (1910, 26). Wright was unaware of the maiden names of either of Hart's wives (Brown, Lamb); if Hughes was brother-in-law to Hart, it must have been by Hart's sister or his wife's sister. For more on Hart's family structure, see Appendix 6.

2. According to Mark Noll, "The usual term in Britain during the eighteenth and early nineteenth centuries was *Independent*, but in North America it was *Congregationalist*" (2003, 20).

3. Also known as "Come, Ye Sinners, Poor and Needy." This hymn, Hart's most popular, is listed as hymn number 100 in his hymnbook and is titled "Come and welcome to Jesus Christ."

example and success, have contributed to enlarge and enrich our fund of sacred poetry: Among these are the respectable names of Doddridge, Newton, Hart, Wesleys, Cowper, Toplady, and Cennick" (1784, iv–v). In *A Selection of Hymns from the Best Authors, Intended to be an Appendix to Dr. Watts's Psalms and Hymns* (1787), Baptist minister John Rippon (1751–1836) included Hart in his compilation of what he considered "the best authors" of the eighteenth century. Strict Baptist William Jeyes Styles (1842–1914) wrote of Hart,

> When at his best, Hart is incomparable. Sententious in expression, tender and melting in sentiment, rich in experimental testimony, and candid without being morbid in laying bare the most secret and solemn exercises of his own soul, he is unapproachable and unique. Words cannot express our personal indebtedness to many of his hymns (Wright: 1910, 98).

The leading early twentieth-century hymnologist Louis F. Benson (1855–1930) remarked,

> The most popular, after Watts, of [eighteenth] century Independent hymn-writers, was Joseph Hart. […] He published in 1759 (119) *Hymns composed on various subjects, with the Author's experience*, to which later supplements added some hundred more. They were introduced in his own chapel in Jewin Street, London, with immediate acceptance, and gained a wide use among Calvinistic Nonconformists of different connections (1915, 212–13).

In his elegy of the first American president George Washington (1732–1799), composer Abraham Wood (1752–1804) quoted Hart's supplemental hymn 45, "Sons of God by blest Adoption," showing Hart's influence in America (Wood: 1800). This hymn, one of Hart's four funeral hymns, was sung at Hart's committal in Bunhill Fields, attended by "more than 20,000 souls" (Hughes: 1768, 43). But despite Hart's popularity during his time, today he is mostly unremembered in the church and academy. In *The English Hymn: A Critical and Historical Study* (1997), a book of over five hundred pages which has become a standard work on English hymnody, J.R. Watson has only devoted two pages to Hart. Jonathan M. Yeager's anthology *Early Evangelicalism: A Reader* (2013)—which includes excerpts from sixty-two well-known and lesser-known evangelical writers—does not include the evangelical Hart. Likewise, *Biographical Dictionary of Evangelicals* (2003), edited by Timothy Larsen, has no entry on Hart.

In fact, there is only one major work on Hart: Thomas Wright's *Joseph Hart* (1910). While this volume is indispensable for Hart research, it is outdated. For instance, Wright was unacquainted with *An Elegy on the Death of the Rev. Mr. Joseph Hart* and thus did not know Hart's ministry as a "faithful guardian to several orphans" (1768, 3). Wright also had no access to Hart's marriage records and so was uninformed of Hart's status as a widower when he married Mary Lamb.[4] He was not even aware of Mary's last name. Others have mistakenly thought Mary's last name was Hughes. Furthermore, Wright had no copy of the letter from Joseph Hart to William Shrubsole, and so was unfamiliar with Hart's connection to Shrubsole. He thought it was due to Shrubsole's conversation with Whitefield that Shrubsole was "able to characterize [Hart] faithfully" (Wright: 1910, 101). That Hart and Shrubsole knew each other personally gives weight to the accuracy of Shrubsole's allegorical portrayal of Hart (Shrubsole: 1776).

In 2015, another biography appeared—*A Prodigal Made a Blessing: The Life and Hymns of Joseph Hart*, compiled and edited by John A. Kingham. But by Kingham's own admission, his book is "not really a new biography" and "most of the rest is taken from Thomas Wright's book, with editing" (11).

Additionally, while Wright's book is a fine account of Hart's life and works, it lacks a thorough examination of Hart's theology and spirituality. Hymnologist Erik Routley's article "Joseph Hart, 1712-68" (1951) studied Hart's hymns as poetry, focusing mainly on their literary style, meter, and rhyme. Peter C. Rae's publication "Joseph Hart and His Hymns" (1988) provided a good exposure to some of the important themes in Hart's hymns, but did not evaluate them at great length. Likewise, Faith Cook's volume, *Our Hymn Writers and Their Hymns* (2005), which has a chapter on Joseph Hart, only briefly examined some of Hart's hymns. Therefore, a need for the critical study of Hart's theology and spirituality still remains.

---

4. See Appendix 3.

1.2 Methodological Considerations

The primary objective of this discourse is to answer the central research question: what role did Hart play in the early British evangelical movement, which emerged out of a series of religious revivals in Britain beginning in the 1730s? The study will show how Hart, after his spiritual conversion in 1757, continued the principles of the Evangelical Revival through his preaching ministry, through social welfare as a guardian to orphans, and most importantly, through his cross-centered hymns. In addition, the research will show how Hart, through his hymnody, defended and promulgated the Calvinistic strain of evangelical theology and piety. His hymnbook, which contains an autobiographical preface and 222 hymns, was an expression of his religious belief and spiritual experience. For Hart, doctrine (what one believes) and spirituality (the personal experience of what one believes) were inseparable.[5] Herbert Buck observed, "No one writes quite like Hart. Others have proclaimed the same truths, but he had his own unique way of expressing them; and they are statements not merely of doctrine but of spiritual experience" (Wright: 1910, 99). The leaders of early British evangelicalism like George Whitefield (1714–1770) strongly believed that true religion was the personal experience of what Henry Scougal (1650–1678) called "the life of God in the soul of man" (1677).[6] This quote is taken from the title of Scougal's book, which was instrumental in Whitefield's spiritual conversion. Commenting on this work, Whitefield said, "I never knew what true religion was, till God sent me that excellent treatise" (Kidd: 2014, 28). Throughout his ministry, Hart, who was directly influenced by Whitefield, advanced this true religion, or what was also referred to during his time as experimental religion or experimental Christianity.

In answering the main research question, the present study employs a historical-theological approach, focusing on Hart's theology and spirituality as expressed in his hymns. As such, the analysis of history, theology, and spirituality will primarily arise from Hart's own works and from

---

5. Alister E. McGrath noted, "Older Protestant writers tended to use terms such as 'piety' or 'godliness' to refer to what is now generally designated as 'spirituality'" (1999, 13). Throughout this present study, I will employ synonymously the terms "piety," "devotion" and "spirituality." For a historical survey of the term "spirituality," see Brian G. Najapfour (2013), Walter H. Principe (1983), and Philip Sheldrake (2000).

6. Cf. Hindmarsh (2018, 3).

descriptions of him in the works of his contemporaries. Compared to the writings of other eighteenth-century evangelical writers, Hart's published works are few, only five in total. They can be sorted into those which came before the experience he identified as his religious conversion, and those which came afterwards. His pre-conversion publications are three:

1) *The Unreasonableness of Religion. Being remarks and animadversions on Mr. John Wesley's sermon on Romans viii. 32* (1741). Siding with Whitefield, this first published work of Hart defends the Reformed doctrine of predestination against John Wesley (1703–1791), who published a sermon called *Free Grace* (1739)—a sermon that argues against predestination. Hart's tract is helpful for understanding his sense of theology against the backdrop of the eighteenth-century Evangelical Revival in Great Britain, especially in relation to Whitefield and Wesley. It is also a source for studying Hart's early antinomianism, inasmuch as his antinomian tendency was already evident during the period when this tract was being written.

2) *Poiema nouthetikon: or, the preceptive poem of Phocylides, translated into English* (1744). Hart's preface to and notes on this translation from Greek into English contribute to the understanding of his life and thought prior to conversion. This work also displays Hart's fluency in Greek.

3) *Herodian's history of his own time: or, of the Roman empire after Marcus, translated into English* (1749). This third work is a translation from Latin into English of Herodian's history of the Roman Empire. Hart's notes and introduction to this translation further illuminate his worldview prior to conversion, as well as his mastery of the Latin language.

His post-conversion works are two:

4) *Hymns, &c. Composed on various subjects. With a preface, containing a brief and summary account of the author's experience, and the great things that God hath done for his soul* (1759). Hart's *Hymns*, including his autobiographical preface, is the main text for the analysis of his theology and spirituality. The advertisements, introductions, prefaces, and memoirs attached to the many editions of his hymnbook also provide some information and context. However, to better understand Hart's doctrine and

devotion, while the discourse focuses on his *Hymns*, an interaction with his other writings and those of his contemporaries will also occur.

5) *The King of the Jews: A Sermon, preached at Jewin Street Meeting, on Christmas-day morning, in the year MDCCLXVIII* (1814). Sadly, this posthumously published sermon is the only one of Hart's sermons to have survived.[7] Preached on December 25, 1767, at Jewin Street Independent Chapel, it was an exposition of the question in Matthew 2:2, "Where is He that is born King of the Jews?" The sermon gives us some insight into Hart as a preacher.

In his foreword to *The Justified Believer* (1997), which contains two treatises on justification, C. Lawrence Dodson attributes to Hart the treatise *A Discourse Upon Justification*. This work, however, is not by Hart, but by the Calvinistic Baptist writer Anne Dutton (1692–1765), published in 1740, along with *A Discourse Concerning the New-Birth* (1740).

In addition to Hart's five published works are five important manuscript artifacts:

1) Letter from Joseph Hart to his nephew, December 29, 1767. Reprinted in *Memorial to Mr. Joseph Hart* (1877), this letter provides some information about Hart's personal life. Until now, this was the only known extant letter from Hart. A transcript of this has been provided in Appendix 2.

2) Letter from Joseph Hart to William Shrubsole, June 10, 1766. Located in John Rylands Library, this letter shows Hart's acquaintance with William Shrubsole (1729–1797), who later wrote an allegorical account of Hart's life. The letter indicates Hart's connection to the Independent church in Chatham (where Whitefield often preached) and the Independent church in Sheerness (where Shrubsole was pastor). It reveals Hart's intent to visit and preach in these two congregations in Kent

---

7. The sermon was taken in shorthand at the time, then later edited and published by G. Terry in London. It was republished by Ebenezer Huntington in 1821 under the title *The King of the Jews*. There is a typo on the title page in which the sermon is said to have been preached on December 25, 1768. Hart died May 24, 1768, so probably the sermon was preached in 1767. In the back of the 1814 edition, there is an advertisement for Hart's *The Unreasonableness of the Christian Religion* (1741), revised and republished by G. Terry under the title *Calvinism and Arminianism, Fairly Stated and Fully Explained (A Scarce and Valuable Work)* (London, 1814).

County, showing how his preaching ministry went beyond his own congregation in London. A transcript of this is available in Appendix 1.

3) Two versions of Joseph Hart's marriage bond to his second wife, Mary Lamb, dated December 27, 1752. These were personally signed by Hart. Transcripts of these are in Appendix 3.

4) Last Will and Testament of Joseph Hart, May 17, 1768. Written eight days before his death, this document further adds to our knowledge of Hart's personal life. A full transcript can be found in Appendix 4.

5) Last Will and Testament of Mary Hart (née Lamb), originally written February 26, 1784, plus codicils of January 8, 1787 and January 27, 1790. These name Hart's surviving children, mention the death of their daughter Mary in 1786, confirm the widow's possession of the Jewin Street meeting house until her death, and name Mercy as the eventual manager of Joseph Hart's hymnal publishing rights. This has been transcribed in Appendix 5.

All the above primary sources on Hart will be examined, along with relevant secondary sources in order to offer a critical appraisal of Hart's theology and spirituality and to argue his importance to the progression of the early evangelical movement. This research will therefore contribute to the understanding of early evangelical theology and spirituality in general, and Hart's theology and spirituality in particular. It will also add to the study of eighteenth-century evangelical hymnody, which according to Mark Noll, was "the most enduring contribution of [the evangelical] movement to world Christianity as a whole" (Schwanda: 2016, xvi).

To better understand Hart's life in the context of his time, this study also requires research into the lives and works of other hymn writers in the eighteenth century, and it requires knowledge of theological developments inside and outside evangelicalism. Key overarching works in the field of hymnology in this regard include Louis F. Benson's *The English Hymn* (1915), Erik Routley's *Hymns and Human Life* (1959), J.R. Watson's *The English Hymn* (1997), and Thomas McCart's *The Matter and Manner of Praise: The Controversial Evolution of Hymnody in the Church of England 1760-1820* (1998). The study of specific hymn writers covered in the third chapter—Isaac Watts, Charles Wesley, Anne Steele, John Newton, and William Cowper—involves more specialized study, and relevant resources are cited as they become particularly significant.

Scholarship surrounding evangelicalism in Hart's time owes much to works of specialists such as Mark Noll's *The Rise of Evangelicalism* (2003) and his article "The Defining Role of Hymns in Early Evangelicalism" (2004), Bruce Hindmarsh's *The Spirit of Early Evangelicalism* (2018), and David Bebbington's *Evangelicalism in Modern Britain* (1989), whose quadrilateral serves as a foundational benchmark for this present study.

1.3 Structure

Chapter one is the book's introduction, which presents the research question, the thesis, the state of literature, and the significance of the research.

Chapter two will provide an updated and critical biography of Hart, especially since none has taken account of the range of sources now available. By studying Hart against the background of the eighteenth-century Evangelical Revival, the chapter will demonstrate Hart's contribution to the growth of evangelicalism through his preaching, his social welfare activity, and most significantly, his hymn writing. This chapter will also survey all of Hart's publications. The goal is to acquaint readers with the historical and theological context of his works.

Chapter three will present Hart's hymns in the framework of eighteenth-century English hymnody by comparing and contrasting them with those of the leading evangelical hymn writers of that era. It will demonstrate how hymnody became a signature of evangelicals as a group. Their movement as a whole was a driving force behind the transition from metrical psalms to hymns in English liturgy, both inside and outside the Church of England. Hart played a role in the hymn explosion experienced by evangelical churches in the eighteenth-century. In fact, as will be substantiated in this chapter, his hymnody represented his endeavor to perpetuate the essence of the Evangelical Revival.

Chapter four will examine Hart's theology and spirituality as deduced from his hymns, especially in light of the religious context of his day and in comparison with his other writings. Consideration will be given to his views on the Trinity, the Scriptures, salvation, and sanctification. Here readers will see how Hart's hymnody was, "A treasury of doctrinal, practical, and experimental Christianity" (Hart: 1796, iii).

The last chapter will contain a general summary of the research in dialogue with scholarship. It will also offer topics for further research and final thoughts on Hart.

CHAPTER 2

The Life, Ministry, and Works of Joseph Hart

2.1 Introduction

Joseph Hart was born in London, about 1712,[1] when there was a noticeable absence of religious fervor in England. Describing his early eighteenth-century world, Hart wrote, "as in former times, so in this degenerate age in which we now live: when darkness has overspread the whole earth, when religion is almost thrown aside, and faith seems in a manner to be banish'd from the world" (1741, 14). During this period, drunkenness in particular became a major problem. Just in England's capital, "one in seven Londoners was addicted to gin" (Olsen: 1999, 239). In his book *A Short History of Drunkenness*, Mark Forsyth remarked, "By the 1720s, people had begun to notice that the streets of London were filled with unconscious drunks who had sold their clothes for gin" (2017, 165). Also rampant were prostitution, gambling, and pickpocketing. However, when a religious movement known as the Evangelical Revival swept England in

---

1. Historians are not of the same mind in their opinion of the year of Hart's birth. Unsure of the exact year of his birth, some use the expressions "*ca.* 1712–1768," "1711/12–1768," or "1712?–1768." See *Oxford Dictionary of National Biography* (2004) and Thomas Wright (1910, 1). Other writers, without hesitation, give 1712 as the year for Hart's birth, although the exact date of his birth is unknown. See *A Dictionary of Hymnology* (1892), *Dictionary of Evangelical Biography 1730–1860* (2004) and *The Canterbury Dictionary of Hymnology* (n.d.). One reason for the difficulty in pinning down the exact date of Hart's birth is the fact that Hart himself did not provide exact dates in the autobiographical preface to his *Hymns*. *The Canterbury Dictionary of Hymnology* noted how Joseph Hart *was baptized at St Botolph Bishopgate, London, May 25, 1712. However, this Joseph Hart was a different person who* died at the age of one on August 20, 1713. Following an email correspondence, the editors admitted this was an error and corrected it on October 28, 2021. In this study, I use "about 1712" as the year of Hart's birth, since his funerary monument in Bunhill Fields informs us of his death on May 24, 1768 at age 56. Based on this information, he could have been born in either 1711 or 1712.

the late 1730s, the nation's spiritual state began to change. Hart witnessed and experienced this change.[2] His life, ministry, and works blossomed against the backdrop of this spiritual revival, surrounded by the development of British evangelicalism[3] and English hymnody. Those intersections will be explored in greater detail in chapters 3 and 4, but first we will consider Hart as a historical person on his own merits.

Although he is not well-known today, Hart was recognized during his time as one of the great preachers among the Calvinistic revivalists. In *An Elegy on the Death of the Rev. Mr Joseph Hart*, Hart was ranked among the other most gifted preachers of his era, such as George Whitefield (1714–1770), Henry Foster (*ca.* 1743–1814), Martin Madan (1725–1790), and William Romaine (1714–1795). To console Hart's mourners, the elegist declared,

> Be that your comfort, nor give way to grief;
> The Gospel Trumpet sounds, not sounds in vain:
> Th' Eternal Father leaves for your relief
> Jose, Whitefield, Foster, Madan, and Romaine (R.W.: 1768, 8).[4]

Remarkably, the elegist, who most likely knew Hart personally, viewed Hart as worthy of being grouped with preachers who played a significant part in the Evangelical Revival of the eighteenth century.

Furthermore, although Hart is not as famous today as other hymn writers who were his contemporaries, such as Charles Wesley (1707–1788), Hart's *Hymns*, first published in 1759, was "widely used, especially by Calvinistic Nonconformists" (Julian: 1892, 492) during the late eighteenth century and nineteenth century. This hymnbook underwent at

---

2. In the American colonies, the "Evangelical Revival" was known as the "Great Awakening".

3. With regard to the origin of evangelicalism, Mark Noll explained, "During the middle third of the eighteenth century, a [...] series of interconnected renewal movements arose in England, Wales, Scotland, Ireland and Britain's North American colonies. These movements were the beginnings of the evangelicalism. [...] They grew out of the Protestant Reformation as it had been experienced in the British Isles, but more was going on than a mere repetition of Reformation beliefs and practices. A series of revivals [...] marked the origin of a distinctly evangelical history" (2013, 18).

4. This author was probably Richard Woodgate (d. 1787), who replaced Joseph Hart's successor John Hughes (d. 1773) at Jewin Street Independent Chapel. "Jose" was very likely Torial Joss (1731–1797) who was a Calvinistic Methodist preacher and George Whitefield's assistant.

least twenty-three editions through 1825. Strict Baptist William Gadsby (1773–1844) considered Hart to be one of "the sweetest and greatest experimental" hymn writers (1838, 4).[5] Yet Hart is significantly overlooked in scholarship past and present, and his life story warrants a fresh review.

2.2 A Biographical Sketch of Joseph Hart: One of "the sweetest and greatest experimental" Hymn Writers

Not much is known about Hart's family and childhood, except according to him he "had the happiness of being born of believing parents" (Hart: 1767, iii).[6] In his *Christian Memoirs*, William Shrubsole (1729–1797), a Calvinistic Nonconformist and contemporary of Hart, assessed Hart "was born in Independent Street, a suburb of the City of Establishment, of religious parents" (1810, 232).[7] In Shrubsole's allegorical description of eighteenth-century religion in England, the City of Establishment is the Church of England, also referred to as the Established Church. Out of this church came many religious groups, which he allegorically called suburbs or streets: (1) High-street—formerly named Orthodox-street but now called Arminian-street—which is the Established Church of England, (2) Presbyterian-street, (3) Independent-street, (4) Quaker-street,

---

5. The entire quote reads, "The pages [of my selection of hymns] gained by the curtailment of my own hymns, as above named, are occupied with a Supplement, consisting of 120 hymns, which have principally been selected from Hart and Berridge, these two men being, I believe, the sweetest and greatest experimental writers that have left any hymns on record." The other writer named here is the Anglican evangelical John Berridge (1716–1793).

6. Besides the Supplement and Appendix, the 5th edition (1767) contains the Author's Experience, (Hart's spiritual autobiography), hereafter referred to as Hart's "Experience." There are many available editions of Hart's hymns. There have been at least twenty-three editions. The one I will use throughout this work is the fifth edition, which appeared in 1767 and was the last edition Hart saw through the press.

7. This work (1776), published only eight years after Hart's death, described allegorically the religious state of England during Hart's time. In 1790, a second edition was published and in the preface Shrubsole noted the difference between the editions: "The additions principally regard one character only; which is of a late faithful Minister of the Gospel, and is drawn from memoirs of his life, written by himself" (xi). Shrubsole was referring to Joseph Hart as an additional character. In chapter 31 of the second edition, the character Mr. Hearty appears, and according to Shrubsole, this is the "late Rev. Mr. Hart of London" (384). The inclusion of Hart in the second edition signifies Hart's importance and popularity during Shrubsole's time. All the quotations in this study are from the 4th edition (1810), which was edited by the author's son and comes with the life of the author.

(5) Baptist-street, and (6) Methodist-lane or Church-street, which has two rows: Calvinistic and Arminian (93–98). Shrubsole's account of Hart indicates Hart's parents were Nonconformists and members of an Independent or congregational church.[8] Thus, Hart grew up in a church practicing paedobaptism like the Presbyterians and exercising a congregational system of government like the Baptists. There Hart would hear what he recounted as "the sound Doctrines of the Gospel" (1767, iii). Andrew Kinsman (1724–1793), a Calvinistic Methodist preacher[9] and Hart's close friend,[10] who on June 5, 1768 delivered an oration at Hart's interment and who knew Hart's parents personally, said Hart was "the son of many prayers" (Hughes: 1768, 41). Addressing the vast crowd of more than 20,000 present at Hart's interment in Bunhill Fields, the great burial ground for Protestant Nonconformists, Kinsman proclaimed,

> I had the pleasure of knowing, and I will say the honour too of preaching the gospel to his aged parents, who both died in the faith. I knew him to be the son of many prayers, years ago; and, from this knowledge, as soon as I read his experience [his spiritual autobiography] and hymns, (believing his tender parents' earnest addresses to the throne of grace for him, in some measure, answered,) I found my heart warmed with the relation, and my soul knit to the author (Hughes: 1768, 41).

When Kinsman said Hart was "the son of many prayers," he might have meant Hart's parents prayed regularly for their son, especially for their son's conversion, which Hart experienced when he was about forty-five years old. Recalling his early life, Hart wrote, "I imbibed the sound Doctrines of the Gospel from my Infancy. [...] But the Impressions were not

---

8. Hart's parents' names might have been Joseph Hart and Mary Grant. See Appendix 6.

9. There is a portrait and biography of Andrew Kinsman (1724–1793) in *The Evangelical Magazine*, August 1793, 45–60, published the same year Kinsman passed away. According to his biographer, Kinsman was converted at the age of seventeen after reading one of George Whitefield's sermons. Later "he became intimately acquainted and closely connected with Mr. Whitefield; for whom he retained the most filial affection to his dying day, frequently travelled with, and consulted him as a father upon all his religious concerns." See *The Evangelical Magazine* (August 1793), 45, 48.

10. According to Kinsman, he and Hart started to become close friends in 1759 (the year Hart published the first edition of his hymnbook). After reading Hart's "Experience" and his hymns, Kinsman sought "a personal interview, and from the year 1759 a religious, literary correspondence ensued. [...] [S]ince that, we have loved as brethren, and servants of the same master" (Hughes: 1768, 41–42).

deep, nor the Influences lasting, being frequently defaced and quenched by the Vanities and Vices of Childhood and Youth" (1767, iii). Hart lived like the prodigal son in Luke 15:11–32, which is how he depicted his pre-converted life:

> Far, far from Home on Husks I fed,
> Puft up with each fantastic Whim.
> With Swine a beastly Life I led:
> And serv'd God's Foe instead of Him.[11]

To further trace Kinsman's connection to the Hart family, it is important to understand his preaching ministry. In 1763, Kinsman was ordained as minister of the Calvinistic Methodist congregation at Plymouth Dock (now Devonport). But it was not until 1771, when Kinsman resigned his grocery business to his son Andrew junior, that he started serving this congregation full time. He remained in this church until his death in 1793. Before his ordination in 1763, Kinsman had been an itinerant preacher, and even when he settled in his congregation at Plymouth Dock, he would still occasionally preach elsewhere (*Evangelical Magazine*: 1793, 54–55, 58). According to his biographer, he "entered fully into a regular course of preaching" in 1750 and eventually was "called out to itinerate frequently in many counties" in England (48). His remarkable gift in preaching impressed even the most famous Calvinistic Methodist preacher George Whitefield, with whom Kinsman "became intimately acquainted and closely connected" and with whom he "frequently travelled" (45, 48). With Whitefield's invitation, Kinsman made several trips to London to preach at the Tabernacle located at Moorfields. This place of worship was built in 1741 by the followers of Whitefield as a counter chapel to the Foundery, the meeting house of the Arminian Methodist society, opened in 1739.[12] Since Whitefield's Tabernacle was not far enough from the Foundery, in 1756 Whitefield's supporters built another facility in London called the Tottenham Court Chapel, where Kinsman was also invited to preach occasionally.[13] Kinsman most likely met Hart's

---

11. Hymn 27, "The Author's own Confession" ("Come hither, ye that fear the Lord").

12. "Whitefield, finding the Tabernacle shed in Moorfields inconvenient and inadequate, took it down and erected on its site a huge hive-shaped building capable of seating 4,000 persons. It was opened with the name unchanged, 10th June 1753" (Wright: 1910, 29).

13. For a history of the Moorfields Tabernacle in London, see introduction to *Two*

parents in the Moorfields Tabernacle[14] and had the honor of preaching the gospel to them. Later in their lives, Hart's parents possibly became members of the Moorfields Tabernacle, where they sat under the preaching of Whitefield and other Calvinistic Methodist preachers. From Hart's spiritual autobiography, it appears Hart was not a member either of the Moorfields Tabernacle or the Tottenham Court Chapel at this time. Yet we know from his own testimony, during his great spiritual turmoil (an event before his conversion in 1757), he would routinely attend these two meeting places. As he recorded,

> While these [spiritual] Horrors [of everlasting damnation in hell] remained [in my mind],[15] I used to run backwards and forwards to Places of religious Worship, especially to the Tabernacle in *Moorefields*, and the Chappel in *Tottenham-Court*, Where, indeed I received some Comfort (which, tho' little, was *then* highly prized, because greatly needed) but in the general almost every Thing served only to condemn me, to make me rue my own Backslidings, and envy those Children of God, who had continued to walk honestly ever since their first Conversion (1767, x–xi).[16]

2.2.1 Hart as a Legalist (from c. 1733 to c. 1740): "thy good Works [cannot] save thy soul. / Renounce them"[17]

Recalling his spiritual state when he was about twenty-one years old, Hart wrote, "[I was] under great Anxiety concerning my Soul. The Spirit

---

Calvinistic Methodist Chapels, 1743–1811: The London Tabernacle and Spa Fields Chapel, ed. Edwin Welch (London: London Record Society, 1975), vii–xix. For Kinsman's association with Whitfield, see Joseph Beaumont Wakeley, *Anecdotes of the Rev. George Whitefield*, 3rd ed. (London: Hodder and Stoughton), 279–83.

14. According to Wright, Kinsman became an honored guest at the house of Hart's parents (1910, 30).

15. This intense spiritual distress took place between about 1756 and May 29, 1757, the day Hart experienced what he called "reconversion." According to Hart, during this period his despair was so deep: "I found in me a Kind of Wish, that I might only be damned with the common Damnation of Transgressors of God's Law. But, oh! I thought the hottest Place in Hell must be my portion. All the evangelical promises were so far from comforting me, that they were my greatest Tormentors; because they would only increase my Condemnation" (1767, x).

16. Shrubsole informs us of the incident in which Hart heard Whitefield preach and "was greatly alarmed by *Mr. Fervidus's* sermon" (1810, 243). Shrubsole's name for Whitefield in this book was Mr. Fervidus.

17. Hymn 27, lines 17:4–18:1.

of Bondage distressed me sore, though I endeavoured (as I believe most under legal Convictions do) to commend myself to God's Favour, by Amendment of Life, virtuous Resolutions, moral Rectitude, and a strict Attendance on religious Ordinances" (1767, iii). Here Hart began to come under conviction to change his sinful living. But the problem with him was that he was trying to be godly without true repentance and a living faith in Christ. Hart was pursuing religious activities without a spiritual conversion or a regenerate heart. His piety was not the fruit of a justified soul, but of a self-righteous spirit. Moreover, Hart performed good works as a means to reconcile himself to God:

> I strove to subdue my Flesh by Fasting, and other rigorous Acts of Penance and Mortification, and whenever I was captivated by its Lusts (which indeed was often the Case) I endeavoured to reconcile myself again to God by Sorrow for my Faults, which, if attended with Tears, I hoped would pass as current Coin with Heaven, and then I judged myself whole again (iii).

In *The Spirit of Early Evangelicalism*, Bruce Hindmarsh observed,

> Evangelicals spoke endlessly about the law. They also disagreed endlessly about the law. Their most serious debates all had to do with the law. If one veered too far in one direction, extolling the unmerited grace of God to undeserving sinners, then one might incur the charge of antinomianism. If one veered too far in the other direction, engaging the human will to exert itself to conform to God's righteous expectations, then one was sure to hear the accusation of legalism (2018, 180).

During this time Hart surely deserved to be charged with legalism. Generally, legalism teaches justification by good works—a doctrine the Apostle Paul refuted in Galatians 2:16. In his well-known work *True Religion Delineated*, American Congregationalist theologian Joseph Bellamy (1719–1790) described a legalist as someone who "thinks that God loves him and will save him for his Duties" (1750, 92). Bellamy's description applies well to Hart, whose merit-based view of salvation caused Hart to boast of his own righteousness before God. Later, in his autobiographical hymn entitled "The Author's own Confession," in which Hart poetically narrated his conversion story, he recorded an imaginary dialogue between himself and God. In this dialogue, God told Hart: "thy good

Works [cannot] save thy soul. / Renounce them."[18] Later Hart would realize, too, how "Self-Righteousness and legal Holiness rather keep the Soul *from*, than draw it *to* Christ" (1767, xv). Hart explained, "they who seek Salvation by them [i.e., by self-righteousness and legal holiness], pursue Shadows; mistake the great End of the Law. [...] No Righteousness besides the Righteousness of Jesus (that is, the righteousness of God) is of any Avail towards Acceptance" (xv–xvi). Hart later came to understand how Christ's righteousness was the only basis for him of divine acceptance. "[T]o be a moral Man, a zealous Man, a devout Man," emphasized Hart, "is very short of being a Christian" (xvi). That is, one's morality does not bring about salvation.

During Hart's time, moralism was prevalent, especially within the Church of England, which was filled with moralistic preachers. According to Jennifer Farooq, author of *Preaching in Eighteenth-Century London*,

> Both Methodists and Dissenters were critical of some Anglican [moralistic] preachers. [...] In 1739, Joseph Stennett, Baptist pastor at Little Wild Street, London, emphasized the futility of this type of preaching, for "it must be a most weak and base expedient to attempt to bring them [deists] back to christianity, at the expense of the fundamental of it; and by reducing the gospel of Christ Jesus only to a few lectures on morality" (2013, 13).[19]

As hinted in Stennett's statement, although deists denied classical Christianity, they found moralistic preaching appealing, for it somewhat fit their "confidence of the day in the sufficiency of rational morality for life and salvation" (Williams: 1988, 190). For this reason, the famous English poet John Dryden (1631–1700) depicted deists as "Rationalists with a heart-hunger for Religion" (Hazard: 1953, 256). As rationalists, they rejected the gospel but they had a desire to conform to the unchanging moral law for their salvation. Therefore, legalists, moralists, and deists all had one thing in common—they all thought salvation could be earned by their obedience to law. But ironically, moralistic preaching led many into

---

18. Hymn 27, lines 17:4–18:1.
19. For Joseph Stennett's quote, see *The Christian Strife for the Faith of the Gospel. A Sermon Preach'd at the Revd Mr. Hill's Meetingplace, in Thames-Street, the 9th of February, 1738. Before a Society of Ministers and Gentlemen, Engaged in a Design for the Encouragement of Young Men, in Their Studies for the Ministry, Whose Hearts God Has Inclined to That Sacred Work* (1739), vii.

immoral living. Exhorting his fellow preachers, the evangelical preacher Thomas Jones (d. 1762) proclaimed, "We have preached Morality so long, that we have hardly any morality left; and this moral Preaching has made our People so very immoral, that there are no Lengths of Wickedness which they are afraid of running into."[20] While it is uncertain how Hart became a legalist, whether it was a result of his struggle to balance the law and the gospel, or whether it was a result of a moralistic sermon he had heard, the problem Jones addressed here happened also to Hart to some extent.

2.2.2 Hart as an Antinomian (from c. 1740 to c. 1751): "Expected to be sav'd by Christ; But to be holy had no Will"[21]

About 1740, when Hart was about twenty-eight years old, he realized he was a "monstrous sinner" and his legalistic religion could not save him. He then looked for a better religion:

> I began to sink deeper and deeper into Conviction of my Nature's Evil, the Deceitfulness and Hardness of my Heart, the Wickedness of my Life, the shallowness of my Christianity, and the Blindness of my Devotion. I saw that I was in a dangerous state, and that I must have a better religion than I had yet experienced, before I could, with any propriety, call myself a Christian (1767, iv).

Unfortunately, the kind of religion he found to replace his old one was still not biblical. If his old religion promoted salvation by good works, his new religion promoted salvation without the fruit of good works. He shifted from being a legalist into being an antinomian—from one extreme to another, or in Shrubsole's parabolic words, Hart left the City of Formality (legalism) to come to the Town of Illumination (antinomianism) (Shrubsole: 1810, 233). As Hart testified,

> [R]ushing impetuously into Notions beyond my Experience, I hasted to make myself a Christian by mere Doctrine, adopting other Men's Opinions before I had tried them; and set up for a great Light in Religion, disregarding the internal Work of Grace begun in my soul by the

---

20. Thomas Jones, *A Sermon Preached at the Visitation of the Reverend Dr. Thackeray, Archdeacon of Surry, on Tuesday, September, 1755, at the Parish Church of St Saviour, Southwark* (1755), 15, cited in Farooq (2013, 13).

21. Hymn 27, lines 2:3–4.

Holy Ghost. This *Liberty*, assumed by myself, and not given by Christ, soon grew to *Libertinism*, in which I took large progressive Strides, and advanced to a dreadful Height, both in Principle and Practice. In a word, I ran such dangerous Lengths both of carnal and spiritual Wickedness, that I even out-went professed Infidels, and shocked the Irreligious and Profane with my horrid Blasphemies, and monstrous Impieties (1767, v).

Previously he had tried to pursue holiness, thinking it would save him. Now he thought he was saved, but had no desire to be holy. As he later admitted,

> The Way of Truth I quickly miss'd;
> And further stray'd, and further still:
> Expected to be sav'd by Christ;
> But to be holy had no Will.[22]

Notably, Hart described this unbiblical notion as libertinism, a term he understood synonymously with antinomianism. In his *Christian Memoirs*, Shrubsole, who was an eyewitness of the religious condition of the eighteenth-century England, said there were many antinomians during Hart's time (1810, 229). These antinomians, wrote Shrubsole, had "very faulty" morals (229). He added,

> Some of the Antinomians are so sottish, as to affirm, that Immanuel has done all for them; not only with respect to his work as mediator and surety; but also as a head of sanctification. That he has repented, believed, and prayed for them; and therefore, that they need not be found in such low and legal duties (230).

What they wanted was not "Immanuel, or holiness, or the New Jerusalem," but "a liberty to sin without punishment, for ever" (230–31). Shrubsole's depiction sheds light on the type of antinomianism Hart ingested. Shrubsole, who knew Hart at this time, further recounted figuratively, "On Sundays, he [i.e., Hart] pretty constantly went to *Saint Nicholas's Church* to hear the celebrated *Dr Decree*, a very popular preacher of that town" (234). Shrubsole took the term Saint Nicholas's Church from Revelation 2:6 and interpreted it to mean any church teaching the doctrine

---

22. Hymn 27, lines 2:1–4.

of the Nicolaitans, a doctrine associated with antinomianism. In this allegory, Dr Decree refers to "any high Antinomian preacher" (384).

Although Shrubsole did not give a specific example of an antinomian church or preacher, his account shows how common antinomian churches and preachers were during this period.[23] Moreover, since Hart resided at Saint Dunstan in the West,[24] on the north side of Fleet Street, it is possible Shrubsole was thinking of William Romaine as Dr Decree, or as one of the high antinomian preachers. Romaine was indeed a very popular Anglican preacher; he converted later to evangelicalism. In 1749, Romaine acquired the afternoon lectureship at the parish church of Saint Dunstan, where the famous Bible translator William Tyndale (d. 1536) once lectured and the Puritan Richard Baxter (1615–1691) once preached. As a parishioner of Saint Dunstan, Hart most likely attended this church. Romaine "first began to declare the doctrine of the [evangelical] revival" in this church (Wood: 2004, 954). His intellectual ability and gift for preaching attracted large crowds. Soon the parish church in Saint Dunstan "became the focal point of London evangelicalism and Romaine was recognized as the capital's principal preacher" (954). Yet, his fellow Anglican evangelical preacher John Newton (1725–1807) was concerned because "Romaine had made many antinomians" (Wilberforce: 1838, 2:136).[25] Romaine's "high Calvinistic doctrines," said Grayson Carter, "includ[ed] an emphasis on the atonement as a 'finished' salvation, with nothing left for the believer to do; all is faith. Predictably, such views set him apart from other leaders of the revival."[26] In his biography

---

23. After Hart's death in 1768, John Fletcher (1729–1785) wrote a series of discourses against antinomianism: *Checks to Antinomianism* (1771–4), *Equal Checks to Pharisaism and Antinomianism* (1774–5) and *Last Check to Antinomianism* (1775). For a brief study of the origin of antinomian controversy among Nonconformists in eighteenth-century England, see chapter 3 of J. Hay Colligan (1915, 9–18).

24. Hart's marriage bond to Mary Lamb, December 27, 1752, reads, "Appeared personally Joseph Hart of the parish of Saint Dunstan in the West, London," etc. See Appendix 3.

25. The quote is taken from William Wilberforce's diary, in which he said, "Wednesday. Dined with old Newton. [...] Newton very calm and pleasing—owned that Romaine had made many antinomians." Similarly, according to Tim Shenton, "True to form, John Wesley thought that most of Romaine's work, *The Walk of Faith*, was deeply coloured with 'antinomianism'. In fact, Wesley thought all Romaine's writings were 'brimful of Antinomianism'" (2004, 264).

26. Grayson Carter, "William Romaine (1714–1795), Church of England clergyman

of Romaine, however, Tim Shenton argued, "But Romaine was not antinomian, far from it, although it must be conceded that his teaching could be perverted to fit in with antinomian thinking" (Shenton: 2004, 265).[27]

Whether or not Romaine was "the celebrated Dr Decree," Hart's antinomianism or libertinism cannot be denied. As Hart further confessed,

> My Actions, were in a great measure, conformable to my Notions. For having (as I imagined) obtained by Christ a Liberty of sinning, I was resolved to make Use of it, and thought the more I could sin without Remorse, the greater Hero I was in Faith. [...] I *committed all Uncleanness with Greediness* (1767, v–vi).

Hart abused the grace of God and thought grace abounds more when one sins more—a misconception the Apostle Paul corrected when he asked, "What shall we say then? Shall we continue in sin, that grace may abound? God forbid. How shall we, that are dead to sin, live any longer therein?" (Rom. 6:1–2).

Hart continued to be a libertine for the next nine or ten years. During this period, he infected "Others with the Poison of [his] Delusions" (1767, vi).

> Abus'd his Grace; despised his Fear;
> And Others taught to do the same.[28]

By his own admission, Hart influenced others with his libertinism by publishing "several Pieces on different Subjects, chiefly Translations of the ancient Heathens; to which [he] prefixed Prefaces and subjoined Notes of a pernicious Tendency, and indulged a Freedom of Thought far

---

and evangelical preacher," in *Oxford Dictionary of National Biography* (2004), https://doi.org/10.1093/ref:odnb/24036

27. In one of his letters, Romaine clarified his view on the matter, "If we do much for, we have nothing to boast of; for he worketh in us both to will and to do. I am for good works as much as any of them; but I would do them to a right end, and upon a right motive; and after all, having done the best that can be done, I would not lay the weight of the least tittle of my salvation—no, not one atom of it, upon them. It all rests on Christ—he is my only foundation—he is my topstone: and all the building, laid on him, growth up into a holy temple in the Lord. He has done all for me: he does all in me: he does all by me. To him be all the glory for ever and ever. Amen" (1830, 195–96).

28. Hymn 27, lines 3:3–4.

unbecoming a Christian" (1767, vi). The works he had in mind include his translation of *Poiema nouthetikon* (1744).²⁹

2.2.3 Hart's English Translation of *Poiema nouthetikon* (1744)

Hart had a "liberal education" (Shrubsole: 1810, 232), a system of education influenced by the Enlightenment, also referred to as the Age of Reason. The Enlightenment's approach to education was humanistic, placing "such a high emphasis upon knowledge through the senses and reason at the expense of faith" (Anthony: 2001, 249). Within this intellectual context, at about thirty-two years of age, Hart translated the Ancient Greek poem *Poiema nouthetikon* from the Ionic dialect (an ancient Greek dialect).³⁰ To help his readers understand the difficult passages found in this work, Hart provided extensive analytical, illustrative, grammatical, and interpretative notes, showing his impressive skill as a classical scholar.³¹ He lamented how "commentators have so grosly mistaken several passages in the works of the ancients, leaving them more obscure after, than they were before, their interpretations" (Hart: 1744, 2).

The *Poiema nouthetikon* (translated as *Preceptive Poem* and also known as *Poem of Admonition*)³² is, in Hart's words, "a collection of excellent precepts for the government of life, through all its stages, and in every state" (1744, iv). For instance, the first ten lines of this poem, as translated by Hart, include the following dictums:

> Let no adult'rous love pollute thy soul.
> Shun man's embrace with man; conjunction soul!
> Plot no deceits, from shedding blood refrain
> And grow not wealthy by dishonest gain.
> But what the hand of justice gives, receive;
> And with thy destin'd lot contented live.
> Abstain from other's goods. Let not thy mouth

---

29. A Greek gnomic poet, Phocylides was born in Miletus about 560 BC.

30. Under the heading "Register of Books for May 1744," Hart's translation appeared in *Gentleman's Magazine* 14 (May 1744): 288.

31. In his translation of *Poiema nouthetikon*, Hart engaged in ancient writers such as Pythagoras, Eusebius, Suidas, Athenaeus, Stobaus, Atticus, Hesiod, Theognis, Pliny, Caesar, and even Erasmus.

32. See *Phocylides' Poem of Admonition; with Introduction and Commentaries*, trans. H. D. Goodwin (Andover: Warren F. Draper, 1879).

Be prone to lies, but always utter truth.
First honour God: And next thy parents too;
And deal to all men their peculiar due (1–4).

Since the poem's "ethical teachings are of the highest, and in entire harmony with Christian and monotheistic doctrines, it was used until the sixteenth century and even later as one of the most popular school manuals of epic style. [...] The importance of the poem lies further in the fact that it was used as a text-book in schools at the time of the Reformation; and with this object in view it was reprinted, annotated, and translated repeatedly after its first edition in 1495."[33] As a classical teacher in one of the schools in London, Hart most likely used this work as a schoolbook.[34] Nevertheless, while the work contains beliefs and practices compatible with Christian morality, it is only a collection of moral and ethical rules devoid of the gospel of Christ.

What is noteworthy here is how Hart's notes on the poem give no indication that he was converted when he translated it, and ironically, Hart translated a poem filled with moral teachings as a libertine.[35]

2.2.4 Hart's English Translation of Herodian's *History of His Own Times, or of the Roman Empire after Marcus* (1749)

Hart also rendered a translation of another classical work, Herodian's *History of His Own Times, or of the Roman Empire after Marcus* (1749).[36] Originally written in Greek, Herodian's work is a contemporary

---

33. "Pseudo-Phocylides" in *Jewish Encyclopedia* (NY: Funk & Wagnalls, 1906), 10:255.

34. His brother-in-law John Hughes noted how Hart "had his livelihood to get at his civil calling; which was that of teaching the learned languages; and writing much in that way" (1768, viii).

35. Today there is a general consensus among scholars that the poem was not written by Phocylides. The first scholar to convincingly disprove Phocylides as the author of the poem was the Jewish-German philologist Jacob Bernays (1824–1881), who published a book in German in 1856 in which he concluded that the poem is "a Jewish-Hellenistic pseudepigraphon" and was written in Alexandria "somewhere between the middle of the second century B.C. and the middle of the first century A.D., a period that also constitutes the hey-day of Jewish pseudepigraphy." Bernays's book's title is *Ueber das Phokylideische Gedicht* (Breslau, 1856). For the quotes, see Pieter Willem van der Horst, *The Sentences of Pseudo-Phocylides: With Introduction and Commentary* (Leiden: E. J. Brill, 1978), 8–9. For a historical study of the research on Pseudo-Phocylides, see chapter one of this book, 3–54.

36. Herodian (or Herodian of Syria, or of Antioch, as he is sometimes known) was a

account, in eight books, of the fifty-eight year history of the Roman Empire from Emperor Marcus Aurelius's death in 180 A.D. to Emperor Gordian III's accession in 238. Although not as reliable as Dio Cassius's history of Rome from 753 BC to 229 AD,[37] Edward C. Echols believed Herodian's work "offers a moralizing account of the downward spiral of the empire" (1961, 6):

> We must credit Herodian with enough sense of history to recognize that the death of Marcus Aurelius signified the end of an era. Herodian's chief concern is with the corruption that accompanied the decline in Rome's world position. That he was not a professional historian is apparent. That he was literate, concerned with the recording of history, aware of the long tradition of Greek historiography [...] is equally apparent (6).

Echols further noted,

> During the Renaissance, Herodian was studied with interest. At the request of Pope Innocent VIII, the Italian humanist Politian prepared, in 1487, and published both at Bologna and Rome, in 1493, so excellent a Latin version of Herodian that it was believed by many to be an original history in Latin (8).

Hart was not the first to translate Herodian's work into English; he was preceded by at least three other attempts.[38] Hart's translation, which most likely was based on Politian's Latin version,[39] appeared in 1749. Hart's goal with respect to this translation was "to give the reader a tolerable knowledge in the Roman affairs, even though [the reader] had never read any other account of them" (xi–xii). Hart had also written a

---

civil servant in Rome, a position "which enabled him to write much of his history from personal experience and observation" (Echols, 1961, 5). Echols' work was the first English translation from the Greek text since Joseph Hart's translation in 1749.

37. *Dio's Roman History: With an English translation by Earnest Cary on the basis of the version of Herbert Baldwin Foster*, 9 vols. (Cambridge, MA: Harvard University, 1914–1955). This is a diglot translation with Greek and English on opposite pages.

38. Nicholas Smyth (*ca.* 1550), J. Maxwell (1629 and 1635), and G. B. Stapylton (1652) (Echols: 1961, 8). Wright noted how Herodian's work was also translated into English in 1698 by "A Gentleman at Oxford." If true, Hart was the fifth to translate the work into English.

39. Hart's notes on his translation indicate he had access to the Greek text. According to Echols, the Politian's Latin version first published in 1493 was reprinted with the Greek text several times over the next two centuries (1961, 8). Thus, in preparing his translation Hart may have used a Latin version and also the Greek text.

forty-two page introduction, which contained "a summary relation of all that was necessary to be known of the Roman state, from its first origin, to the time whence Herodian's history commences" (xii). And because Hart thought the reign of Emperor Gordian III was not "a very proper period at which to end the Roman history," he had "added, by way of appendix, a general account of the most remarkable transactions under each of the subsequent emperors, to the reign of Constantine the Great" (xiii). Additionally, since according to Hart, "no history can be well understood, much less retained, unless the right time be fix'd to each incident, chronology must be allowed to be one of the most material ingredients in historical compositions" (xiii). Thus, he had also prepared a chronological table "from the best ancient historians" (xiv). This chronological table along with his lengthy introduction, appendix, and notes on his translation, prove him to be a diligent and accomplished scholar, well-informed about ancient history and well-versed in Latin.

2.2.5 Hart's *The Unreasonableness of Religion. Being Remarks and Animadversions on Mr. John Wesley's Sermon on Romans viii.32* (1741)

During the same time period when Hart was a libertine he wrote his more well-known work *The Unreasonableness of Religion. Being Remarks and Animadversions on Mr. John Wesley's Sermon on Romans viii.32* (1741).[40] To better understand this treatise, we need to read it in light of the eighteenth-century Evangelical Revival in England and more specifically in light of the rift between John Wesley (1703–1791) and George Whitefield. These two men were key preachers who worked together to advance this revival. But the Calvinist Whitefield broke with the Arminian Wesley over the issue of predestination. The division between them started when Wesley published in August 1739 his sermon *Free Grace*,

---

40. This work was later advertised in *The Charter* (May 5, 1839): 239; *Bents Monthly Literary Advertiser* (September 10, 1838): 105, and again in *Bent's Monthly Literary Advertiser* (May 10, 1839): 70; *London Conservative Journal and Church of England Gazette* (July 7, 1838): 1, and on (September 15, 1838): 1, and again on (February 23, 1839): 1. This shows how one hundred years after the publication of Hart's tract, some people were still interested in reading it. The tract was also revised and republished in 1812 by George Terry under the title *Calvinism, and Arminianism, fairly stated, and fully explained by a learned layman, who afterwards became an eminent preacher: published in the year 1741* (London, 1812).

which he originally preached at Bristol. Attached to this sermon was a thirty-six stanza hymn entitled "Universal Redemption," by his brother Charles Wesley.[41] Wesley's *Free Grace*, which Whitefield repeatedly referred to as "a sermon on predestination," contained several arguments against that Calvinistic doctrine. For Wesley, this doctrine, which he called "the horrible decree" (10), is "not a doctrine of God" (25). Speaking of predestination, Wesley averred,

> Call it therefore by whatever name you please, "election, preterition, predestination or reprobation," it comes in the end to the same thing. The sense of all is plainly this. By virtue of an eternal, unchangeable, irresistible decree of God, one part of mankind are infallibly saved, and the rest infallibly damn'd: It being impossible, that any of the former should be damn'd, or that any of the latter should be saved (10).

Wesley believed such doctrine "directly tends to destroy that holiness, which is the end of all the ordinances of God" (11). It destroys, he insisted, "several particular branches of holiness. Such are meekness and love" (12). As Wesley saw it, predestination "directly tends to destroy our zeal for good works" (16). In short, Wesley thought predestination tends to promote antinomianism. As he explained:

> that the doctrine itself, "That every man is either elected or not elected from eternity, and that the one must inevitably be saved, and the other inevitably damn'd," has a manifest tendency to destroy holiness in general. For it wholly takes away those first motives to follow after it, so frequently propos'd in Scripture, the hope of future reward and fear of punishment, the hope of heaven and fear of hell. That *these shall go away into everlasting punishment, and those into life eternal* is not motive to him to struggle for life who believes his lot is cast already. It is not reasonable for him so to do, if he thinks he is unalterably adjudged either to life or death (10).

In March 1741, Whitefield published his counterattack against Wesley—*Free Grace Indeed! A Letter to the Reverend Mr. John Wesley, Relating to His Sermon against Absolute Election; Published under the Title of Free Grace* (1741). "[T]he publication of his reply to Wesley," states Iain Murray, "was an inevitable separation. Henceforth the evangelical

---

41. The hymn "Universal Redemption" also appeared in *Hymns and Sacred Poems* (1740), 136–42.

forces engaged in the revival movement were divided and a new party of Arminian evangelicals emerged for the first time in British church history" (Whitefield: 1965, 567). Indeed, the difference between Wesley and Whitefield was such that it damaged their relationship, and "led them to build separate chapels, form separate societies, and pursue, to the end of life, separate lines of actions. [...] Thus the gulf between Wesley and Whitefield was immense" (Tyerman: 1870, 1:313).

Hart, considering himself a Calvinist and siding with Whitefield on the issue of predestination, took time to write against Wesley's *Free Grace* in defense of the Reformed teaching on predestination. In *The Unreasonableness of Religion*, Hart mentioned that among the opponents of this teaching was

> a Zealot, who has drawn after him a number of followers to hear the old Arminian errours. [...] The person, I mean, is Mr. John Wesley: Who in a sermon lately come to my hands, preach'd at Bristol, and published the year before last, under the specious title of *Free Grace*, has [...] debased, and vilified the glorious doctrine of God's eternal love to elected sinners; bespattering it with all the slander and calumny, that the devil, and his own wicked heart could invent, in the forementioned sermon (1741, 14–15).

In his defense of the doctrine of predestination, Hart contended

> that the glory of God is the ultimate and only end of all his works: and that as *even the wicked made for the day of evil* [Prov. 16:14] shall be instruments of setting forth this glory in their destruction, which they are utterly unable by any means to avoid: So on the other hand, *those who are predestinated to the adoption of sons* [Eph 1:5], shall be irresistibly wrought on by the Spirit of God; and shall infallibly receive the grace given them here, and enjoy the glory prepared for them in Christ before the foundation of the world, in a state of eternal union with God hereafter (7–8).

Whitefield's *Free Grace Indeed!* and Hart's *The Unreasonableness of Religion* were both published in 1741, when Hart was about twenty-nine. Hart opened his tract by reminding his readers that although

> the publication of the following sheets was occasion'd by the reading of the sermon [of John Wesley], in answer to which they are written: Yet there are, I am perswaded, some things contain'd in them, which will be

relish'd and own'd by every experienc'd Christians. To whose consideration I desire to offer them: tho' seemingly spoken to an unbeliever (3).

Ironically, though Hart wrote as if already converted, he actually penned his tract while still unconverted, a Christian in name only, as will be clear later. Given Hart's spiritual condition, it was also ironic how Hart regarded Wesley as unsaved:

> As I have no hatred to him as a man; so I confess I have no love to him as a Christian. For brotherly love, and gospel-charity is in me confined to those only, whom I esteem believers. Consequently I can have none for him, out of whose own mouth I can gather nothing to perswade me he is a Christian (17).

In *The Advantage of Correct Thoughts on the Sinfulness of Sin. A Sermon. With an Appendix, Containing Observations on Antinomians and Arminians* (1795), Particular Baptist John Martin (1741–1820) showed how Antinomians and Arminians viewed each other during this period: "At present, Antinomians contend, that all Arminians are under the covenant of works; that they are enemies to the doctrines of grace, and that they seek to be justified in the sight of God by the merit of their own personal obedience" (42). Hart thought of Wesley in this way, which was most likely the reason he perceived him as an unbeliever. As Hart said,

> The next objection brought by Mr. *Wesley* against this Doctrine, [of predestination] is, That it tends to Destroy *all Holiness.* [...] To which I readily make this Reply. That it Really does So. It Effectually cuts off all Hope of Reward to Those, who are Working for Life Under *Terms of Acceptance.* [...] It utterly Damns all zealous Work-mongers: Who are for patching up a Filthy Garment out of the Nasty Rags of Legal Holiness, joining it (if it were possible) to the Pure and Spotless Robe of the Mediator's Righteousness, freely given to all the Elect; for whom it was prepared before the Foundation of the World (1741, 36–37).

"On the other side," added Martin, "Arminians contend, that Antinomians are an abandoned set of people; that they will not allow the moral law to be a rule of their behaviour; that they do what they can to turn the grace of God into lasciviousness" (1795, 42).

Hart's main thesis in *The Unreasonableness of Religion* was that "religion and reason are not only widely different, but directly contrary, the one to the other" (1741, 5).[42] For instance, he explained,

> Reason bids me expect acceptance from the almighty in a future state, according to the moral justice, equity, and goodness of mine actions in the present. On the contrary, religion teaches me, that I shall be acquitted, justified, and accepted of God, by the righteousness of another freely bestow'd, and given me, without the least regard to my own personal either merit, or demerit (6).

Hart further differentiated religion and reason by saying:

> So again reason tells me, that in order to secure an interest in eternal life, I must by mine own natural strength, strive, struggle and labour; and pray for the assistance of God, to enable me so to please him here, that I may shun his wrath, and enjoy him in bliss hereafter. But religion plainly shews me, that when I was in my natural state, it was impossible for me to move one step towards heaven; no, not so much as to implore the divine assistance aright; but was utterly *dead in trespasses and sins* [Eph 2:1]; and as incapable of exerting the least power, or motion towards any spiritual good, as a dead carcass is of performing any action of natural life (6).

Hart's explanation implied two crucial doctrines: first, the Calvinistic doctrine of total depravity, which teaches man by nature is utterly unable to save himself. Man cannot even repent and believe unless God grants him faith and repentance. Thence, recalling the days when Hart was yet an antinomian, he wrote in his "Experience:"

> How often did I make my strongest Efforts to call God *my God*! But alas! I could no more do this, than I could raise the Dead! I found now, by woful Experience, that Faith was not in my Power, and the Question with me now was, not whether I *would* be a Christian or no, but whether I *might*, not whether I should repent and believe, but whether God would give me true Repentance, and a Living faith (1767, iv).

---

42. Hart explained the difference between religion and reason this way: "As by religion I mean, the knowledge of the true God, the right way of worshipping him here, and the sure and certain means of enjoying him in endless glory hereafter: So by reason I understand, the natural dictates of the human mind; whereby every man in this fallen state is capable of making rational deductions, and argumentations; and so advancing himself by degrees, in what is generally called knowledge."

The second doctrine implied in Hart's explanation was the Reformed doctrine of justification by faith alone. Previously, when Hart was a legalist, he had believed in a salvation obtained by good works. Now he was convinced of a salvation apart from good works. With respect to these doctrines Hart would not meet with opposition from Whitefield. However, he understood and defended these two doctrines, along with predestination, from the perspective of an antinomian theology—with which Whitefield would not agree.

Hart's antinomianism in the treatise can be seen in the way he argued against those who claimed it was their duty as converted to stir up the gift inside them (2 Tim 1:16), to pray to the Lord to increase their faith (Luke 17:5), and to grow in grace and in the knowledge of their Lord and Savior Jesus Christ (2 Pet 1:16). In short, Hart opposed the idea that as Christians we "must exert all [our] natural powers, and abilities to be more and more acquainted with God, and make greater progress in faith, and higher advancement in knowledge" (1741, 8). Hart did not think it was his duty to perform these biblical imperatives. Even "to pray to God" for help to do these commands, Hart stressed, "is so far from falling under the notion of a duty":

> [M]y hardest work in religion is (if I may so express it) to do nothing. My greatest labour, to lie quiet. My strongest struggling, to sit still. And my most active endeavours to apprehend my self entirely passive in God's hand; a creature meerly recipient of whatsoever measure of good he shall please to infuse into me: and to know, and see, my only business is to glorify God; which is done by believing, trusting, depending, relying wholly upon him, without any regard to my own frame, or disposition of mind at all (9).

As can be observed, Hart's antinomianism was born out of his genuine desire to exalt God's sovereign grace in his life at the expense of any moral duty toward God. Although he never called himself a hyper-Calvinist, his being antinomian was both the cause and effect of his hyper-Calvinistic theology. His emphasis on divine sovereignty to the exclusion of human responsibility is a classic mark of hyper-Calvinism.[43] For example, the hyper-Calvinistic Baptist minister John

---

43. For a study of hyper-Calvinism during the eighteenth-century, see Peter Toon (2011).

Brine (1703–1765), who was converted under the preaching of Hart's contemporary, John Gill (1697–1771), opposed

> other Calvinists who thought that unconverted people had a moral responsibility to hear and respond to the gospel. His teaching elevated the initiative of God in salvation, to the extent of believing that God adopted and justified the elect even before their own experience of faith. Preachers therefore had no right to 'offer' Christ to their hearers, as this challenged the sovereign actions of God.[44]

A comparable tendency is seen in Hart when he said man

> has not the least share, or part in the work of salvation: no, not so much as to accept it when offered, or forward it, when began: but it is entirely indebted, from the beginning, carrying on, and accomplishing the whole work to him, *who worketh all things according to the counsel of his own will* [Eph 1:11] (1741, 12–13).

Similarly, by focusing too much on God's eternal decree and man's inability, Hart failed to see the importance of human responsibility not only in the context of justification but also in sanctification. As he proclaimed,

> I plainly see, and experimentally feel, that, as before conversion I could not move one hairs breadth towards God and goodness: so since I am new created in Christ Jesus, the old man in me is as rebellious, and stubborn as ever. I have as great, or rather seemingly greater inclination to sin, and hatred to God, than before (1741, 8).

And what Hart stated just previously—"the question with me now was [...] not whether I should repent and believe, but whether God would give me true repentance, and a living faith"—also has a hyper-Calvinistic tone.

Hart's antinomianism was not just the cause and effect of his hyper-Calvinism, it was also a result of his overreaction to Arminianism, which tends to emphasize the role of the human will in salvation more than divine grace. In his attempt to defend the doctrine of sovereign grace against the Arminian view of human free will, Hart fell into antinomianism.

---

44. S.L. Copson, "John Brine (1703–1765), Baptist minister," in *Oxford Dictionary of National Biography* (2004), https://doi.org/10.1093/ref:odnb/3436

Describing the antinomians during Hart's time, Shrubsole said, "They have disputed on grace and predestination, until they have thrown off all respect to the holy laws of our King" (1810, 229). They "imagine, that our dear Lord by dying for sin, has excused them from any obligation to the moral law; being under gospel grace, they say, that no sin, however indulged, can hurt them" (229–30). Here Shrubsole well described the antinomianism of Hart, who toward the end of his tract concluded, the believers' "sins do not destroy, but often increase their comfort even here" (1741, 59). In the words of Jude 1:4, Hart "turn[ed] the grace of our God into lasciviousness." Or in Hart's own admission at a later time, he had abused God's grace, using it as a license to sin:

> Abus'd his Grace; despis'd his Fear;
> A forward Fool, a willing Drudge,
> I acted for the Prince of Hell:
> Did all he bid without a Grudge;
> And boasted, I could sin so well.[45]

Here is antinomianism in its highest form. This abuse is why antinomianism is often associated with libertinism. Not only was Hart an antinomian in theory but also in practice.

Later Hart would publicly repent of having written *The Unreasonableness of Religion*. And in his message "To the Reader" of his *Hymns*, he would warn of the great danger of libertinism:

> I charge them therefore in the name of God to beware of any such diabolical delusion; for they who say, let us sin that grace may abound, their damnation is just. And the damnation which men incur by a presumptuous wilful abuse and contempt of the gospel, is worse than that of Sodom and Gomorrah: For our God is a consuming fire.

"Pharisaic Zeal [or legalism], and Antinomian Security," said Hart, "are the two Engines of Satan with which he grinds the Church in all Ages" (1767, xiv).

According to Shrubsole, it was Whitefield who challenged Hart to leave the Town of Illumination (antinomianism). Shrubsole's allegorical story of Hart's departure from antinomianism is worth citing here, for he knew both Hart and Whitefield:

---

45. Hymn 27, lines 3:3, 5:1–4.

Mr. Fervidus [i.e., Mr. Whitefield] determined to go and preach in that town [of illumination or antinomianism]. I accompanied him. He was peculiarly awful there. He preached in the market-place, on a market-day, and had a very large congregation. He stood in the midst of them, and blazed like another Mount Sinai, with lightnings and thunders; and his voice was like a dreadful trumpet; so that whole town rang, and I myself trembled and quaked. Some of the townsmen [i.e., antinomians] were affected while he preached, but the impressions soon wore off.

Mr. Hearty [i.e., Mr. Hart], however, was greatly alarmed by Mr. Fervidus's sermon; and soon after came to my house, and declared, he would no more return to that town. At that time, he gave me the account of himself, which I have related, and manifested all the signs of a sincere repentance of his sins. He abode here several weeks, and chiefly spent his time in deep reflection, by the side of the river and among the adjacent trees: but he was distressed with great horrors and terrors (1810, 234–35).

Whitefield made a fourth visit to America in 1751 and returned to England in 1752, probably the year Hart heard Whitefield preach the gospel and was convinced to abandon antinomianism. This was also probably the year Hart began visiting Tottenham Court Chapel more regularly. But before Hart experienced what he called "reconversion," he had gone through two spiritually painful stages. The first of these was mere outward reform.

2.2.6 Hart's Mere Outward Reform (from *ca.* 1752 to 1756)

On December 28, 1752, Hart married Mary Lamb (*ca.* 1726–1790) at St. Benet Paul's Wharf, London.[46] Interestingly, although both Hart and his fiancée were still residents of Saint Dunstan, they did not get married at the parish church there but at St. Benet Paul's Wharf, whose rector at this time was the eloquent preacher John Thomas (1696–1781) (Ward: 2004). In their marriage bond, we discover Hart was a widower when he married Mary, about fourteen years younger than himself: "Appeared personally

---

46. For their marriage records, see Appendix 3. There is also a record indicating Mary (Lamb) Hart was buried on February 17, 1790, at the age of 64 and she was living on Chriswell Street at the time of her death. Chriswell was less than a quarter mile from the church Hart served on Jewin Street. See *General Register Office: Registers of Births, Marriages and Deaths Surrendered to the Non-Parochial Registers Commissions of 1837 and 1857*. Class Number: RG 4; Piece Number: 3987. The National Archives, Kew, England. Accessible via Ancestry.com.

Joseph Hart of the parish of Saint Dunstan in the West, London, Widower, and Alledged that he intends to intermarry with Mary Lamb of the same parish, aged twenty-five years, a Spinster." John Hughes, Hart's brother-in-law, depicted Mary as "a loving, virtuous woman" (1768, 29).

Hart remained an antinomian until about this time. Now about forty years old, Hart "began by degrees to reform a little, and to live in a more sober and orderly Manner" (1767, vi). Then he thought because he was "not only sound in Principles, but sober and honest in Practice," he could not "but be in the right Way to the Favour of God" (vi).

But later, writing in his "Experience," Hart acknowledged he was still not yet truly converted. "The fountains of the great deeps of my sinful nature," admitted Hart, "were not broken up!" (vii). He was then just experiencing reform not rooted in being truly saved—a similar experience he had when he was a legalist. The only difference being he was now aware of the doctrine of justification by faith in Christ, though he confessed he "was so far from seeing, or owning that there was such a Necessity for [Christ's] death" (vii). As he disclosed:

> And now, as I retained the Form of sound Words, and held the Doctrines of Free-Grace, Justification by Faith, and other orthodox Tenets, I was tolerably confident of the Goodness of my State, especially as I could now add that other Requisite, a moral Behavior. [...] I looked on his Death indeed as the grand Sacrifice for Sin, and always thought on him with Respect and Reverence; but did not see the inestimable Value of his Blood and Righteousness clearly enough to make me abhor myself, and count all Things else but Dung and Dross (vi–vii).

Hart's experience is not uncommon. For instance, John Bunyan (1628–1688) had gone through a similar experience. In his *Grace Abounding to the Chief of Sinners* (1666), Bunyan mentioned how before he knew Christ savingly, he had experienced "some outward reformation" (1962, 12–13).[47] But because this outward change was not rooted in the gospel, it did not last. Bunyan's book, which is his spiritual autobiography, was to some extent comparable to Hart's "Experience." Their accounts of conversion were remarkably similar to some degree. As Arthur Gregory noted, "Contemporary with Watts and Doddridge, but having closer spiritual affinity with John Bunyan was Joseph Hart. [...] Again and again this

---

47. Quoted here from the edition by Roger Sharrock (1962).

narrative [Hart's 'Experience'] recalls Grace Abounding, though Hart has little of the vigour, and none of the humour, of Bunyan" (1904, 147).

2.2.7 Hart's Deep Despondency (from *ca.* 1756 to May 29, 1757)
The second stage Hart went through immediately prior to what he accounted his reconversion was a severe gloom caused by the absence of Christ. Now about forty-four years of age, Hart "fell into a deep Despondency of Mind, because [he] had never experienced grand Revelations and miraculous Discoveries" to indicate he was among the elect (Hart: 1767, vii–viii). Although Hart had already left hyper-Calvinism, he still retained some of its beliefs, such as "grand revelations" from God and "miraculous discoveries" of election found outside Scripture. In his study of hyper-Calvinism during the 'Long Eighteenth Century,' Paul Helm explained how in hyper-Calvinism the

> object of faith is not simply "Christ, and him crucified," announced indiscriminately to sinners, but something additional that will provide to the one who has it the evidence that he is already justified. What could that be? Since the New Testament does not list the names of those who are elected and eternally justified, it must be some *datum* that goes beyond divine special revelation in Scripture (2018, 135).

Hence, at this time Hart constantly besought Christ to reveal himself to him "in clearer Manner" (1767, viii). By this plea, Hart was asking Christ to reveal to him directly (outside the Scriptures) his status as one of the chosen. He still struggled with whether he would just be "content with trusting" Christ, or would look for "the visionary Revelations, of which [he] had formed some wild idea" (viii). The absence of this direct revelation from Christ caused him to be "very melancholy." He added,

> [I] shunned all Company, walking pensively alone, or sitting in private, and bewailing my sad and dark Condition, not having a Friend in the World, to whom I could communicate the Burden of my Soul; which was so heavy, that I sometimes hesitated even to take my necessary Food (viii).

Some Baptists before Hart also dealt with melancholy. John Bunyan, for example, also suffered deep depression before and even after his conversion.[48] Moreover, the Presbyterian Timothy Rogers (1658–1728) had to resign from the ministry because of this predicament. In his book *Trouble of Mind and the Disease of Melancholly* (1691), Rogers called melancholy "the worst of all distempers; and those sinking and guilty fears which it brings along with it, are inexpressibly dreadful" (3). Nevertheless, all these pastors, Bunyan and Hart in particular, did not allow their melancholy to stop them from pursuing Jesus. The week before Easter of 1757 (which fell on April 10), Hart was spiritually comforted by having "an amazing View of the Agony of Christ in the Garden." He was "lost in Wonder and Adoration, and the Impression it made was too deep" (1767, ix). Shortly after this experience, he penned the first part of his hymn number one, called "On the Passion."[49] The hymn has fourteen stanzas, the first of which clearly reflects Hart's experience during this period:

> Come, all ye chosen Saints of God,
> That long to feel the cleansing Blood,
> In pensive Pleasure join Me,
> To sing of sad *Gethsemane*.

Notice Hart's longing "to feel the cleansing blood" of Christ. He knew only this blood could cleanse him from sin and guilt and bring him comfort.

But the comfort of Christ's blood was soon replaced with terror. As Hart related, "I looked on myself as a Gospel-Sinner, one that had

---

48. Richard Greaves felt Bunyan's description of his spiritual struggles in *Grace Abounding to the Chief of Sinners* was more than spiritual in nature. He believed Bunyan was suffering from depression, which was also known in Bunyan's time as melancholy. He concluded, "The evidence strongly suggests that Bunyan suffered from recurrent, chronic dysthymia ['sometimes referred to as reactive, mild, neurotic, or psychogenic depression'] on which a major depressive episode was imposed about late 1653 or early 1654. The onset of the illness would have occurred about early 1651 and terminated, by Bunyan's reckoning, in approximately late 1657 or early 1658. There would be at least one further apparent recurrence, triggered by anxiety about late 1663 or 1664 during his imprisonment. During his illness in the 1650s, he suffered from pronounced dysphoria, marked feelings of worthlessness, impaired rational ability at times, apparent insomnia, and diminished pleasure in normal activities. He thought periodically about death, even to the point that he was 'a terror to myself,' yet he was afraid to die because of the judgment he expected in the afterlife" (2002, 57–58).

49. Hart informs us he "afterwards mutilated and altered" this hymn (1767, ix).

trampled under Foot the Blood of Jesus, and for whom there remained no more Sacrifice for Sin" (ix). Hart thought he was destined to be everlastingly damned. He was so horrified with this thought he could not sleep and would not dare close his eyes, even when he was sleepy, lest he "should awake in Hell" (x). For many days, he went back and forth from despair to hope and hope to despair. The struggle Hart shared here seems common among those who had adopted the hyper-Calvinistic mindset. Later, in his autobiographical hymn, Hart would observe how other Christians had gone through the same struggle:

> Oh! What a dismal State was this!
> What Horrors shook my feeble Frame!
> But, Brethren, surely you can guess:
> For you, perhaps, have felt the same.[50]

2.2.8 Hart's Reconversion Experience (May 29, 1757): "sweet Peace in my Soul"[51]

Hart continued to suffer great spiritual turmoil until Whit Sunday (or Pentecost Sunday), May 29, 1757, when he "happened to go in the Afternoon to the *Moravian* Chappel in *Fetter-Lane*, where [he] had been several Times before" (1767, xi). There the unnamed minister preached a sermon on Revelation 3:10, which the Lord used for Hart's conversion. His own words best describe what he called his reconversion story:

> Tho' the Text, and most of what was said on it, seemed to make greatly against me; yet I listened with much Attention, and felt myself deeply impressed by it. When it was over, I thought of hastening to *Tottenham-Court* Chappel; but presently altering my Mind, returned to my own House (xi).[52]

Then Hart recounted,

> I was hardly got home, when I felt myself melting away into a strange Softness of Affection; which made me fling myself on my Knees before God. My Horrors were immediately dispelled, and such Light and Comfort flowed into my Heart, as no Words can paint. The Lord by

---

50. Hymn 27, stanza 12.
51. Hart: 1767, xii.
52. Probably at this time the Tottenham Court Chapel became Hart's regular place for corporate worship.

his Spirit of Love came,—not in a visionary Manner into my Brain, but with such divine Power and Energy into my soul, that I was lost in blissful Amazement (xi).

The Moravian Chapel in Fetter Lane, where Hart experienced conversion, was less than 1,000 feet from his home in St Dunstan-in-the-West, London. This chapel was the meeting place of the Fetter Lane Society, organized in 1738 by the Moravian missionary Peter Boehler (1712–1775) and his disciples. The Wesley brothers and Whitefield were once part of this society before they broke from the Moravians.

A cardinal belief among the Moravians was "true faith is always accompanied by a sense of assurance and evidenced by freedom from sin, fear, and doubt, three fruits which inseparably attend assurance and attest to a proper faith. Any doubt or fear, therefore, is a sign of unbelief" (Heitzenrater: 2013, 85). Given Hart's spiritual struggle at this time, this teaching might have attracted Hart to attend the Moravian chapel, where he finally experienced the assurance of pardon for which he had been longing. As a result, Hart could now face death with no fear of going to hell. Augustus M. Toplady (1740–1778), known today as the writer of the hymn "Rock of Ages," recorded Hart's confident, death-bed declaration, "I know myself to be a child of God, and an heir of glory. Judas was lost, that the scripture might be fulfilled: but the scripture would not be fulfilled, if I should not be saved" (Toplady: 1825, 4:169).

Awestruck by an amazing change in his life, Hart could only wonder why such a holy God would save a wicked sinner like him:

> What an amazing Change was here!
> I look'd for Hell; he brought me Heav'n.
> Chear up, said he; dismiss thy Fear;
> Chear up, thy Sins are all forgiv'n.
>
> I would object; but faster much
> He answer'd Peace. What Me?—*Yes, Thee.*
> But my enormous Crimes are such—
> *I give thee Pardon full and free.*[53]

---

53. Hymn 27, stanzas 15 and 16.

With this new-found assurance of forgiveness, Hart could now enjoy peace and joy in his soul:

> He said. I took the full Release.
> The Lord had sign'd it with his Blood.
> My Horrors fled; and perfect Peace
> And Joy unspeakable ensu'd.[54]

However, not long after his conversion (or reconversion as he called it), he was "terribly infested with Thoughts so monstrously obscene and blasphemous, that they" could not be described (xiii). Yet he was "sensible that most of God's Children are sometimes attacked in like Manner," though he felt his thoughts "were foul and black beyond Example, and seemed to be the Master-pieces of Hell" (xiii). Thankfully, this horrifying experience did not endure. As he narrated,

> I soon began to be visited by God's Spirit in a different Manner from whatever I had felt before. [...] I now believed my Name was sculptured deep in the Lord Jesus's Breast, with Characters never to be erased. I saw him, with the Eye of Faith, stooping under the Load of *my* Sins, groaning and grovelling in *Gethsemane* for *Me* (xiii).

It appears Hart did not have full assurance of salvation, until after this event—when the Spirit had visited him in a different manner from anything he had experienced before. Although Hart did not tell how the Spirit visited him, one may deduce it was not in "a visionary manner." In Hart's mind, the major work of the Spirit is to bring sinners to Christ, so they may see by faith his precious blood, in which Hart found peace and comfort. Indeed, after his encounter with the Spirit, he could testify,

> The incarnate God was more and more revealed to me, and I had far other Notions of his Sufferings, than I had entertained before. Now I saw that the Grief of Christ was the Grief of my Maker; that his Wounds were the wounds of the Almighty God; and the least Drop of his Blood now appeared to me more valuable than ten Thousands of worlds. As I had before thought his Sufferings *too little*, they now appeared to me to be *too great* (xiii–xiv).

---

54. Hymn 27, stanza 19.

One of the early hymns Hart wrote was on the Holy Spirit. In this hymn he prayed,

> Come, Holy Spirit, come;
> Let thy bright Beams arise,
>
> Dispel the Darkness from our Minds;
> And open all our Eyes.
>
> Convince us of our Sin;
> Then lead to Jesu's Blood:[55]

This atoning blood, shed on the cross, to which Hart again and again fled for comfort, especially in time of Satan's assault, became one of the major themes of his hymnody. And this emphasis on Christ's atoning sacrifice, or crucicentrism as David Bebbington styles it, became one of the hallmarks of early evangelicalism (Bebbington: 1989, 14–17).

The complex narrative of Hart's conversion accorded to some degree with his view of conversion in *The Unreasonableness of Religion*, published sixteen years before his reconversion experience. Here he presented different stages that sinners would go through on the way to true conversion. These steps can be organized into eight points:

[1] The first thing generally done by the Spirit in the Conversion of a Sinner, is to shew him, that he is lost in himself and must die Eternally without the Free Grace and Mercy of God in the Mediator. The Man now hangs as it were between Heaven and Hell. In his own Apprehension there is but one Step between him and Endless Misery.

[2] Thus is he Continually Distress'd, and Unsatisfied, reaping no Comfort from any thing he reads or Hears: till God shall shine in upon him by his Spirit, Opening his Understanding to Understand the Scriptures. [...]

[3] He now begins to see a Marvelous Light in the Sacred Writings, unknown to him before by the Letter. Christ is Exhibited clearly in the Word; and he is enabled to view him with Spiritual Eyes, and to Close in with him Savingly [...] feeling Raptures and Transports of inexpressible Joy and Comfort. [...]

---

55. Hymn 4, "To the Holy Ghost" ("Come, Holy Spirit, come"), lines 1:1–4, 4:1–2.

[4] But this Light of Revelation must be clouded; and Faith must Combat with Difficulties and Dangers. For without Opposition it lies Unactive; and not to be distinguished from a False, and Dead Faith.

[5] The Believer has now a more Amazing Sight of his own Vileness, and Deformity, Sees, that every thing he thinks, and acts, is Sin. Yet Faith tells him, he shall notwithstanding be saved.

[6] Anon his Corruptions grow more Prevalent; Temptations to Infidelity Assault; his Lusts and Vices become Predominant, and he falls into Sins as Gross and as Frequent as before; and perhaps more now than ever.

[7] Yet God in the very midst of his Rebellions, or immediately after his Acts of Iniquity, breaks in upon his Soul with new Discoveries of his Unchangeable Love to him in his Son.

[8] This greatly strengthens his Faith, and plainly shews him, that as nothing could Move God at first to place his Love upon him; so nothing can provoke him to take it from him. Nay, the Viler he is, he finds the Lord the More Kind and Merciful to him. And where Sin abounds, Grace to him does Superabound. And his Iniquities are no Hinderers, but Helpers of his Faith (1741, 29–31).

Hart's concept of conversion in point one—that God ordinarily begins the work of conversion by first showing sinners how apart from divine mercy they are miserable endlessly—resonated with the teaching of most Puritans regarding their doctrine of preparation for grace.[56] In *Prepared by Grace, for Grace: The Puritans on God's Ordinary Way of Leading Sinners to Christ*, the authors asserted, "in general the Puritans' view was that conviction of sin and active seeking of God's mercy usually preceded conscious resting and relying upon Christ" (Beeke/Smalley: 2013, 10).[57] Written in light of his defense of the doctrine of predestination against Arminianism, Hart's goal in his morphology of conversion was like that of the Puritans, namely, to show how "God's eternal predestination of a

---

56. For instance, see William Ames (1639), 8–9. In response to the question: "How the sinner ought to prepare himselfe to conversion," Ames wrote, there must be "a conviction of Conscience," followed by "a despare of salvation," resulting in "a true humiliation of heart, which consists in griefe and feare because of sin, and doth bring forth confession."

57. For differing interpretations of the Puritan doctrine of preparation, see Perry Miller (1943) and Norman Pettit (1966).

sinner to eternal life unfolds in personal experience according to a discernible pattern of events and experiences" (10). In point four, Hart's notion of saving faith as attaining assurance only after a season of combat also resembled in some ways the teaching of William Perkins (1558–1602).[58] However, Hart's statement in point six that a person who has closed in with Christ savingly, later "falls into Sins as Gross and as Frequent as before; and perhaps more now than ever" was somewhat inconsistent with a normal post-conversion experience as the Puritans understood it,[59] though exceptions appeared in the Reformed tradition for backsliding. For instance, George Marsden identified three main stages toward genuine conversion in New England minister Timothy Edwards (1669–1758), the second of which included backsliding. As Edwards saw it, after sinners were convicted or awakened (first step), they underwent humiliation (second step). Marsden explained,

> Normally, following the first enthusiasm of their awakening, they would experience a backsliding into sin that would lead them to realize the terribleness of their sins and that God would be entirely just in condemning them to hell. Sometimes this stage was described as involving a sense of "terror" (2003, 27).

Then, following the second stage was true repentance and faith, resulting in a changed life in Christ (third step).[60]

---

58. Perkins wrote, "[God] kindle[s] in the heart some seeds or sparks of faith, that is, a will and desire to believe, and grace to strive against doubting and despair. Now, at the same instant, when God begins to kindle in the heart any sparks of faith, then also He justifies the sinner and withal begins the work of sanctification. [...] so soon as faith is put into the heart, there is presently a combat, for it fights with doubting, despair, and distrust. And in this combat, faith shows itself by fervent, constant, and earnest invocation for pardon; and after invocation follows a strengthening and prevailing of this desire" (Yuille: 2019, 142). Notice how both Perkins and Hart used the word "combat" to refer to spiritual struggle.

59. Moreover, what Hart said in point eight—that "his Iniquities are no Hinderers, but Helpers of his Faith"—departed from an orthodox Puritan view because of its antinomian character. One must remember Hart wrote his morphology of conversion when he was increasingly becoming antinomian. For a treatment of antinomianism in the seventeenth and eighteenth centuries, see Whitney G. Gamble (2018), David D. Hall (1990), Curt Daniel (1997 and 2004).

60. For a study of Timothy Edwards's morphology of conversion, see Kenneth P. Minkema (1988), 80–95.

Taking into consideration Hart's conversion experience, Erik Routley has observed how Hart's account of himself presents him "to be a typical product of early eighteenth-century Calvinism; educated, intelligent, sensitive, and, as it happens with him, introspective as well" (1951, 200). Routley has pointed out,

> Calvinism starts the young Christian on his way with a sense of sin. Its august dogma is the Sovereignty of God and the helplessness of man. Except the Christian pilgrim be able to appropriate also the other dogma, that the promises of God are sure, he is doomed either to cast off his faith and live in negligent sloth or to take it seriously and despair. All depends on that other appropriation, and whereas the dogma of sin is objective enough to be thrust at him as a certainty with which he must reckon, the dogma of the promises makes no sense to him until it is engrafted in his soul by personal experience (200).

2.2.9 Hart's Ministry: "Some Service might by Me be done / To Souls that truly trust in Him"[61]

Delivered from misery, Hart was filled with joy. Out of his gratitude for the great things God had done for his soul, he wanted to serve him in a public capacity: "I threw my Soul willingly into my Saviour's Hands; lay weeping at his Feet, wholly resigned to his Will, and only begging that I might, if he was graciously pleased to permit it, be of Some Service to his Church and People" (1767, xii). Before entering the ministry, Hart first became a hymn writer.

In 1759, two years after his conversion, Hart published the first edition of his *Hymns Composed on Various Subjects*, which included a preface containing a brief summary account of his conversion experience and the great things God had done for his soul. "This publication," said hymn writer Henry Fowler (1779–1838), "most likely drew him into the notice of many godly persons, and was the means, under God, of calling him into the ministry" (Hart: 1851, 7).[62] Indeed, in 1760, a year after the publication of his hymnbook, he became minister of the Independent congregation at Jewin Street, east of Aldersgate Street, London. Probably around this time Hart and his family moved from

---

61. Hymn 27, lines 20:3–4.
62. The author of this memoir drew some of his information from one of Hart's grandsons, whose name was also Joseph Hart, music seller, Hatton Garden.

St. Dunstan-in-the-West to St. Martin-in-the-Fields, as their last three children were born in the latter place, which was closer to Jewin Street, about a quarter mile away.[63]

In *The History and Antiquities of Dissenting Churches and Meeting Houses*, Walter Wilson (d. 1847) noted how Jewin Street "was anciently called the Jew's garden, and was the only burial place allowed them in England" until 1177 when King Henry II "allowed them to have such a ground in any part where they dwelt. [...] In process of time, this ground became built upon, and thence was derived the name Jewin-street" (1810, 3:327).[64] The history of the meeting house at Jewin Street goes back to 1662, when a large group of Puritan ministers were expelled from the Church of England for not conforming fully to the *Book of Common Prayer*, as required in The Act of Uniformity 1662. The event came to be known as the Great Ejection. One of the ejected ministers was the Presbyterian William Jenkyn (1613–1685) under whose ministry the meeting-house at Jewin Street was erected. He pastored here from 1672 (when the Royal Declaration of Indulgence was issued) to 1682 (when a period of severe persecution of the Nonconformists commenced). During this period, reported Wilson, "the meeting-houses were every where shut up, and both the ministers and people proscribed the worship of God in public, under pain of fine and imprisonment" (1810, 3:335). This caused the meeting house to be unoccupied until 1692 when the Presbyterian minister John Shower (1657–1715) and his growing congregation occupied the meeting house from their old small building at Curriers' Hall (Mercer: 2004).

The meeting house at Jewin Street became unoccupied again when it got too small for Shower's fast growing congregation. In 1701, this congregation vacated the chapel and moved into their newly built and bigger meeting house in the Old Jewry (Mercer: 2004). The worship place at Jewin Street was afterward used by a group of Independents under the ministry of Thomas Powell (b. 1656?). Upon Powell's death, his congregation broke up and another congregation took over the chapel under the care of Daniel Neal (1678–1743) who served the church until his retirement

---

63. Their last three children, Thomas Hart (b. 1758), Benjamin Hart (1759–1836) and Mercy Hart (1767–1801), were all baptized at St Martin in the Fields, Westminster, London.

64. This book has an entire section on the history of the meeting house at Jewin Street, including the ministers who served on this street.

in 1742 (Okie: 2004). Neal was then succeeded in 1743 by Roger Pickering (d. 1755), under whose pastoral oversight the congregation split into two groups and eventually dissolved (Wilson: 1810, 3:104, 341). This was the time in England when Presbyterian churches were somewhat in decline (Helm: 2018, 128). The meeting house at Jewin Street being now vacant was occupied by a group of Particular Baptists in 1756 under the care of Thomas Craner (d. 1773), who eventually moved his congregation elsewhere in 1760 (Wilson: 1810, 3:320, 341). Finally, soon after the meeting house once again became unoccupied, Hart took possession of it in 1760, and "preached there to a church of his own gathering" (3:342). Hart proved to be a gifted preacher. Many came to hear him preach, resulting in the growth of his congregation.

2.2.9.1 "Many refreshed under the preached word from his lips"[65]

Hart "did not begin to preach till towards the year 1760; and is said to have delivered his first sermon at the old meeting-house in St. John's [or King John's] court, Bermondsey," northeast of Jewin Street (Wilson: 1810, 3:347). Isaac Mauduit (1662/3–1718), father of the political writer Israel Mauduit (1708–1787), was "the first dissenting minister" of this congregation (Schweizer: 2007). Perhaps in the course of time this congregation had lost their minister and called Hart to replace him; after which, they moved into the meeting house at Jewin Street by 1760.

Sadly, only one of Hart's sermons has survived—*The King of the Jews*, published posthumously (1814). This message, preached on December 25, 1767, at Jewin Street Independent Chapel, is an exposition of the question in Matthew 2:2: "Where is He that is born King of the Jews?" Reading this sermon, one notices how Hart was a man of intellect, yet his style of preaching was down-to-earth.[66] His words were spoken at a level readily understood by the illiterate members of his congregation, as illiteracy during this time was still high. By the time Hart became a pastor in 1760, the population of London was approximately three-quarters of a million,[67]

---

65. Hart (1851), 9.

66. Although there is only one surviving sermon of Hart, his remarks on preaching as well as testimonies on his preaching by his contemporaries contain enough conclusions on the content and style of Hart's sermons, even more so if this one sermon is taken as exemplary for his other pulpit messages.

67. See Clive Emsley, Tim Hitchcock and Robert Shoemaker, "London History: A

and while London had the highest literacy rate in England, many Londoners were still unable to read and write. One factor contributing to Hart's popularity as a preacher was his ability to connect effectively with the uneducated—a gift not all preachers have. In his sermon, he showed his disappointment with preachers of his day who only confused their hearers by making their sermons complex rather than simple:

> I could heartily wish, that expositors of scripture, in this our day, were more heartily agreed, and confirmed, in this one thing: and instead of laying so many stumbling-blocks in the way of people as they do, by caviling and pretended criticisms at the translation [of Scripture], they would rather labour to smooth the way of the illiterate, than make it rough, by attempting to remove pretended difficulties that appear on some occasion where there are none (1814, 8).

Hart also preached with organizational skill and application. At the beginning of his message, after introducing his three main points, he declared it was his "wonted manner" to "proceed to a suitable word of application from the whole" (10).[68] That is, it was his practice to provide practical applications at the end of the sermon. Hart also preached discriminatingly, addressing unbelievers and believers both. As he came to the conclusion of his message, Hart spoke to the unbelievers, pleading with them to come to Christ for mercy:

> I shall address myself to the unconverted, who take pleasure in anything that is sinful, if it will but satisfy their senses for a moment. I would ask you, in the midst of your mirth and jollity, in the midst of your sensual pleasures, "Where is He that is born King of the Jews?" There are principally but two kings that reign in this world: the one is God, the only rightful sovereign of the earth; the other is the devil, a usurper. Therefore remember, you are a subject either in the kingdom of God, or of the devil. [...] If you will not be subjects of his [Christ's] mercy now, you must be subjects of his wrath hereafter—there is no medium (26–28).

Population History of London," *Old Bailey Proceedings Online*, www.oldbaileyonline.org. See also Jennifer Farooq (2013).

68. His three points come in a question form: (1) "in what sense and how Jesus Christ is King of the Jews?" (2) "How it is, that he is thus said to be born King of the Jews?" and (3) "Where he is, that is so born King of the Jews?"

Then, addressing the believers, especially those who struggled with assurance of salvation, Hart proclaimed with passion:

> But some, perhaps, may be dejected and distressed on account of the weakness of their faith, and may be tempted to argue and conclude that they are not believers because their faith is so weak and small. I would ask you, my brother believer, how was Christ first born? Was he made a perfect man at once? no, as I told you before, he himself was once a little, weak, feeble babe, although he was, at the same time, the mighty God that held up heaven and earth. Why are you, then, cast down? If you have the least grain of true divine faith, you are as truly one of his members, as if you had faith to do all miracles; and you are as much a believer now, as if you were sitting with him in glory; for his weakness was no bar to his deity and sonship (30).

Earlier in the sermon, Hart told his congregation "the way to heaven is not by mere visionary revelation, but by divine faith, believing in Christ, receiving life from him, and depending on the promises of God" (7). This statement was a clear attack on hyper-Calvinism; and it perhaps implied hyper-Calvinists were present in Hart's congregation. These hyper-Calvinists were not content with what God revealed in Scripture, but were looking for an extra-biblical revelation for the assurance of their salvation. Possibly some of those who were struggling with assurance of salvation had this hyper-Calvinistic attitude. They felt they could not be saved until God himself had revealed this to them in a visionary revelation. But as Hart argued in his sermon, "no mere revelation, dream, or vision, though it be ever so singular, or great, is in itself sufficient to constitute any one a child of God" (7). Hart emphasized a salvation by faith alone in Christ and an assurance of salvation by the gospel promise.

We also know from his brother-in-law John Hughes, in the institution of the Lord's Supper, Hart demonstrated extra "power and presence of the dear Lord Jesus" (Hughes: 1768, vi). Hart's practical, discriminating, passionate, powerful preaching, backed up by his personal piety, and empowered by the Lord's presence, drew many people to come to hear him preach. The number of people who attended was often greater than the meeting house could accommodate. Many were "refreshed under the preached word from his lips" (Hart: 1851, 9). His popularity as a preacher went beyond his congregation in London, as indicated in his letter to

Shrubsole, minister of Bethel Chapel in Sheerness. From London, Hart wrote to Shrubsole on June 10, 1766,

> As I intend (the Lord permitting) to visit the Chatham Brethren [at Ebenezer Chapel] next Lord's Day Se'nnight [seven-night, a week from now], I intend likewise to reach you [in Sheerness] the Monday following (viz. 23d Inst.) [namely the 23rd of this month] and Preach Monday and Tuesday Evenings and Administer the Lord's Supper on one of the Days, as shall be judged most convenient, and so take my Leave of you on the Wednesday Morning. If this be [agre]eable and your Pulpit vacant for me at those times, let me know by a Line from you as soon as you can; and withal acquaint me whither I must go; for if Mr. Bishop has left his Cabbins, I shall not know where to find him.
>
> Give my kind Love to the Brethren; and exhort them to join with you in Prayer to the Lord for a Blessing on my Visit.[69]

The letter expressed Hart's planned visit to minister, first to Ebenezer Chapel in Chatham, an Independent congregation, where Whitefield often preached, and then to Shrubsole's Independent congregation in Sheerness.[70] Shrubsole's allegorical account of Hart's itinerant preaching revealed how Whitefield was deeply impressed by the impact of Hart's powerful preaching. "*Mr. Hearty* [i.e., Hart]," wrote Shrubsole, "with a small quantity of his wonderful composition, which he calls *Philippian Powder* [referring to the 'force of the doctrines of grace'], threw down the inn and the houses which stood in *Boasting-street*, which were some of the highest and best built in the place, and shook the whole city. […] *Mr. Fervidus* [i.e., Whitefield] was highly pleased with this exploit of Mr. Hearty's" (1810, 301–2, 385).

2.2.9.2 "I will keep my pulpit as chaste as my bed"

The Calvinist Hart was always on guard, watching over his flock, ensuring they received sound teaching. To protect his congregation from defective doctrine, said Calvinist Augustus Toplady, Hart "made it his inviolable rule, not to let an Arian, an Arminian, or any unsound preacher, occupy his pulpit, so much as once. His usual saying on those occasions was, I will keep my pulpit as chaste as my bed" (1825, 4:134). Hart strove to preach

---

69. For a full transcription, see Appendix 1.
70. For a history of these two congregations, see "Records of the Independent Churches in Kent," in Thomas Timpson (1859), 322–26, 482–88.

nothing but the pure Word of God. Not only did he guard his congregation from false doctrine, he also refuted false teachers. With all his strength, declared Hughes, Hart stoutly defended "the doctrines of the gospel, viz. the Trinity in unity; the electing love of God; the free justification of the sinner by the imputation of Christ's righteousness, and salvation alone by his precious blood; the new birth and final perseverance of the saints" (1768, 28). In *An Elegy on the Death of the Rev. Mr. Joseph Hart* (1768) by R.W., he was likened to Samson, and the false teachers to the Philistines. As Samson defeated the Philistines, so did Hart defeat the false teachers of his day:

> Let the Philistines of this day rejoice,
> And vainly sport at our great champion's fall;
> Sing, O ye Christians, with triumphant voice,
> Hart laid their vineyard waste, expos'd to all.
>
> His nervous arm did wield the two-edg'd sword,
> And cut the pillars of their Babel down;
> Arians, Socinians, felt the pow'rful word,
> And Deists, Atheists, sunk beneath his frown (4–5).

Hart was not just concerned with his church's doctrinal purity, he also firmly maintained the necessity of moral purity. Hart always entreated his congregation to live according to the gospel (Hughes: 1768, 28), because he had personally learned how true piety emanates from the gospel. Apart from the gospel, no true piety could exist. Any form of righteousness not stemming from the righteousness of Christ is artificial. Hart wanted to see his flock with sound heads and pure hearts.

Entering the ministry at age forty-eight, Hart made a commitment to use all his energy for the advancement of Christ's kingdom. Describing how industrious Hart was, Hughes likened him to a "laborious ox that dies with his yoke on his neck" (1768, 29). And according to Kinsman, Hart specifically "labored hard [...] for the conversion of souls," proclaiming "the glories of the incarnate Saviour, and his finished redemption" (Hughes: 1768, 39). Hart, added Kinsman, frequently warned his congregation "to flee from the wrath to come, to renounce [their] own righteousness, and put on the Lord Jesus Christ" (39). This earnest, gospel-centered preaching, coupled with God's benediction, resulted in the conversion of many souls.

2.2.9.3 "A faithful guardian to several orphans"[71]

Beyond his pastoral work, Hart was also "a faithful guardian to several orphans." Eighteenth-century England saw many abandoned children in the streets. Philanthropist Thomas Coram (1668–1751), observing this social ill, in 1739 launched the Foundling Hospital in London—a charitable institution for providing unwanted children with basic needs such as shelter, food, clothing, and education.[72] Hart sought to alleviate the problem by caring for several orphans as their guardian. In his *Commentaries on the Laws of England*, written between 1765 and 1770, the judge Sir William Blackstone (1723–1780) described what Hart's responsibilities as a guardian looked like. "The guardian," explained Blackstone, is

> only a temporary parent: that is, for so long time as the ward [a child under a guardian's care] is an infant, or under age [...and] performs the office both of the *tutor* [teacher] and *curator* [guardian] of the Roman laws; the former of which had the charge of the maintenance and education of the minor, the latter the care of his fortune (1915, 1:460–461).[73]

In *An Elegy on the Death of the Rev. Mr. Joseph Hart* (1768) by R.W., we learn how Hart faithfully kept these responsibilities. To comfort Hart's orphans, the elegist uttered these words:

> Now mourn the widow—now the orphans weep;
> Their kind protector—he's, alas! No more—
> Whose charge of trust for them did sacred keep;
> Whose friendly hand oft made their cup run o'er (3).

Hart might have been inspired by Whitefield, who established the Bethesda Orphanage in 1740 in the newly founded colony of Georgia. Regardless, early evangelicals were known for their active involvement in social welfare. They saw it as part of their duty and as an opportunity for them to help the destitute not only with their physical needs but more

---

71. R. W., *An Elegy on the Death of the Rev. Mr. Joseph Hart*, 3.
72. For a study of the Foundling Hospital, see Gilliam Pugh (2007), Ruth K. McClure (1981), and Marthe Jocelyn (2005).
73. Blackstone's work contains four books written between 1765 and 1770 and originally published by the Clarendon Press at Oxford. Book 1 details the rights of persons. Book 2 enumerates the rights of things. Book 3 handles private wrongs. Book 4 is a discussion of public wrongs. Blackstone has an entire section on the relationship between guardian and ward; see Book 1, Chapter 17, "Of Guardian and Ward," 460–69. The work is helpful in understanding the common law of eighteenth-century England.

so with their spiritual needs (Edwards: 1999, 370–405). Their activism, which Bebbington regarded as one of the four defining characteristics of evangelicalism (1989, 1–17),[74] arose from their recognition of what God had done for them in the gospel.

2.2.9.4 "Labouring under many deep temptations" and trials

If one word best describes Hart's ministry, it is *suffering*. His brother-in-law Hughes attested,

> [Hart] came into the work of the ministry in much weakness and brokenness of soul; and laboring under many deep temptations, of a dreadful nature; for though the Lord was pleased to confirm him in his everlasting love to his soul; yet [...] he was at times so left to the buffetings of Satan, for the trial of his faith, and to such clouds and darkness on his soul, that he has been oftentimes obliged to preach to the church with sense and reason flying in his own face; and his faith at the same time like a bruised reed; insomuch that he has often done by the church, as the widow of *Zarephath* did to the prophet Elijah, who made him a cake of that little she had, when herself seemed at the very point of starving (1768, 27).

Hart faced challenges at home as well. He had six children, one of whom, named after him, was epileptic.[75] This child was only about six years old when Hart entered the ministry. On August 18, 1763, his son Daniel died at about the age of three. In their article "Social Capital and the History of Mortality in Britain," Peter Razzell and Christine Spence stated, "In London mortality peaked in the middle of the eighteenth century. [...] Approximately two-thirds of the children under the age of five died in the 1750s" (2005, 447). Razzell and Spence think the increase in mortality "was probably a result of the growth in the virulence of smallpox,

---

74. The three other main features of evangelicalism are conversionism, biblicism, and crucicentrism. By conversionism Bebbington refers to the evangelicals' strong emphasis on the necessity of personal faith in Jesus. By biblicism he intends their high regard for the authority of Scripture. And by crucicentrism he indicates that central to their theology and spirituality was Christ's atoning work on the cross. For Bebbington, these four features are the defining features of the Evangelical movement. Later, this fourfold definition of evangelicalism came to be known as the Bebbington quadrilateral, which for many became a standard definition of evangelicalism.

75. For more on Hart's family structure, see Appendix 6.

typhus, and other infectious diseases during this period" (447). This was one of the contexts in which Hart raised his children.

In addition to the trial with respect to his children, his wife was also sickly, as was Hart himself. When Hart died in 1768 it was said that his "widow has been for some months in a bad state of health, and is now incapable of doing any thing" (Hughes: 1768, i). Hart's own poor health is evident in an autobiographical hymn on sickness:

> When pining Sickness wastes the Frame,
> Acute Disease, or tiring Pain;
> When life fast spends her feeble Flame,
> And all the Help of Man proves vain;
>
> Med'cines can't ease, nor Cordials chear,
> Nor Food support, nor Sleep refresh.
>
> When Flesh decays; and Heart thus fails;
> He shall thy Strength and Portion be:
> Shall take thy Weakness, bear thy Ails;
> And softly whisper, "Trust in me."[76]

Yet, according to Hughes, God "so ordered it [i.e., all Hart's suffering], that it was a means of making him through the super-abundant grace of God, experimentally wise and humble" (20–21). Hart's afflictions did not shake his faith; rather, they strengthened it. Nor did they stop him from preaching Christ; instead, they encouraged him more to preach Jesus—so much so that according to Hughes, Hart "preached Christ [...] with the arrows of death sticking in him" (29).

Nevertheless, in all these trials, Hart expressed,

> Trials may press of ev'ry Sort;
> They may be sore; they must be short.
> We now *believe*, but soon shall *view*,
> The greatest Glories God can shew.[77]

One cannot but feel Hart's longing to be free from pain and see that glory in heaven. When composing this hymn, he must have had in mind Romans 8:18, "[T]he sufferings of this present time are not worthy to be

---

76. Supplement Hymn 40, "[Sickness]," lines 1:1–4, 2:3–4, 5:1–4.
77. Hymn 21, "The wonders of Redeeming Love" ("How wond'rous are the Works of God"), stanza 9.

compared with the glory which shall be revealed in us," and 1 Peter 1:6, "[T]hough now for a little while, if necessary, you have been grieved by various trials." Reflecting on Hart's personal acquaintance with suffering, biographer Thomas Wright commented, "Few hymnists can approach Hart when he is upon the subject of sorrow" (1910, 44).

2.2.10 Hart's Hymns: "a treasury of doctrinal, practical, and experimental Christianity"[78]

As an erudite translator and poet, it was unsurprising for Hart to compose hymns. The first edition of his *Hymns*, released on July 7, 1759, contained 119 hymns. According to Hart, these hymns "were begun almost two years ago [i.e., 1757]; but have been greatly impeded and often interrupted by disorder and darkness of soul, afflictions and temptations of various kinds, and other hindrances" (i). Hart continued, "They are published not only in the same *Order*, but almost in the same *Manner* in which they were first written" (i). With this information, we can make informed suggestions as to the dates of Hart's hymns.[79] For instance, hymns numbered 4, 5, and 6 (all hymns on the Holy Spirit) were likely written in connection with Pentecost Sunday, May 29, 1757, the day he experienced evangelical conversion. Hymns numbered 12, 13, and 14 (all hymns on Christ's nativity) are therefore thought to have been written for Christmas of 1757. Then hymn number 16, called "New Year's Day," was probably written on or around January 1, 1758.

After the first edition, he continued to compose hymns. This resulted in his *Supplement* (82 hymns written between 1760 and 1761) and *Appendix* (13 hymns written between 1761 and 1765). So all-in-all, including his 7 doxologies and "Fast Hymn," Hart had 222 hymns. These "simple, but experimental and comfortable hymns," pronounced Hughes,

> have been a means of refreshing the souls of many, who have been ready to give up all soul affairs for lost; and many poor prodigals, who have long fed on husks, and have been almost starved, have ventured with him, to arise and go to their father; and say: father, I have sinned against heaven, and in thy sight, and am no more worthy to be called thy son; and with him have received their father's kiss; and have had their poor

---

78. John Towers, Advertisement in Joseph Hart, *Hymns*, 14th ed. (1799), iii.

79. I follow Wright's dating of Hart's hymns. See his table of dates of Hart's hymns for more information about the dates. *The Life of Joseph Hart*, 42.

wandering feet shod with the gospel-shoes; and the best robe (even that of Christ's righteousness) put on them; and on the right hand of their faith, the ring of everlasting Love (1768, vii).

This statement was an answer to Hart's humble wish, expressed in the preface to his *Hymns*. He desired only that through his hymns,

> Jesus of *Nazareth*, the mighty God, the Friend of Sinners, would be pleased to make them, in some Measure (weak and mean as they are) instrumental in setting forth his Glory, propagating and enforcing the Truths of his Gospel, chearing the Hearts of his People, and exalting his inestimable Righteousness, upon which alone the unworthy Author desires to rest the whole of his Salvation (ii).

Hart's expressed reason for writing hymns reveals three general features of his hymnody. First, much like other eighteenth-century Evangelical hymn writers, Hart viewed his hymns as a vehicle for evangelism. This evangelistic emphasis is best seen in his most celebrated hymn, "Come and welcome to Jesus Christ," also known by its first line, "Come, ye sinners, poor and wretched."[80] This hymn, through which many people today are familiar with Hart's name, was a means of outreach to those of his day who were influenced by hyper-Calvinism. The hyper-Calvinists, having argued that since the unregenerate are unable to believe and therefore have no duty to believe in Jesus for salvation, concluded it is unbiblical to urge the unregenerate to come to Christ by faith. By overemphasizing God's sovereignty and man's total depravity, hyper-Calvinists undermined the universal call and free offer of the gospel in evangelism.[81] J.I. Packer, in his classic book *Evangelism and the Sovereignty of God*, appealed to Hart's hymn by way of illustrating how the "belief that God is sovereign in grace does not affect the *genuineness* of the gospel invitations, or the truth of the gospel promises" (1961, 100). Packer went on to say, "The whole hymn is a magnificent statement of the gospel invitation" (100), as one can see below:

> Come, ye Sinners, poor and wretched,
> Weak and wounded, sick and sore.

---

80. Hymn 100; often altered as "Come, ye sinners, poor and needy."
81. Among the noted hyper-Calvinists of the eighteenth-century were Joseph Hussey (1660 –1726), Lewis Wayman (d. 1764), and John Brine (1703–1765). For a helpful study of hyper-Calvinism in eighteenth century England, see Gerald L. Priest (2004).

> Jesus ready stands to save you,
> Full of Pity join'd with Pow'r.
> He is able, he is able, he is able;
> He is willing: doubt no more.
>
> Ho! ye needy, come, and welcome;
> God's free Bounty glorify;
> True Belief, and true Repentance,
> Ev'ry Grace that brings us nigh,
> Without Money, without Money, without Money,
> Come to Jesus Christ, and buy!

In his advertisement to the fourteenth edition of Hart's *Hymns* (1799), the Independent minister John Towers (*ca.* 1747–1804), who knew Hart personally, commented, "Hart's hymns so exactly describe the preaching of the late Mr. Hart, that it may justly be said, in them 'he being dead, yet speaketh'" (iii). Therefore while Hart believed in God's sovereignty and man's total depravity, Hart did not hesitate in his preaching to call sinners indiscriminately to come to Jesus by faith for salvation. This shows the hymn writer Hart was not a "high-Calvinist," as Bruce Hindmarsh labeled him (2005, 245),[82] or his hymns were not "of an ultra-Calvinistic tone," as James Rigg (1891) claimed.[83]

The second important feature of Hart's hymns is that they are not only doctrinally biblical but also eminently "experimental" (or in modern parlance, experiential). This point was well explained by Towers: "Herein the doctrines of the gospel are illustrated so practically, the precepts of the word enforced so evangelically, and their effects stated so experimentally, that with propriety it may be styled, 'a treasury of doctrinal, practical, and experimental Christianity'" (1799, iii). When we analyze

---

82. In his book about John Newton, Hindmarsh identified the following six elements of high-Calvinism during the mid-eighteenth century: "[1] Election is unconditional, based on supralapsarian scheme of divine decrees; divine grace is irresistible; [2] Limited, particular atonement; [3] Eternal Justification; Christ's righteousness imputed to the elect from eternity, before the actual exercise of faith; [4] Final perseverance a corollary of election, doctrinal antinomianism sometimes implied; [5] Free offer of gospel constrained or even repudiated; faith is not properly the duty of unbelievers; [6] Charged by Arminians and other Calvinists as Antinomians" (1996, 125). The last four points do not properly apply to Hart as a hymn writer.

83. For a helpful description of ultra-Calvinism, see Grayson Carter (2001).

Hart's experiences, one cannot help but think of how his spiritual journey was an important factor in his becoming an experimental hymnist—the reason why William Gadsby highly esteemed Hart as a hymn writer (cf. Ruhl: 2013).

Hart's past painful experience in seeking and entering into a genuine conversion enabled him to relate well to those struggling with the same problem. His hymn 24, entitled "A Dialogue between a Believer and his Soul," which has an autobiographical tone, illustrates this point. In the first stanza of the hymn the believer says:

> Come, my Soul, and let us try,
> For a little Season,
> Ev'ry Burden to lay by:
> Come, and let us reason.
> What is this that casts thee down?
> Who are those that grieve thee?
> Speak, and let the worst be known;
> Speaking may relieve thee.

The second stanza is the troubled soul responding:

> *Oh! I sink beneath the Load*
> *Of my Nature's Evil;*
> *Full of Enmity to God;*
> *Captiv'd by the Devil:*
> *Restless as the troubled Seas;*
> *Feeble, faint, and fearful;*
> *Plagu'd with ev'ry sore Disease;*
> *How can I be chearful?*

This stanza echoes Hart's past experience: overburdened by sin and without hope of forgiveness, he found comfort in Christ, particularly by reflection on the Savior's suffering. Thus in stanza three, Hart aimed to encourage distressed souls, and specifically pointed them to Christ's suffering in Gethsemane as well as Golgotha:

> Think on what thy Saviour bore
> In the gloomy Garden,
> Sweating Blood at ev'ry Pore
> To procure thy Pardon!
> See him stretch'd upon the Wood,
> Bleeding, grieving, crying,

> Suff'ring all the Wrath of God;
> Groaning, gasping, dying!

This theme of Christ's suffering is a repeated motif in Hart's hymns. Whenever he felt cast down, he looked up to the cross and there found relief. Faith Cook thus rightly observed, "Perhaps more than any other hymn-writer, Hart would become the poet of the cross, and the word 'Gethsemane' occurs time and time again in his writings. The very first hymn he wrote set the theme" (2005, 154).

> Come, all ye chosen Saints of God,
> That long to feel the cleansing Blood,
> In pensive Pleasure join with Me,
> To sing of sad *Gethsemane*.
>
> In *Eden's* Garden there was Food,
> Of ev'ry kind for Man, while good;
> But, banish'd thence, we fly to Thee,
> O garden of *Gethsemane*![84]

The third and final important feature of Hart's hymns is "the practical godliness they insist upon" (*Memorial*: 1877, 4). Not only did Hart pen his hymns to promote the gospel and comfort the weary, he also intended to encourage believers unto a holy life. He desired for singers to know Christ more through his compositions. However, as he had learned himself, knowing Christ was not the only goal. The redeemed must also long to become more like their Lord and Savior, more conformed to his likeness. As Hart expressed in supplemental hymn 63, "But 'tis a Blessing few can boast / To know the holy Son." Then Hart prayed:

> Lord, help us by Thy mighty Pow'r
> To gain our constant View;
> Which is, that we may know thee more,
> And more resemble too.[85]

Not surprisingly, Hart's hymns endeared themselves to many people of his own time. His adherents were so many that more than 20,000 came to his interment. Hart died on May 24, 1768 at the age of fifty-six. After his

---

84. Hymn 1, "On the Passion," stanzas 1 and 14.
85. Supplement Hymn 63, "[Christ is holy]" ("God is a high and holy God"), lines 2:3–4, 6:1–4.

death, his brother-in-law John Hughes, who was a Baptist, succeeded him at Jewin Street Independent Church. Hart was not a Baptist as Lawrence Dodson mistakenly suggested (1997, iii), so the congregation's decision to call Hughes as their new pastor caused a split. Those who did not want to have a Baptist minister, one of them being Hart's widow, left and started a new congregation with the Independent minister John Towers as their pastor (Wilson: 1810, 3:342–43).[86] They "leased the Presbyterian meeting-house in Bartholomew Close, where he [Towers] was ordained in 1769" (Gordon/Mercer: 2004). In 1784, they moved to a chapel in the Barbican, where Towers's ministry "proved remarkably successful" (2004).[87] Towers also delivered a funeral sermon upon Hart's death, but his sermon, which was based on Job 19:21, was not printed. Hart's body was buried in Bunhill Fields, alongside the other great Nonconformists such as Thomas Goodwin, John Owen, and John Bunyan. In this graveyard, declaimed Kinsman, "the precious remains of a dear husband, an indulgent and affectionate father, pastor and friend" are deposited (Hughes: 1768, 40).

2.3 Summary

Hart's life is a gripping story of spiritual struggles, sufferings, and success. Although he grew up in a Christian home, he did not experience conversion and assurance of faith until he was about forty-five. He first became a legalist and then an antinomian; and even after his conversion, he continued to struggle with assurance of salvation, or "had many Bunyan like temptations" (Gregory: 1904, 148). Yet, once he underwent evangelical conversion in 1757, he became actively and faithfully involved in God's kingdom, continuing the spirit of the Evangelical Revival movement through his ministry, by preaching the gospel, caring for orphans, and most notably, hymn writing.

---

86. See also Hart (1851), 14.

87. From the advertisement in the tenth edition of Hart's *Hymns* (1784), we are informed Hart's widow also moved to Barbican and lodged "at No. 6. Princess Street, Barbican."

CHAPTER 3

Joseph Hart and Eighteenth-Century Evangelical Hymnody

3.1 Introduction

One of the gifts of eighteenth-century evangelicalism to Christendom is its hymns. In Mark Noll's words, hymnody is "the most enduring contribution of this movement to world Christianity as a whole" (Schwanda: 2016, xvi). In fact, the congregational singing of hymns should be added to David Bebbington's quadrilateral as one of the defining features of early evangelicalism (Bebbington: 1989, 14–17). As Noll remarked, "Eighteenth-century evangelicalism was always most characteristic when believers joined their voices in song" (Schwanda: 2016, xvi). Communal hymn-singing though is not original to evangelicals. It was practiced by the earliest Christians.[1] However, in the fourth century the Council of Laodicea decreed, "No others shall sing in the Church, save only the canonical singers, who go up into the ambo and sing from a book."[2] Original compositions by private individuals were also forbidden.[3] While the Council of Laodicea was not accepted as ecumenical and thus ought not to be viewed as universally binding, its decree gradually caused church music and singing to become an exclusive right of the clergy or professional

---

1. For an analysis of early Christian hymnody, see Ruth E. Messenger (1942), Everett Ferguson (2004), Anthony Ruff (2019), Mark A. Lamport/Benjamin K. Forrest/Vernon M. Whaley, vol. 1 (2019).

2. Synod of Laodicea (4th cen.), canon 15, trans. Henry Percival, in *Nicene and Post-Nicene Fathers*, vol. 14, ed. Philip Schaff and Henry Wace (Buffalo, NY: Christian Literature Publishing Co., 1900). See also Henry Hugh (1908).

3. Synod of Laodicea, canon 59: "No psalms composed by private individuals nor any uncanonical books may be read in the church, but only the Canonical Books of the Old and New Testaments." After the Council of Laodicea, many new songs were composed, but typically would need the approval of the bishops before being sung in the congregation.

musicians. All other forms of religious singing were done informally outside the walls of the church.[4]

During the medieval period, despite the prohibition for the laity to participate in church-singing, Jan Hus (d. 1415) encouraged all to sing together with the clerical choir. He himself composed hymns.[5] In the fifteenth century, the Council of Constance, which condemned Hus as a heretic, reiterated the Laodicea decree and sternly warned laypeople not "to sing publicly in the churches."[6] Without regard to the warning, in 1501 Hus's followers, known as Bohemian Brethren, published a collection of eighty-nine hymns, which was considered "the first Protestant hymnal" (Frank/Knouse: 2008, 44).[7]

Opposing the predominant reticence toward singing in public worship, and believing in the priesthood of all believers, Martin Luther (1483–1546), who was regarded by Ernest Ryden as "the father of evangelical hymnody," reintroduced corporate singing into the worship service in Germany (Ryden: 1959, 57).[8] In 1524 he published what came to be known as "the first reformational songbook" (Selderhuis: 2017, 261).[9] He continued producing hymns, "and thus congregational singing would be established as a permanent characteristic of Protestantism" (261).

---

4. The dominance of the Catholic church over congregational singing was not universal. The Catholic church did not always have strict control over the liturgy in all territories, leading to exceptions to rules and local variations, which is partly why, in the counter-reformation, the Pope asserted greater control and more consistent uniformity across Catholicism. See, for instance, Anthony Ruff (2019), 9–12.

5. "Of the many attributed to [Hus] probably, at least, six are his genuine works" (Schwarze: 1944, 165).

6. The entire quote reads, "If laymen are forbidden to preach and interpret the Scriptures, much more are they forbidden to sing publicly in the churches" (Ryden: 1959, 58). I could not locate the original source of the quote.

7. Cf. Helen A. Dickinson and Clarence Dickinson (1917), 129.

8. Erik Routley explained, "Hymnody as it is now understood throughout Christendom began with Martin Luther. [...] What we mean when we ascribe this historical role to Luther is that it was he who successfully propagated the idea that the communal singing of Christian songs could be an integral part of public worship. People had plenty of religious songs before his time; but not at the Mass, not at the center of worship, and not songs known all over Europe" (Richardson/Routley: 2005, 1).

9. The title of Luther's hymnal is *Etlich Cristlich lider / Lobgesang und Psalm* [Some Christian songs / Canticle and Psalm] (Wittenberg, 1524). This hymnbook contains eight hymns, four of which are by Luther. For a treatment of Luther and his hymnody, see Christopher Boyd Brown (2005) and Robin A. Leaver (2017).

The French reformer Jean Calvin (1509–1564) also exhorted his whole congregation to sing. While pastoring the French-speaking church in Strasbourg, he published the first metrical psalter in French in 1539, drawn largely from Clément Marot's work.[10] This psalter contained versifications of eighteen psalms, the Ten Commandments, the Song of Simeon, and the Apostles' Creed, all set to music.[11] Hence, although he favored metrical psalmody and did not promote hymns, he allowed the singing of songs with words taken from biblical texts other than the Psalms.[12]

In England, influenced by Calvin rather than Luther, Anglicans developed their own Psalter and generally eschewed hymns. Seventeenth-century Puritans carried over this practice.[13] For some Puritans, such as John Cotton (1585–1652), noncanonical hymns could be sung only in private worship.[14] Later, some Nonconformists made efforts to incorporate hymns in congregational singing. Richard Baxter (1615–1691) led "a movement to introduce hymns among the ejected Presbyterians (Benson: 1915, 82)."[15] Benjamin Keach (1640–1704) established congregational hymn

---

10. *Aulcuns pseaulmes et cantiques mys en chant* [Some psalms and songs arranged for singing] (Strasburg, 1539). This psalter became the basis for the Genevan Psalter of 1562. For a study of this psalter, see Richard R. Terry (1930), Cecil Mizelle Roper (1972), and Waldo Selden Pratt (1935).

11. Louis F. Benson observed, "But even at Geneva, the fountain head of Metrical Psalmody, the addiction to psalms was not absolutely exclusive" (1915, 27). Karin Maag wrote, "Following Calvin's practice, which he developed in Strasbourg, Genevans sang in unison only unaccompanied Psalms and other key scriptural texts such as the Ten Commandments (in French) in church" (2016, 21). Concerning the Apostles' Creed, it never appeared in the table of songs that were actually used in the Genevan church. That table was followed in the Reformed churches of Europe in subsequent generations. This shows how the Creed was not sung in the worship services of the Genevan church. Cf. Pierre Pidoux (1962, 134–35).

12. For a study of Calvin's view of the Psalms, see Herman J. Selderhuis (2007).

13. In the words of Cotton, "Not onely the Psalmes of David, but any other spirituall Songs recorded in Scripture, may be lawfully be sung in Christian Churches, as the song of Moses, and Asaph, Heman and Ethan, Solomon and Hezekiah, Habacuck and Zachary, Hanna and Deborah, Mary and Elizabeth, and the like" (1647, 15).

14. Cotton put it this way: "Wee grant also, that any private Christian, who hath a gift to frame a spirituall Song, may both frame it, and sing it privately, for his own private comfort" (1647, 15). Cotton left England in 1633 for New England, where he operated as a Congregationalist no longer within the Church of England, and hence his views expressed in a book published in 1647 about the use of various songs beyond the psalter would have limited relevance to what had been or would be permitted or practiced in the Church of England.

15. See Richard Baxter (1692). This book includes *Te Deum*.

singing among Particular Baptists.[16] But it was through the effort of the Independent Isaac Watts (1674-1748) that church hymn-singing became widely spread throughout England and into the British colonies, such as found in New England. After the publication of his *Hymns and Spiritual Songs* in 1707, England began to witness a hymn explosion among evangelical churches. Joseph Hart (1712-1768) contributed to this explosion. If Watts's hymns helped ignite the flames of the Evangelical Revival, which during this time affected many denominations, Hart's hymns continued to fuel the revival. In his article "The Defining Role of Hymns in Early Evangelicalism," Noll stated, "Nothing was more central to the evangelical revival than the singing of new hymns written in praise of the goodness, mercy, and grace of God" (2004, 4).

Hart's most significant contribution to the evangelical movement was his hymnody. Although some scholars have studied Hart's hymns before,[17] this chapter will examine his hymns in light of eighteenth-century English hymnody by comparing and contrasting him with some key representatives of the evangelical hymn writers of this period. The study will begin with Isaac Watts, often regarded as the father of English hymnody, not in the sense of being the first to write hymns but the first to effectively establish hymn singing among English speaking Protestant churches. Then the following hymn writers—Charles and John Wesley (Methodist hymnody), Anne Steele (Baptist hymnody), and William Cowper and John Newton (Anglican hymnody)—will be treated, showing their similarities and differences with Hart. The chapter will conclude with William Romaine to demonstrate how not all early evangelicals were supportive of hymn singing in the church. Nonetheless, the study will show how hymnody became an earmark of evangelicals as a group. Hart was a part of this group and his hymns were his undertaking to continue the quintessence of the Evangelical Revival.

---

16. See Benjamin Keach (1691). For a study of his hymnody, consult James P. Carnes (1984), Allan Clifford (1985), and Hugh Martin (1961).

17. See Erik Routley (1951), Peter C. Rae (1988), Robert W. Oliver (2000), and Faith Cook (2005).

3.2 "The Golden Age of Hymns": Eighteenth-Century Evangelical Hymnody

The century into which evangelicalism emerged has been dubbed "the golden age of hymns" (*Golden Age*: 1991) or "the century of divine songs" (Sampson: 1943, 37). The term evangelicalism came from the word "evangelical," which became virtually synonymous with the appellation "Protestant," or more specifically "Lutheran," during the sixteenth-century Protestant Reformation.[18] In the eighteenth century, however, the designation "evangelical" came to be associated with the Evangelical Revival, which started in the 1730s. Eventually, it became "the standard description of the doctrines or ministers of the revival movement, whether inside or outside the Church of England" (Bebbington: 1989, 1). In his monumental work *Evangelicalism in Modern Britain: A History from the 1730s to the 1980s*, Bebbington identified four defining characteristics of the evangelical religion:

> *conversionism*, the belief that lives need to be changed; *activism*, the expression of the gospel in effort; *biblicism*, a particular regard for the Bible; and what may be called *crucicentrism*, a stress on the sacrifice of Christ on the cross. Together they form a quadrilateral of priorities that is the basis of Evangelicalism (2–3).

While Bebbington's quadrilateral is "the most serviceable general definition of 'evangelical'" (Noll: 2001, 185) and has been widely accepted as "the standard definition of evangelicalism" (Larsen: 2007, 1), it lacks a sufficient description of evangelicals. For instance, as will become apparent in this chapter, his quadrilateral needs to be expanded to include communal hymn singing. Many of these evangelicals were hymn writers, and their movement as a whole was a major reason for the shift from metrical psalms to hymns in English liturgy, both inside and outside the Church of England. Brian Wibberley credited the Tractarian (Oxford) Movement for this shift within the Anglican Church, arguing how "it was not until the Oxford Movement originated, that hymnody began to be fostered within the Establishment" (1934, 131). But Robin Leaver has argued, "the transition from metrical psalmody to hymnody was affected not so

---

18. *The New Cassell's German Dictionary* defines *evangelisch* as "evangelical, Protestant, Lutheran" (New York: Funk & Wagnalls, 1971), 145. For a discussion of the definition of "evangelical," see Mark A. Noll (2003), 16–21 and Jonathan M. Yeager (2013), 1–4.

much by the ideals of nineteenth-century Tractarians as by the practice of eighteenth-century Evangelicals, who were innovative with regard to the liturgical use of hymns" (McCart: 1998, vii).

To stress the importance of hymns in the early evangelical movement, Noll wrote,

> It is difficult to discover any significant event, person, or structure of early evangelicalism that did not involve the singing of hymns. It is likewise difficult to discover any significant experience of singing where the hymns had not been freshly written by the evangelicals themselves (or by Isaac Watts who befriended them and whose hymns they embraced enthusiastically from the start) (2004, 4).

Watts in particular is the poet to whom all "subsequent hymn writers, even when they surpass him, are indebted" (Eskew/McElrath: 1980, 119), and thus provided an important model for Hart. He was called "the liberator of English hymnody" by Erik Routley (1959, 64), but he can also be seen as the reformer of English metrical psalmody.

3.2.1 Isaac Watts: the Reformer of English Metrical Psalmody

Watts was born and raised in a nonconformist family. His parents were members of an Independent church in Southampton, England. During the sixteenth and seventeenth centuries, the singing of metrical translations of the Psalms in congregational worship was prevalent in the Church of England and among Calvinistic dissenting churches.[19] The psalter in general use at this time was that of Thomas Sternhold and John Hopkins. The completed edition of 1562, while containing mostly metrical psalms, also included canticles and hymns, such as *Veni Creator Spiritus* ("Come, Creator Spirit") and *Te Deum* ("We praise thee, O God"), revealing the early adaptation of Latin hymnody into English liturgy. After Nahum Tate and Nicholas Brady published their *New Version of the Psalms of David* in 1696, churches gradually began to use their new metrical psalter, while Sternhold and Hopkins became the "Old Version." Starting in the *Supplement to the New Version* (1700), this psalter was accompanied by a limited number of hymns, including the Christmas carol "While Shepherds watch'd their Flocks by Night," a paraphrase of Luke 2:8–15. Nevertheless, during Watts's adolescence both the Church of England and Calvinist

---

19. "There are some churches," wrote Watts, "that utterly disallow singing" (1707, 233).

dissenting churches were psalm singing as a whole. The shift from psalm singing to hymn singing can be attributed to Watts's successful "Reformation of Psalmodie amongst the Churches" (Watts: 1707, xiii). His "version of the psalms became very popular and was in a large measure responsible for the decline in the use of the older metrical psalters" (Leaver: 1978, 59).

In 1707, the year England and Scotland officially became Great Britain, Watts published his *Hymns and Spiritual Songs*, to which he attached an epilogue, "A Short Essay Towards the Improvement of Christian Psalmody: Or, An Enquiry how the Psalms of *David* ought to be translated into Christian Songs, and how lawful and necessary it is to compose other Hymns according to the clearer Revelations of the Gospel, for the Use of the Christian Church." As evident in the essay's title, the first improvement had to do with translation. Watts complained about the way English psalmody contained "something in it so extremely Jewish and cloudy that darkens our Sight of God the Saviour" (v). This was why for him "the greatest part of Christians find but little Edification or Comfort in it" (233). His solution to this imperfection, as he called it, was to Christianize part of the psalmody. That is, the "cloudy and typical Expressions of the legal dispensation should be turned into Evangelical Language, according to the Explications of the New Testament" (246). And wherever one "finds the Person or Offices of our Lord Jesus Christ in Prophecy, they ought rather to be translated in a way of History, and those Evangelical Truths should be stript of their Vail of Darkness, and drest in such Expressions that Christ may appear in 'em to all that sing" (247). To that end, Watts produced his own psalter in 1719, *The Psalms of David Imitated in the Language of the New Testament*, which included "Joy to the World," his paraphrase of the second part of Psalm 98, labeled as "The Messiah's Coming and Kingdom."

In Joseph Hart's hymn called "All my springs are in Thee," a direct quote from Psalm 87:7, Hart employed Watts's method of Christologizing Psalms:

> O my Jesus, thou art Mine,
> With all thy Grace and Pow'r;
> I am now, and shall be Thine,
> When Time shall be no more.
> Thou reviv'st me by thy Death;
> Thy Blood from Guilt has set me free;

> My fresh Springs of Hope, and faith,
> And Love, are all in Thee.[20]

Here singers can notice the liberty Hart took to interpret the pronoun "thee" in Psalm 87:7 to refer to Christ, when the context suggests the antecedent of that pronoun to be "Zion," which Watts understood as Christ's church.[21]

Believing congregational songs should be relevant to our present circumstances, Watts proposed to contemporize metrical psalms. He thought the Psalms "ought to be translated in such a Manner as we have reason to believe David would have compos'd 'em if he had lived in our day" (1707, 252). By way of example, "*Judah* and *Israel* may be called *England* and *Scotland*, and the Land of *Canaan* may be translated into *Great Britain*" (1707, 246).[22] This "Method of translating ancient Songs into Christian Worship" (245) is noticeable in Watts's paraphrases of Psalms 67 and 100:

> Shine Mighty God, on *Britain* shine
> With beams of healing Grace,
> Our waiting Eyes would fain behold
> Thy reconciled Face.
>
> Sing to the Lord with joyful Voice,
> Let every Land his Name adore,
> The *British-Isles* shall send the Noise
> Across the Ocean to the Shore.[23]

For Watts, the Psalms "are given as a Pattern to be imitated in our Composures, rather than as the precise and invariable Matter of our

---

20. Hymn 72, "All my Springs are in thee. Psal. lxxxvii. 7" ("Bless the Lord, my Soul; and raise"), stanza 3. All of Hart's hymns are quoted from *Hymns, &c. Composed on Various Subjects*, 5th ed. (London, 1767), the last edition before his death.

21. Compare Hart's hymn 72 to Watts's paraphrase of Psalm 87 in *The psalms of David Imitated in the Language of the New Testament* (1719). For other instances in which Hart Christologized portions of Psalms, see his hymns 43, 69, 81, 108, and supplement hymn 71.

22. "Where there are Sentences, or whole Psalms, that can very difficulty be accommodated to our Times," explained Watts, "they may be utterly omitted. Such is Psal. 150. part of the 38, 45, 48, 60, 68, 81, 108, and some others, as well as a great part of the Song of Solomon" (247).

23. Respectively, "The Churches Increase and Prosperity" (Psalm 67) and "Praise to the Lord from Nations" (Psalm 100), in *Hymns and Spiritual Songs* (1707).

Psalmody" (1707, 252). By "imitated" Watts "meant that he sought to write words which would do the same thing for people of his time and for his nation" (Stackhouse: 2019, 205). Hart applied Watts's principle of imitation to his hymn writing. His three hymns on death, 41 to 43 in the Supplement, were occasioned by the sudden death of King George II in 1760, the year Hart became pastor of the Independent congregation at Jewin Street. His biographer Thomas Wright explained,

> Hart was probably a spectator of the funeral solemnities, and heard the herald at arms proclaim the many illustrious titles and honours with which the deceased sovereign had been invested. Funeral sermons of the laudatory sort fluttered from the Press like the leaves of Vallombrosa (1910, 64).

Hart used this occasion to warn his people:

> Ye Sons of Men, the Warning take.
> A Moment brings us all to Dust.
> Awake from Sin; from Sloth awake.
> Reflect, in what you put your Trust.
>
> Life is a Lilly, fair today;
> Tomorrow into th' Oven thrown.
> Health soon will fail, and Strength decay.
> No Help in Pow'r; in Riches none.
>
> Ah! what avail the pompous Pall?
> The sable Stoles, the plumed Herse?
> To rot within some sacred Wall;
> Or wound a Stone with lying Verse?[24]

Undoubtedly King George had a splendid pall and well-decorated hearse, but Hart wanted the singers of his hymns to realize this fancy funeral had no value without Christ. For Hart,

> Blessed are They, and only They,
> Who in the Lord the Saviour, die.
> Their Bodies wait Redemption's Day;
> And sleep in Peace where e'er they lie.[25]

---

24. Supplement Hymn 41, "Death," stanzas 1-3. Sable stoles are black robes.
25. Supplement Hymn 41, stanza 5.

Concerned too with the poetry of metrical psalmody, Watts felt Psalms ought to be translated not as though they are to be read but to be sung. He reasoned,

> If it be the Duty of the Churches to sing Psalms, they must necessarily be turn'd into such a sort of Verse and Metre as will best fit them for the whole Church to join in the Worship: Now this will be very different from a Translation of the Original Language word for word; for the Lines must be confin'd to a certain Number of Syllables, and the Stanza or Verse to a certain Number of Lines, that so the Tune being short the People may be acquainted with it, and be ready to sing without difficulty. [...] Where there are any dark Expressions, and difficult to be understood in the Hebrew Songs, these should be left out in our Psalmody, or at least made very plain by a Paraphrase (1707; 241, 246).

The "basic hermeneutic" of the metrical psalters in use before and during Watts's time was "to reproduce as closely as possible in meter and rhyme the vocabulary and meaning of Scripture" (Leaver: 1978, 57). The Puritans in New England, with their desire to generate a more accurate metrical translation of the Psalms, published *The Whole Booke of Psalmes Faithfully Translated into English Metre* (1640), commonly known as *The Bay Psalm Book*. The translators' preface to this psalter provides a context for Watts's concern:

> Neither let any think, that for the meetre sake wee have taken liberty or poeticall licence to depart from the true and proper sense of Davids words in the Hebrew verses, noe; but it hath beene on part of our religious care and faithfull indeavour, to keepe close to the originall text.

> If therefore the verses are not always so smooth and elegant as some may desire or expect; let them consider that Gods Altar needs not our pollishings: Ex. 20. For wee have respected rather a plaine translation, then to smooth our verses with sweetness of any paraphrase, and soe have attended Conscience rather then Elegance, fidelity rather then poety, in translating the Hebrew words into English language, and Davids poetry into english meetre (Preface, n.p.).

In light of this quote, Benjamin Kolodziej asserted, "Although *The Bay Psalm Book* was an American Puritan publication, these sentiments reflect a general English piety which 'attended Conscience rather than Elegance'" (Kolodziej: 2004, 237). Concerned more with the aesthetics of metrical psalmody than its accuracy to the original, Watts presented a new system of versifying the Psalms in much freer translations. Consequently, many of his metrical psalms from 1719 can be properly categorized as hymns, such as "Jesus shall reign where'er the sun" (based on Psalm 72:5–19) and "Our God, our help in ages past" (drawn from Psalm 90:1–6).

Although Hart did not produce psalms as Watts did, he followed this hermeneutical principle whenever he devised a hymn based either on a particular verse in the Psalms or on a scriptural text in general. For instance, notice how Hart loosely and aesthetically paraphrased Psalm 34:10, "The young lions do lack, and suffer hunger: but they that seek the LORD shall not want any good thing":[26]

> Proud Lions, that boast
> When lusty and young,
> Soon find, to their Cost,
> Self-Confidence wrong:
> Tormented with Hunger
> They feel their Strength vain;
> For Famine is stronger,
> And gnaws them with Pain.
>
> But Lambs are preserv'd,
> Tho' helpless in Kind;
> When Lions are starv'd,
> *They* Nourishment find
> Their Shepherd upholds them,
> When faint, in his Arms;
> And feeds them, and folds them;
> And guards them from Harms.[27]

Finally, Watts's view of singing as chiefly speaking "our own Hearts and our Words to God," led him to compose "Hymns of Humane Composure according to the Spirit and Doctrines of the Gospel" (1707; 243, 270).[28] In total he produced "nearly 700 hymns and psalm paraphrases" (Crookshank: 2013). He believed songs should "speak our own Experience

---

26. All Scripture quotations in this chapter, unless otherwise noted, are taken from the King James Bible, the version Joseph Hart utilized in his writings.
27. Hymn 81, "The young Lions do lack, and suffer Hunger […]" ("Ye Lambs of Christ's fold"), stanzas 4–5.
28. "The Church of England approves this Practice [of singing hymns of human composure], as appears in those spiritual Songs at the End of the old Translation of the

of divine Things, especially our religious joy" (Watts: 1707, 257). Here he differed from Calvin who saw singing primarily as God speaking to us in his word and us speaking his word back to him in song. For Watts, songs "are generally Expressions of our own Experiences, or of [God's] glories" (243). Commenting on the substance of Watts's hymns, hymnologist Louis Benson observed, "The great theme of the Hymn proper became the Gospel in the full width of its range, including man's deliverance from the terrors of the law. The Hymn thus became primarily an expression of Christian experience" (1915, 208).

This emphasis on the Christian experience of the gospel attracted leaders of the Evangelical Movement to Watts's hymns. Methodist preacher George Whitefield (1714–1770) employed Watts's hymns in his revival meetings. His *Collection of Hymns for Social Worship* (1753), which was particularly designed for the use of his Tabernacle congregation in London, contained hymns by various writers, such as Watts, whose hymns dominated the collection (cf. Noll: 2016). Joseph Hart, who occasionally attended Whitefield's Tabernacle, would have been familiar with Watts's hymns through this collection.

In New England, churches influenced by the Great Awakening also embraced Watts's hymns, which were "more in consonance with the revival preaching and more expressive of the evangelical fervor" (Benson: 1915, 163). Writing on May 22, 1744, the Congregationalist minister Jonathan Edwards (1703–1758), a key leader of the awakening, recounted his Northampton congregation's warm reception of Watts's hymns in a letter to Rev. Benjamin Colman, May 22, 1744:

> It has been our manner in this congregation, for more than two years past, in the summer time, when we sing three times upon the sabbath, to sing an hymn, or part of a hymn of Dr. [Isaac] Watts', the last time, viz.: at the conclusion of the afternoon exercise. I introduced it principally because I saw in the people a very general inclination to it. Indeed, I was not properly he that introduced it: they began it in my absence on a journey; and seemed to be greatly pleased with it (1998, 144).

While consenting to the singing of Watts's hymns, Edwards was concerned when he returned to his congregation from a long journey,

---

Psalm-Book [i.e., the Sternhold and Hopkins psalter], and some Churches among the Dissenters" (273).

and he learned they "sang nothing else [but Watts's compositions], and neglected the Psalms wholly" as found in the *New England Psalm Book* (1651),[29] which during this time was the standard song book of New England Congregational churches. Edwards voiced his frustration this way: "When I came home I disliked not their making some use of the hymns, but did not like their setting aside the Psalms (1998, 144)." Whereas the customary practice of the time was to sing psalms only, his congregation, on the other hand, had tended to sing hymns only in his absence. Taking the middle ground, Edwards favored the singing of both psalms and hymns and thereby became one of the first Congregational ministers in New England to use hymns for corporate worship. George Claghorn noted, "Edwards took an active interest in music, particularly because singing then as now, often went hand in hand with revivalism" (143). For Edwards "music, especially sacred music, has a powerful efficacy to soften the heart into tenderness" (1992, 224). No wonder therefore why Edwards took great interest in Watts's hymns, whose hymns underlined the significance of human affections in Christian life. Eventually, Watts "over took the Bay Psalm Book in popularity among New England congregations" (Stackhouse: 2019, 201).

Watts's hymns also appealed to the Anglican priest John Wesley, who while in Colonial America as a missionary, published his first hymnal, *A Collection of Psalms and Hymns* (1737). Designed for mission work in the colony of Georgia, this hymnbook contained seventy songs, half of which were by Watts. Regarded by Methodist scholar Carlton Young and others as "the first Anglican hymnal,"[30] this collection did not include any of Charles Wesley's hymns, simply because Charles did not start hymn writing until after his conversion in 1738. Because during this time congregational hymn singing was "an unofficial, and, if anybody cared to press the point, an illegal activity in the Church of England" (Routley: 1959, 79),[31] John was charged with "introducing into the church

---

29. Or *The Psalms Hymns and Spiritual Songs of the Old and New Testament, Faithfully Translated into English Metre* (1651). The *Bay Psalm Book* (1640) was extensively revised in 1651 by Henry Dunster and Richard Lyon, and this became the standard edition during Edwards's time.

30. Carlton Young, "John Wesley's Collection of Psalms and Hymns (1737)," in *The Canterbury Dictionary of Hymnology*, http://www.hymnology.co.uk/j/john-wesleys-collection-of-psalms-and-hymns-(1737) (accessed February 9, 2021).

31. McCart argued, "The central issue regarding the introduction of hymns was their

and service [...] compositions of Psalms and Hymns not inspected or authorized by any proper judicature" (Ward/Heitzenrater: 1998, 555). Hymnologist Erik Routley explained, "The rubrics provided for canticles, psalms, and anthems, but not for hymns in the services of public worship appointed in the Book of Common Prayer" (1959, 79). However, when Thomas Robinson (1749–1813) was questioned by his fellow Anglicans as to why he allowed the singing of hymns in the church service when he was a curate in Cambridgeshire, he replied and argued, "Where there is no law, there is no transgression. Our cannons and rubrics prescribe no exclusive matters for singing" (Vaughan: 1816, 50). In other words, for Robinson the Book of Common Prayer's silence regarding hymn singing did not mean churches were forbidden to sing hymns. Despite the restriction, out of the needs of their congregants some Anglican clergy composed hymns for the use of their people.[32] The Wesley brothers, taking up the banner of Watts, greatly contributed to the development of hymn singing in the Church of England, especially among the congregations Hart knew and attended.

3.2.2 John and Charles Wesley: Methodist Hymnody

Unlike Watts, the Wesley brothers were trained and ministered in the Established Church. In 1729 John (who was just ordained a priest in the previous year) and his brother Charles started the Holy Club.[33] Members of this religious society, including Whitefield, who underwent a conversion experience in 1735, came to be known as Methodists because of

---

legal status in the tires of the Book of Common Prayer. Although the use of metrical forms (psalms, canticles, and hymns) in congregational worship had been a part of the liturgical life of the Church of England since the early days of the Reformation, toward the end of the eighteenth century many began to question whether specific collections had been duly authorized for such use" (1998, xv).

32. McCart noted, "The blatant disregard of the rubrics of the Book of Common Prayer and the Injunctions of 1559, with regard to the use of hymns within the liturgy of the church, by a considerable number of clergy indicates that the needs of the congregation exceeded the legal demands for conformity to the established formularies of the church and that the clergy willingly attempted to meet those needs rather than blindly obeying the formularies" (1998, 117). See also the three exceptions to the restriction identified by Routley (1959), 79–80.

33. A religious organization, the Holy Club promoted piety through Bible study, prayer, fasting, Communion, and other religious activities. For a background study of the Holy Club, see John Wesley (1774).

their methodical approach to spiritual disciplines. In 1735, the same year Charles was ordained to priesthood, he and John went to the Georgia colony to minister to the colonists and spread Anglicanism especially among the Native Americans. Their mission work did not turn out successfully, forcing them to return to England—first Charles in 1736, followed by his brother in 1738. Yet, during this mission trip they met the Moravians, who profoundly impacted their pursuit of personal conversion and passion for hymns. For these Moravians hymn singing was "an expression of the state of their hearts as well as a means to strengthen fellowship" (Peuker: 2011, 623).

Back in England, on May 21, 1738, Charles experienced a gospel conversion, which he expressed this way: "I now found myself at peace with God, and rejoiced in hope of loving Christ."[34] Three days later, John had the same experience. Following the example of Whitefield, in 1739 the Wesley brothers began preaching justification by faith alone in the open air. That same year, two places of worship were established for their followers: the New Room in Bristol (the very first Methodist worship place) and the Foundery in London. This event marked the beginning of Methodism, a spiritual renewal within the Anglican Church. One needs to realize that during "Charles's lifetime and the majority of John's, Methodism was not its own denomination but rather an evangelical movement rooted in the Church of England" (Stalcup: 2019, 210). Although the split started in 1784, Methodism did not officially separate from the Anglican Church until after John's death (1791).

One of the peculiarities of the Methodist movement was "the lively singing of new hymns" (210). Thus, in a sense Methodism was a liturgical reformation to introduce hymns into Anglican worship. With no intent to disaffiliate from the Established Church, the Wesley brothers encouraged their followers to attend not only the Methodist societies but also the local parish churches. As a result, their members had "two distinct types of singing." Thomas McCart wrote,

> In the societies, the faithful sang the powerful hymnody of the Wesleys and other evangelical authors. At the Sunday parish service, however,

---

34. *The Journal of Charles Wesley* (May 21, 1738), *Wesley Center Online*, http://wesley.nnu.edu/charles-wesley/the-journal-of-charles-wesley-1707-1788/the-journal-of-charles-wesley-may-1-august-31-1738/ (accessed February 2, 2021).

they sang the metrical psalms of either the 'Old Version' or the *New Version*. Such could not continue for long, and by 1757 the use of hymns had expanded beyond the meeting house to the Church of England (1998, 28).[35]

Early Methodism did not really differ so much from the Established Church in theology as in emphasis. Given what John and Charles had gone through, they stressed the necessity for personal conversion and assurance of faith, two underscorings which would become hallmarks of evangelicalism (Stalcup: 2019, 211). These emphases are clearly reflected in Charles's hymns. He wrote more than 6,500 hymns, many of which are evangelistic. His hymn "Before Preaching to the Colliers in Leicestershire" (known by its first line, "Jesu, thou all-redeeming Lord") captures well his evangelistic passion. Urgently calling sinners to believe in Jesus for their salvation, Charles proclaimed:

> The God of love, to earth he came,
> That you might come to heaven;
> Believe, believe in Jesu's name,
> And all your sins forgiven.
>
> Believe, that Jesus died for thee;
> And sure as he hath died,
> Thy debt is paid, thy soul is free,
> And thou art justified.[36]

In another hymn, Wesley urged sinners to come to Christ with the following words:

> For you the purple Current flow'd,
> In Pardons from his wounded Side;
> Languish'd for you th' Eternal God,
> For you the Prince of Glory dy'd;
> *Believe*; and all your Guilt's forgiven,
> *Only Believe*—and yours is Heaven![37]

---

35. While more and more local parishes were using hymns, hymn singing did not become officially approved until 1820.

36. The hymn first appeared in *Hymns and Sacred Poems*, vol. 1 (Bristol, 1749). For a textual study of the hymn, see John Julian (1907), 602, and Randy L. Maddox, *Charles Wesley's Published Verse*, https://divinity.duke.edu/initiatives/cswt/charles-published-verse.

37. "Christ the Friend of Sinners" ("Where shall my wond'ring Soul begin?"), as in

The line "Jesus died for thee" and the repeated phrase "for you" implies the author's Arminian view of the atonement—that Christ died for all.[38] This doctrine distinguishes him from Calvinist Hart, who like Charles, used hymns for evangelistic purposes but was careful in his offer of the gospel, avoiding such an Arminian expression like "Jesus died for thee." In his hymn labeled "Salvation by Christ alone," the contrast with Wesley is evident in the way Hart presented the gospel to sinners:

> Fly then, awaken'd Sinners, fly;
> Your Case admits no Stay;
> The Fountain's open'd now for Sin.
> Come, wash your Guilt away.
>
> See how from Jesu's wounded Side
> The Water flows, and Blood!
> If you but touch that purple Tide,
> You make your Peace with God.
>
> Only by Faith in Jesu's Wounds
> The Sinner gets Release:
> No other Sacrifice for Sin
> Will God accept but this.[39]

With Zechariah 13:1 in mind, Hart pleaded with sinners to fly in repentance to the fountain where they can wash their guilt away by Jesus' blood. "If you but touch that purple Tide" is probably an allusion to the woman suffering from chronic bleeding who said, "If I may but touch his [Jesus'] garment, I shall be whole" (Matt 9:21). Hart's point is this: sinners cannot have peace with God until they believe in Christ, or until they touch by faith that "purple Tide," which in this context refers to Christ's blood.[40] In his article "Joseph Hart and His Hymns," Peter Rae observed,

---

John and Charles Wesley, *Hymns and Sacred Poems* (1739), 101. For an analysis of this hymn, see Fenner/Najapfour (2020), 3–10.

38. Charles Wesley's Arminian theology is evident in many of his hymns, some of which were published in the periodical his brother John founded in 1778, *The Arminian Magazine: Consisting of Extracts and Original Treatises on Universal Redemption*. But for a theological counterpoint, see Charles Spurgeon's contrasting assessment of Wesley's hymns in "Exposition of the Doctrines of Grace," delivered April 11, 1861 in *Metropolitan Tabernacle Pulpit*, vol. 7 (London: Passmore & Alabaster, 1862), 297–304.

39. Hymn 8, "Salvation by Christ alone" ("How can ye hope, deluded Souls"), stanzas 5–7.

40. The word "purple" appears three times in Hart's hymns and it always refers

"Hart is often wrongly accused of being an extreme [or hyper] Calvinist, but he has a well-developed sense of the need to invite sinners to accept Christ and close with the offer of salvation" (1988, 36).[41]

When addressing his fellow believers, however, Hart did not hesitate to say, "Now look up with Faith, and see / Him that bled for you and me,"[42] or

> Saints, from the Garden to the Cross
> Your conqu'ring Lord pursue.
> Who, dearly to redeem your Loss,
> Groan'd, bled, and died for You;[43]

A similar utterance is found in Hart's hymn on the Lord's Supper, which is intended for Christians:

> This pure and heav'nly Gift
> Within our Hearts to move;
> The dying Saviour left,
> These Tokens of His love:
> Which seem to say, "While this ye do,
> Remember Him that died for you."[44]

Likewise, his hymn on Christ's Ascension, directed to believers, has this stanza:

> Sinners! rejoice; He died for you;
> For you prepares a place;
> Sends down His Spirit to guide you through,
> With every gift of grace.[45]

---

to Christ's blood. See hymn 59, "The High-Priest," and supplement hymn 9, "[For the Lord's Supper]."

41. Hart's most familiar gospel invitation hymn is number 100, "Come, and welcome, to Jesus Christ" ("Come, ye sinners, poor and wretched").

42. Hymn 39, "The Sinner's Hope" ("Come, ye humble Sinner-Train"), lines 2:1–2.

43. Supplement hymn 73, "Salvation to the Lamb" ("Poor sinner, come, cast off thy Fear"), lines 2:1–4.

44. Supplement hymn 16 ("When Jesus undertook"), stanza 4. Hart has twenty hymns on the Lord's Supper in the Supplement. None of these hymns have given titles. See also supplement hymn 7 ("Join ev'ry tongue to sing").

45. Supplement hymn 35, "Christ's Ascension" ("Now for a Theme of thankful Praise"), stanza 5.

Early Methodists also stressed assurance of faith, or what Charles Wesley referred to as "the Moravian doctrine that a man cannot have peace without assurance of his pardon."[46] Wesley's "Hymn to the Holy Ghost" vividly demonstrates this doctrine by which believers can know they are saved:

> Thou art Thyself the Seal;
> I more than Pardon feel,
> Peace, Unutterable Peace,
> Joy that Ages ne'er can move,
> Faith's Assurance, Hope's Increase,
> All the Confidence of Love![47]

One can notice how Wesley felt more than pardon, because he also felt the results of divine forgiveness such as peace, joy, and faith's assurance. While this hymn communicates Charles's own experience, it is designed to be sung by all Christians. This, then, is another distinct feature of his hymns: they are generally self-aware, as is seen in his frequent use of the personal pronouns "I," "my," and "me" throughout his hymnody. As James Sallee pointed out,

> Charles Wesley's hymns are also basically autobiographical. They portray in a simple and direct way his own spiritual history, which was similar to the experience of thousands of people of all times. In essence, his hymns relate the spiritual unrest of a convicted soul bound by sin, an instantaneous release through conversion, and the assurance of salvation (1978, 14).[48]

Two days after Charles's conversion in 1738, he wrote what he called "an hymn upon my conversion."[49] That autobiographical hymn, which he left untitled in his journal, was "Christ the Friend of Sinners," best known by its opening words "Where Shall My Wondering Soul Begin?"[50] The following year, to celebrate the first anniversary of his conversion, he penned "For the Anniversary Day of One's Conversion," published in hymnals today beginning with the line "O for a Thousand Tongues to

---

46. *The Journal of Charles Wesley* (May 1, 1738).
47. *Hymns and Sacred Poems* (London, 1739), 112 ("Hear, Holy Spirit, hear").
48. See also Benson (1915), 249.
49. *The Journal of Charles Wesley* (May 23, 1738).
50. *Hymns and Sacred Poems* (1739), 101.

sing."⁵¹ Although Wesley made this hymn primarily to commemorate his conversion, he intended it to be sung by others. It begins with a doxology, "Glory to God," and continues with a testimony of Charles's new life in Christ:

> I felt my Lord's atoning blood
> Close to *my* soul applied;
> *Me, me* he lov'd—the Son of God
> For *me*, for *me* he died!
>
> I found, and own'd his promise true,
> Ascertain'd of *my* part,
> My pardon pass'd in heaven I *knew*
> When written on my heart.

The simultaneous occurrence of the words "felt" and "knew" are characteristic of much of Charles's hymnody. These twin words appear also in his hymn of conversion: "Should know, should feel my Sins forgiven."⁵² For Wesley, who was described by Donald Davie as "a poet of vehement feeling" (1993, 57), one should not merely know the gospel but also feel it. That is, the knowledge of God's truth and experience of its effects must go together. So to feel, in this context, is to experience the effects. This experiential emphasis is not only typical of early Methodist hymnody but of evangelical hymnody in general. The same stress occurs in Hart's hymn on "Praying for Fruitfulness,"

> But I from Month to Month complain.
> I feel no Warmth; no Fruits I see.
> I look for Life; but dead remain:
> 'Tis Winter all the Year with Me.⁵³

Hart saw in his own life the danger of having head knowledge of the gospel without heart-felt experience of its power. Hence, in one of his hymns, Hart prayed to the Holy Spirit,

---

51. *Hymns and Sacred Poems* (1740), 120–23, originally beginning "Glory to God, and praise, and love"; later truncated to begin with stanza 7.
52. "Where Shall My Wondering Soul Begin?" in *Hymns and Sacred Poems* (1739).
53. Appendix hymn 5, "[Praying for Fruitfulness]" ("Jesus, to Thee I make my Moan"), stanza 5.

> Warm our cold Hearts with heav'nly Heat,
> And set our Souls on Fire.
>
> Pray, thou for Us; that we thro' Faith
> May feel th' Effects of Jesu's Death:
> Thro' Faith that works by Love.[54]

Interestingly, Hart's account of his conversion in 1757 resembled those of Charles and John, all drawing special attention to their experience of the effects of their rebirth. First, Charles: "I felt great peace and joy";[55] second, John: "I felt my heart strangely warmed";[56] then Hart: "I felt myself melting away into a strange Softness of Affection. […] I enjoyed sweet Peace in my Soul" (1767, xi–xii). Later, their testimony would "be seen as a description of a typical experience of evangelical conversion, although there has been considerable discussion as to whether it should rather be seen as an expression of assurance of salvation" (Randall: 2006, 205).[57] The resemblance between the three was no doubt due in part to their mutual conversion under the ministry of the Moravians, who contributed tremendously to "the spiritual origins of English Evangelicalism" (Sheldrake: 2005, 447). Descendants of the Bohemian Brethren, the Moravians were shaped by the Pietism of their leader Nikolaus Ludwig von Zinzendorf (1700–1760), who was himself a hymn writer. Reacting to the dead orthodoxy or formalism within the Lutheran church, Pietism reclaimed "the experiential dimension of the Christian faith" (Carlson: 2011, 673). Zinzendorf's "theology of the heart" became central to the Moravians, "according to which a personal experience of faith was more important than a rational understanding of dogma" (Peuker: 2011, 623).[58] In light of this background, it is not surprising therefore to see a strong emphasis on the necessity of personal, heart-felt experience of faith in the hymns of both Wesley and Hart.

---

54. Hymn 6, "Another [hymn to the Holy Spirit]" ("Descend from Heav'n, celestial Dove"), lines 1:5–6, 5:4–6.

55. *The Journal of Charles Wesley* (May 25, 1738).

56. *The Journal of the Reverend John Wesley*, vol. 1 (New York: Carlton and Phillips, 1855), 74.

57. Here, Randall is referring to John's conversion but his statement can be well applied to Charles's and Hart's conversion.

58. For a treatment of Zinzendorf's "theology of the heart," see chapter 2 of Craig D. Atwood (2004).

Their insistence that the gospel truth must be both known and felt might have been occasioned also by rationalism, which regarded "reason as the ultimate authority in religion."[59] Originating in the seventeenth century, rationalism privileged philosophical reason over religious experience for arriving at certainty in knowledge. It would thus reject Wesley's claim that God's truths can be known and felt. In contrast to this epistemological position, Wesley as well as Hart maintained the imperative coexistence of the mind (reason) and heart (experience) in religion. As Hart wrote in his hymn on faith and repentance,

> True Religion's more than Notion;
> Something must be known and felt.[60]

Following the style of Wesley, Hart also wrote an autobiographical hymn called "The Author's own Confession," wherein Hart told of God's saving work in his soul:

> Come hither, ye that fear the Lord,
> Disciples of God's suffering Son;
> Let me relate, and you record,
> What he for my poor Soul has done.[61]

Like Wesley's autobiographical hymns, this hymn was expected to be used for public singing, because Hart believed some of those who sang his hymn could relate to his spiritual experience:

> Pangs of remorse my conscience tore;
> Hell opened hideous to my view;
> And what I only heard before
> I found by sad experience true.
>
> Oh! what a dismal state was this!
> What Horrors shook my feeble Frame!
> But, Brethren, surely you can guess;
> For you, perhaps, have felt the same.[62]

---

59. "Rationalism," *Oxford English Dictionary Online* (Oxford University Press), https://www.oed.com/view/Entry/158504?redirectedFrom=rationalism

60. Hymn 56, "Another [hymn on Faith and Repentance]," Part 1 ("Let us ask th' important Question"), lines 1:5–6.

61. Hymn 27, stanza 1.

62. Hymn 27, stanzas 11–12.

Here Hart spoke about the spiritual struggle he had prior to what he called his reconversion. He suffered from severe despondency caused by Christ's absence. What is noteworthy in the hymn is Hart's supposition that some of his original audience might have had the same struggle: "For you, perhaps, have felt the same." Indeed, many of Hart's hymns are personal accounts of his own life and experience which other Christians can share. This manner of writing autobiographical hymns would become a common practice among evangelical hymnists.[63] John Newton's "Amazing Grace!" is one good example.[64]

Another important facet of early Methodist hymnody was its pedagogical use. Wesley saw his hymns as vehicles for spreading the teachings of Methodism. Universal redemption (i.e., unlimited atonement) and Christian perfection were two peculiar doctrines of this movement. In his *Hymns and Sacred Poems* (1740), Charles wrote three hymns on universal redemption, which teaches that Jesus died for all:

> For *me*, for *me* the Saviour died!
> Surely Thy Grace for all is free:
> I *feel* it now by Faith *applied*:
> Who died for All, hath died for *me!*[65]

Wesley also had hymns expressing his belief in Christian perfection or entire sanctification in this life. His hymn "Pleading the Promise of Sanctification," which had been attached to his brother John's sermon on Christian perfection,[66] concludes with this prayer:

> Now let me gain Perfection's Height!
> Now let me into Nothing fall!
> Be less than Nothing in thy Sight,
> And feel that Christ is all in all.[67]

---

63. For some autobiographical hymns, see chapter 8 of Hezekiah Butterworth (1875).

64. The hymn was first published in *Olney Hymns* (London, 1779), 53.

65. "Universal Redemption" ("Saviour of all, by God design'd"), in *Hymns and Sacred Poems* (1740), 132–33. Italics as in the original.

66. Beginning "God of all Power, and Truth and Grace," in John Wesley, *Christian Perfection: A Sermon* (London, 1741), stanza 28. I owe this reference to Randy L. Maddox. See his editorial introduction to "Promise of Sanctification" (1741), http://divinityarchive.com/bitstream/handle/11258/449/08_Promise_of_Sanctification_%281741%29.pdf?sequence=1

67. "Pleading the Promise of Sanctification," in John and Charles Wesley, *Hymns and Sacred Poems* (1742).

In their preface to *Hymns and Sacred Poems* (1742), the Wesley brothers explained what they meant by one who is perfect: "We mean, one in whom is 'the mind which was in Christ,' and who 'so walketh as he walked'; a man that 'hath clean hands and a pure heart'; or that is 'cleansed from all filthiness of flesh and spirit'; one 'in whom there is no occasion of stumbling,' and who accordingly 'doth not commit sin.'"

As already noted, Hart disagreed with universal redemption. As a Calvinist, he believed Christ died only for a particular group of people chosen by God for salvation. With regard to Christian perfection, in his hymn on "Difference and Degrees of Faith," Hart maintained believers cannot find perfection in this life:

> Tho' we are sav'd from Guilt and Wrath,
> Perfection is not found.
> Lord, make our Union closer yet;
> And let the Marriage be complete.[68]

Nonetheless, believers should not doubt how one day God will bring their Christian lives to full perfection:

> Doubt not; he will carry on
> To its full Perfection,
> That good Work He has begun.
> Why then this Dejection?[69]

This stanza is unquestionably based on Philippians 1:6, "Being confident of this very thing, that he which hath begun a good work in you will perform it until the day of Jesus Christ." Hart found support from this verse for his view that Christians cannot attain perfection until Jesus returns. But for Hart this truth did not mean believers should not pursue perfection:

> Forward press towards Perfection;
> Watch, and pray; and all Things prove.
> Seek to know your God's Election,
> Search his everlasting Love;[70]

---

68. Hymn 79, "Difference and Degrees of Faith" ("He that believeth Christ, the Lord"), lines 4:3–6.

69. Hymn 24, "A Dialogue between a Believer and his Soul" ("Come, my Soul, and let us try"), lines 5:5–8.

70. Appendix hymn 11, ["Treasure in Heaven"] ("Lukewarm Souls, the Foe grows stronger"), lines 4:1–4.

The first line of this stanza probably has Philippians 3:14–15 as its scriptural background, where Paul said, "I press toward the mark for the prize of the high calling of God in Christ Jesus. Let us therefore, as many as be perfect [...]"

In theological content, therefore, Hart was closer to Watts than Wesley. But as for their style in hymnody, Hart was more like Wesley than Watts. Like Wesley, Hart showed more emotion in his hymns than Watts. As a matter of fact, Watts was "somewhat suspicious of Methodism, not wanting to associate with the more emotional forms of evangelicalism" (Yeager: 2013, 5). Because of the Arminian theology contained in Wesley's hymns, particular Baptists hesitated to use his hymns,

> though this resistance eased as the Calvinism of Particular Baptists became more open to evangelism and missions. Those writers, such as Augustus Toplady (1740–1778), Joseph Hart [...] and John Cennick (1718–1755), who shared the style and fervor of the Wesleys, while retaining a more traditional Calvinism after the manner of George Whitefield, became sources for Baptist congregations more quickly (Music/Richardson: 2008, 23).

In 1769, John Ash (1724–1779) and Caleb Evans (1737–1791), both Particular Baptists, compiled and edited *A Collection of Hymns Adapted to Public Worship*. Regarded as "the first congregational Baptist hymnbook" (Hayden: 2004), this collection contained more than 400 hymns, many of which are by Anne Steele (1717–1778), the best known and greatest Baptist hymnwriter of the eighteenth century, whose theological convictions, excepting baptism, would have been closer to Hart's than Wesley's.

3.2.3 Anne Steele: Baptist Hymnody

Anne Steele grew up in a Particular or Calvinistic Baptist family. In 1739, her father William Steele (1689–1769) became pastor of the Baptist church at Broughton, Hampshire, where she attended her entire life. By this time, the customary practice among Particular Baptists was to sing both metrical psalms and hymns for worship services. In the latter part of the previous century Benjamin Keach had already established hymn singing as normative in public worship among Particular Baptist churches. *The breach repaired in God's worship, or, Singing of psalms, hymns, and spiritual songs* (1691) became the definitive refutation of the major arguments against congregational singing in general and hymn singing in particular.

In *A Brief Discourse Concerning Singing* (1690), Particular Baptist Isaac Marlow (1649–1719) objected not only to the practice of hymn singing but also to congregational singing, even of psalms. Marlow explained how "the vocal Singing together, either of David's Psalms, or any humane pre-composed Forms, is a corrupting of the pure Worship of Jesus Christ, in mingling of Law and Gospel, or humane and divine things together" (48). In contrast, Keach viewed the congregational singing of psalms, hymns, and spiritual songs as "an Ordinance of God," or a part of God's ordained worship (1691, vi). Keach also produced two hymnals, *Spiritual melody, containing near three hundred sacred hymns* (1691) and *A feast of fat things full of marrow containing several Scripture songs taken out of the Old and New Testaments* (1696). The latter hymnbook was republished in 1700 as *Spiritual songs being the marrow of Scripture in songs of praise to Almighty God from the Old and New Testament: with a hundred divine hymns on several occasions as now practised in several congregations in and about London*. As the last part of the title of this reprinted hymnbook suggests, "By the close of the seventeenth century, the use of hymns was well on its way to become a generally recognized part of public worship among the Particular Baptists" (Haykin/Robinson: 2011, 308). Because of his successful introduction of hymns into public worship, Keach was considered a "Pioneer of Congregational Hymn Singing" (Martin: 1961). That said, "If Benjamin Keach was the liberator of Baptist hymnody, Anne Steele was its biggest voice" (Fenner: 2015, 21).

Using the pen name "Theodosia", Steele's hymns were first published in two volumes in 1760 as *Poems on Subjects Chiefly Devotional*. One of the recurring themes in her hymnody is suffering, which was due to her own personal experience. In 1720, at age three, her mother died, although her father remarried three years later. "Her health was never firm," said Caleb Evans in his preface to Steele's posthumous *Miscellaneous Pieces in Verse and Prose* (1780, vii). In their article "Anne Steele's Health: A Modern Diagnosis," Michael Dixon and Hugh Steele-Smith sketched a more detailed and accurate picture of Steele's maladies, believing Steele "suffered from malaria for most of her life" and "from chronic intermittent fever until her death" (1988, 353). Steele also endured "peptic ulcer disease" (354). Sharing her health condition with her stepmother, Anne Cator Steele, in a letter written in 1745, Steele mentioned a "frequent pain in my head and [...] disorder in my stomach."[71] In 1760, her stepmother died, and the death of her father in 1769, "to whom she was united by the strongest ties of affectionate duty and gratitude, gave such a shock to her feeble frame, that she never entirely recovered it" (Steele: 1780, vii). Toward the end of her life she had "uncommon and agonizing pains," causing her to be bedridden for "some years before her death" (ix). She died unmarried in 1778. Yet in all her trials, she learned to turn "her sorrow into song" (Watson: 2004). Her hymn "Desiring Resignation and Thankfulness" beautifully illustrates this point.[72] The word "resignation" here has the idea of surrendering oneself to God's sovereign will in the midst of suffering. Cynthia Aalders identified this theme as predominant in Steele's hymnody (2009, 136). For Steele, the believer's proper response to trials is humble resignation to God:

> When present suff'rings pain my heart,
> Or future terrors rise,
> And light and hope almost depart
> From these dejected eyes,
>
> Thy pow'rful word supports my hope,
> Sweet cordial of the mind!
> And bears my fainting spirit up,
> And bids me wait resign'd.
>
> And O, whate'er of earthly bliss
> Thy sov'reign hand denies,
> Accepted at thy throne of grace,
> Let this petition rise:
>
> "Give me a calm, a thankful heart,
> From ev'ry murmur free;
> The blessings of thy grace impart,
> And let me live to thee" (sts. 6–9).

Earlier in the hymn, Steele also expressed her longing for heaven, where suffering is no more:

> Lord, teach me to adore thy hand,
> From whence my comforts flow;

---

71. Steele to Anne Cator Steele, 30 December 1745, STE 3/7, ix, cited in Aalders (2009), 106n16.
72. Beginning "When I survey life's varied scene," in Steele (1760), 1:134–36.

> And let me in this desert land
> A glimpse of Canaan know (st. 2).

Here one can feel Steele's yearning to be in "Canaan," which represents a place of eternal rest and absolute peace. Thus, as Aalders pointed out, "As much as Steele's spiritual identity can be described with reference to her faithful resignation to the will of God, it can also be characterized by her hopeful longing for God." Both "resignation and longing informed Steele's spirituality, and together they shaped her work as a hymnwriter" (2009, 147). The concept of this twofold emphasis is also present in the hymnody of Joseph Hart, who was sometimes mistakenly thought of as a Particular Baptist.[73]

Like Steele, Hart's life was marked by great difficulties. He lost his first wife, Mary Brown, possibly in childbirth, within the first three years of their marriage. In 1752, he remarried, but his second wife, Mary Lamb, seemed not to be in good health, especially toward the end of her life, because when Hart died in 1768 it was said of her that she "has been for some months in a bad state of health, and is now incapable of doing any thing" (Hughes: 1768, 1). Furthermore, one of Hart's children died at about age three and another was epileptic. And based on his two autobiographical hymns on sickness, written in 1760, Hart himself was poor in health:[74]

> When pining Sickness wastes the Frame,
> Acute Disease, or tiring Pain;
> When Life fast spends her feeble Flame,
> And all the Help of Man proves vain;
>
> Joyless and flat all Things appear;
> The Spir'ts are languid, thin the Flesh;

---

73. F.F. Bruce called Hart "a Particular Baptist minister of London" in "The Psychology of St. Paul's Epistles" *Journal of the Transactions of the Victoria Institute* 87 (1955): 111.

74. In Hart's preface to his hymnal, he said his hymns "are published not only in the same *Order*, but almost in the same *Manner* in which they were first written." Since the two hymns on sickness (hymns 39 and 40) in the Supplement are immediately followed by the three hymns on death (hymns 41 to 43), which were occasioned by the death of King George II in October of 1760, we can safely assert the hymns on sickness were written in 1760.

> Med'cines can't ease, nor Cordials chear,
> Nor Food support, nor Sleep refresh.[75]

In fact, in his preface to the first edition of his *Hymns, &c. Composed on Various Subjects*, he informed his readers that his hymns "were begun almost two years ago [i.e., in 1757, the year of his reconversion]; but have been greatly impeded and often interrupted by disorder and darkness of soul, afflictions and temptations of various kinds, and other hindrances" (i). Hart's dealing with physical problems along with spiritual struggles is worthy of note. It seems in his mind the two were inseparable. For example, in his hymn on sickness, he simultaneously addressed infirmity and sin:

> Lord, hear a restless Wretch's Groans.
> To Thee my Soul in secret moans.
> My body's weak, my heart's unclean;
> I pine with sickness, and with sin.
>
> Thou know'st what 'tis, Lord, to be sick:
> And, tho' Almighty, hast been weak.
> Sin thou hadst none; and yet didst die
> For guilty Sinners, such as I.
>
> Sin's rankling Sores my Soul corrode.
> Oh! heal them with thy balmy Blood.
> And if Thou dost my Health restore;
> Lord, let me ne'er offend thee more.
>
> Or if I never more must rise;
> But Death's cold Hand must close my Eyes.
> Pardon my Sins; and take me Home:
> O come, Lord Jesus, quickly come.[76]

In the last stanza, Hart exhibited his resignation to God: "If I never more must rise [from the bed of sickness]...take me Home." Hart is not doubting God's ability to heal him but expressing his submission to God's perfect will. Elsewhere he entreated God, "May we all our Wills resign, / Quite absorpt and lost in thine."[77] This prayer echoes what

---

75. Supplement hymn 40, "[Sickness]," stanzas 1–2.
76. Supplement hymn 39, "Sickness," stanzas 1, 3–5.
77. Hymn 87, "Christ the Christian's only Hope" ("Gracious God, thy Children keep"), lines 10:1–2.

Jesus uttered at the Mount of Olives, "Father, if thou be willing, remove this cup from me: nevertheless not my will, but thine, be done" (Luke 22:42). Just as Jesus submitted to his father's will, so did Hart desire to surrender his will to God. Such was Hart's spirituality of resignation to God. Hart ended another hymn with a longing to be with Jesus in heaven,

> Where Saints are free from ev'ry Load
> Of passions, or of Pains.
>
> Heav'n is that holy happy Place,
> Where Sin no more defiles.[78]

With these thoughts, one understands why Hart concluded his hymn on sickness with the petition: "take me Home:/O come, Lord Jesus, quickly come."[79] For Hart, he can either be with Jesus by death (when Christ takes him home) or by Parousia (when Jesus takes him to himself when he returns).

When compared, Hart and Steele both saw resignation to God as the appropriate response to their loss and pain in life. With their Calvinistic theology, they found peace in entrusting their lives to God's sovereign will, knowing in the end whatever God ordained was for their spiritual profit. As Hart wrote,

> Every state, howe'er distressing,
> Shall be Profit in the End;
> Ev'ry Ordinance a Blessing;
> Ev'ry Providence a Friend.
>
> All Things for our Good are given,
> Comforts, Crosses, Staffs, or Rods.[80]

Or in Steele's words,

---

[78]. Supplement hymn 55, "Heaven," ("Ye Souls that trust in Christ, rejoice"), lines 5:1–2, 2:1–2.

[79]. Supplement hymn 39, lines 5:3b–4.

[80]. Supplement hymn 77, "Hymn, at recommending a Minister" ("Holy Ghost, inspire our Praises"), lines 3:5–8, 5:5–6. Similarly, Hart wrote in hymn 21, "The Wonders of redeeming Love" ("How wound'rous are the Works of God"): "All Things to Us must work for Good, / For whom the Lord hath shed his Blood," lines 8:3–4.

> Prest with affliction, let me then conclude,
> That storms and sunshine, (kind vicissitude!)
> Are mingled blessings, meant to work my good.[81]

The scriptural backdrop for their texts is certainly Romans 8:28, "And we know that all things work together for good to them that love God [...]" While submitting to God, Hart and Steele also found comfort in reflecting on the future glory awaiting them. They knew their suffering was only temporary and someday they would receive perfection in their bodies. This eschatological note sustained them in their life's journeys despite difficulties. Few hymn writers in the eighteenth-century can equal Steele and Hart on the subject of suffering. Perhaps the one who came closest to them was the poet William Cowper (1731–1800), who was known for his bouts of suicidal depression and who collaborated with John Newton to produce the *Olney Hymns* (1779). The following discussion will consider these two evangelical Anglicans: first, Cowper who had much in common with Joseph Hart in his spiritual struggles, and then Newton who like Hart was once a libertine.

3.2.4 William Cowper and John Newton: Anglican Hymnody

Hinting at the difficulty of his life, William Cowper described himself "as a stricken deer" (1785, 96). His father, John Cowper (1694–1756), a rector in the Church of England, wanted him to become a lawyer, although his love was poetry. To please his father he pursued law, even when he felt unfit for this profession, causing the beginning of a downward spiral in his life. He fell in love with his cousin Theodora Jane Cowper (1734?–1824). They had a mutual feeling for each other, but due to Cowper's financially unstable situation, Theodora's father did not approve of their marriage. In 1753, Cowper had his first bout of melancholy, followed by a period of suicidal depression in 1763, which John Baird put this way:

> About a week before the examination [at the bar of the House of Lords] he bought a half-ounce of laudanum. Unable to swallow the fatal dose, he prepared for flight to France, then decided to drown himself, then attempted to stab himself with his penknife (the blade broke), and

---

81. "A Simile" ("Oft have I view'd the flow'rs while bright and gay"), lines 17–19 (1760, 1:217).

finally hanged himself with a garter which snapped just as he lost consciousness (2013).

His cousin Martin Madan (1726–1790), who in 1760 produced *A Collection of Psalms and Hymns, Extracted from various Authors*, tried to help him but with no success. Eventually, Cowper moved to St Albans, a mental asylum, where he stayed from December 1763 to June 1765. Here he was treated by Dr Nathaniel Cotton, an evangelical physician, who became instrumental in his conversion in 1764. At last he experienced a "peaceful serenity" in his soul and had "the sweet sense of mercy and pardon, purchased by the blood of Christ" (Greatheed: 1814, 13).

Yet even after his conversion, Cowper continued to periodically experience psychological breakdowns. Moreover, with a sensitive heart and frail mind, Cowper was prone to doubting his own salvation. Sometimes he felt deserted by God, as explicitly seen when he had a relapse in 1773 during which he crashed into "the horrible abyss of absolute despair" (33). Suddenly "he considered himself as cast off for ever from the hope of mercy (32)." He thought "the Lord, after having renewed him in holiness, had doomed him to everlasting perdition" (33). He was a committed Calvinist, but as Arthur Pollard observed, Cowper "interpreted Calvinism to his own terrible disadvantage" (Lewis: 2004, 1:263). Against this backdrop, Cowper penned one of his most celebrated hymns, "Light shining out of Darkness", known by its first line, "God moves in a mysterious way." This hymn, said his biographer Samuel Greatheed, expressed his "faith and hope, which he retained at the time [...] of his severe distress" (1814, 32):

> God moves in a mysterious way,
> His wonders to perform;
> He plants his footsteps in the sea,
> And rides upon the storm.
>
> Judge not the Lord by feeble sense,
> But trust him for his grace;
> Behind a frowning providence
> He hides a smiling face.
>
> Blind unbelief is sure to err,
> And scan his work in vain:

> God is his own interpreter,
> And he will make it plain.[82]

Speaking of Cowper, Andrew Pratt noted,

> There is, perhaps, no more enigmatic writer, who feels at once the sense of divine providence and damnation so intimately intermingled; who feels hope and despair in equal measure; who cries to the God whom he believes cannot accept him in spite of that selfsame God's immense grace. His words speak of a whirlwind of change and uncertainty, of the inward struggle for faith (Larsen: 2003, 163).[83]

Just like Cowper, Joseph Hart also sank into deep depression but not to the same degree. Writing in April of 1759, Hart recounted,

> About three or four Years ago [i.e., 1755 or 1756], I fell into a deep Despondency of Mind. [...] I was very melancholy, and shunned all Company, walking pensively alone, or sitting in private, and bewailing my sad and dark Condition [...] which was so heavy, that I sometimes hesitated even to take my necessary Food (viii).

Hart was transparent about the cause of his mental and spiritual agony. In his own words, it was because he "had never experienced grand Revelations and miraculous Discoveries" (vii). That is, he was hoping to experience an extraordinary discovery that he was one of the elect by receiving a direct revelation from God outside Scripture. This mindset was typical of hyper-Calvinists, and Hart himself was once one of them. Although by this time Hart had already decided to abandon his hyper-Calvinism, he still manifested some of its teachings, such as looking for assurance of faith through "visionary Revelations" outside God's revealed Word. The cause, therefore, of Hart's "Gloom of Mind and Dejection of Spirit" was his strong sense of God's absence in his life (viii).

Worsening Hart's condition was his perception that he was a reprobate: "I looked on myself as a Gospel-Sinner, one that had trampled under Foot the Blood of Jesus, and for whom there remained no more Sacrifice

---

82. As in John Newton, *Twenty Six Letters on Religious Subjects to Which Are Added Hymns, &c.* (London, 1774), 215–16, stanzas 1, 4, and 6. Five years later this hymn was included in *Olney Hymns* (1779), 328.

83. A modern psychologist would have diagnosed Cowper with acute clinical depression.

for Sin." "For so deep was my Despair," he added, "that I found in me a Kind of Wish, that I might only be damned with the common Damnation of Transgressors of God's Law, But, oh! I thought the hottest Place in Hell must be my Portion" (ix–x). These "Clouds of Horror" continued to overwhelm him until his conversion on May 29, 1757:

> My Horrors were immediately dispelled, and such Light and Comfort flowed into my Hearts, as no Words can paint. The Lord by his Spirit of Love came,—not in a visionary Manner into my Brain, but with such divine Power and Energy into my Soul, that I was lost in blissful Amazement. I cried out, "What Me, Lord?" His Spirit answered in me, *Yes Thee*. I objected; "But I have been so unspeakably vile and wicked"—The Answer was; *I pardon thee fully and freely. Thy own Goodness* [...] *cannot save thee, nor shall thy Wickedness damn thee. I undertake to work all thy Works in thee and for thee, and to bring thee safe through all* (xi–xii).

Stanzas 16 through 18 of Hart's autobiographical hymn basically repeat what he said in the latter part of the quote:

> I would object; but faster much
> He answer'd, Peace. What, Me?— *Yes, Thee.*
> But my enormous Crimes are such—
> *I give thee Pardon, full and free.*
>
> But for the future, Lord—*I am*
> *Thy great salvation, perfect, whole.*
> *Behold, thy bad Works shall not damn,*
> *Nor can thy good Works save thy Soul.*
>
> *Renounce them both. Myself alone,*
> *Will for thee work, and in thee too.*
> *Henceforth I make the Cause My own;*
> *And undertake to bring thee thro'.*[84]

Though his horrors had not returned "with equal Violence" after this experience, not long after his conversion, Hart struggled with assurance of salvation. He did not disclose in detail the nature of his struggle, but the way he described it indicates it was serious. "I was terribly infected

---

84. Hymn 27, "The Author's own Confession" ("Come hither, ye that fear the Lord"), stanzas 16–18.

with Thoughts," he wrote, "so monstrously obscene and blasphemous, that they cannot be spoken [...]. They haunted me some Months; and used to make me weep bitterly, and cry earnestly to my God to remove them" (xii–xiii). Possibly Hart's thought of being a reprobate came back because later he said, "I now believed my Name was sculptured deep in the Lord Jesus's Breast, with Characters never to be erased" (xiii). What gave him full assurance of faith was his new understanding of Christ's sufferings:

> the least of Drop of his Blood now appeared to me more valuable than ten Thousands of Worlds. As I had before thoughts his Sufferings *too little*, they now appeared to me to be *too great*; I often cried out, in Transports of blissful Astonishment, "Lord, 'tis too much, 'tis too much, surely my Soul was not worth so great a Price" (xiv).

The second part of his first hymn, "On the Passion," was doubtlessly written on this occasion:

> And why, dear Saviour, tell me why,
> Thou thus would'st suffer, bleed, and die?
> What mighty Motive could thee move?
> The Motive's plain; 'twas all for Love.
>
> For Love of whom? Of sinners base,
> A harden'd Herd, a Rebel-Race;
> That mock'd and trampled on thy Blood,
> And wanton'd with the Wounds of God.
>
> O Love of unexampled Kind!
> That leaves all Thought so far behind;
> Where length, and Breadth, and Depth, and Height,
> Are lost to my astonish'd Sight.[85]

Hart seemed to have struggled with doubts the rest of his life. His hymn "The Doubting Christian"[86] is self-descriptive, and his hymn "A dialogue between a believer and his soul" vividly reveals the painful battle within his soul:

---

85. Hymn 1, "On the Passion," part 2, stanzas 1, 2, and 9.
86. Hymn 3, beginning "If Unbelief's that Sin accurst."

> Soul. *Oh! I sink beneath the Load*
> *Of my Nature's Evil;*
> *Full of enmity to God;*
> *Captiv'd by the devil:*
> *Restless as the troubled Seas;*
> *Feeble, faint, and fearful;*
> *Plagu'd with ev'ry sore Disease;*
> *How can I be chearful?*
>
> *Bel[iever]. Think on what thy Saviour bore*
> *In the gloomy Garden,*
> *Sweating Blood at ev'ry Pore,*
> *To procure thy Pardon!*
> *See Him stretch'd upon the Wood,*
> *Bleeding, grieving, crying;*
> *Suff'ring all the Wrath of God;*
> *Groaning, gasping, dying!*
>
> Soul. *This by faith I sometimes view;*
> *And those Views relieve me:*
> *But my Sins return anew;*
> *These are they that grieve me.*
> *Oh! I'm leprous, stinking, foul,*
> *Quite throughout infected.*
> *Have not I, if any Soul,*
> *Cause to be dejected?*
>
> *Bel[iever]. Think how loud thy dying Lord*
> *Cry'd out, "It is finish'd!"*
> *Treasure up that sacred Word*
> *Whole and undiminish'd.*
> *Doubt not; He will carry on,*
> *To its full perfection,*
> *That good work He has begun.*
> *Why then this Dejection?*[87]

Hart's brother-in-law John Hughes, explained:

> it is well known, to many, that he came into the work of the ministry in much weakness and brokenness of soul; and laboring under many deep temptations, of a dreadful nature; for though the Lord was pleased to confirm him in his everlasting love to his soul; yet (to my knowledge)

---

87. Hymn 24, beginning "Come, my Soul, and let us try," stanzas 2–5.

he was at times so left to the buffetings of Satan, for the trial of his faith, and to such clouds and darkness on his soul (1768, 27).

Yet as Hart wrote, "tho' I am often sorely distrest by spiritual internal Foes, afflicted, tormented, and bowed down almost to Death, with the Sense of my own present Barrenness, Ingratitude, and Proneness to Evil, he [i.e., Christ] shews me his bleeding Wounds" (xx). Elsewhere he said, "thou[gh] I have many sore Trials and Temptations in my Soul; yet it pleases the Lord to reveal himself often in me, to open the Mysteries of his Cross, and give me to trust in his precious Blood" (xiii). This atoning blood, in which Hart found comfort in the Christian life, became the controlling theme of his hymns, so much as that if one were to cut the vein of his hymnody, it would figuratively bleed with Christ's blood. This is the blood, wrote Hart, that "can cleanse the blackest Soul; / And wash our Guilt away."[88]

Similarly, Cowper, who often struggled to see himself as God's child, drew much comfort from "a fountain fill'd with blood / Drawn from Emmanuel's veins." "And there," sang Cowper, "have I […] Wash'd all my sins away."[89] In another place he wrote,

> Jesus, whose blood so freely stream'd
> To satisfy the laws demand;
> By thee from guilt and wrath redeem'd,
> Before the Father's face I stand.[90]

Early evangelicals were known for their "int'rest in the Saviour's blood," to borrow Charles Wesley's words from his hymn "And can it be."[91] They "aimed at bringing back, and by an aggressive movement, the Cross, and all that the Cross essentially implies" (Gladstone: 1879, 1879). Sometimes they used graphic images to emphasize the importance of Christ's atonement in Christian life. See for example Cowper's "fountain fill'd with blood," and Hart's "Amaz'd to find him [i.e., Jesus] bath'd

---

88. Hymn 7, "Christ very God and Man" ("A man there is, a real man"), lines 6:1b–2.
89. As in Richard Conyers, *Collection of Psalms and Hymns, from various authors* (London, 1772), 187–88. The hymn later appeared in *Olney Hymns* (1779), where it was titled "Praise for the fountain opened. [Zechariah] Chap. xiii.i," 98–99.
90. Cowper, "Jehovah-Shalem," in *Olney Hymns* (1779), 29, stanza 1.
91. As in *Hymns and Sacred Poems* (1739), headed "Free Grace."

in Blood."[92] However, not all regard such expressions as appropriate for corporate worship. Finding Cowper's line offensive and thus improper for congregational singing, the poet James Montgomery (1771-1854) changed it to say "From Calvary's cross, a fountain flows."[93] Montgomery reasoned, "I entirely rewrote the first verse of that favourite hymn, commencing—'There is a fountain filled with blood,' &c. The words are objectionable as representing a fountain being filled, instead of springing up: I think my version is unexceptionable" (Holland/Everett: 1855, 4:70). But as Elizabeth Cosnett explained, the point Cowper wanted to communicate to "contemporaries was not of gruesome amounts of blood but of boundless mercy" (Canterbury, n.d.). Furthermore, in Ray Palmer's judgment, Montgomery's criticism

> takes the words as if they were intended to be a literal prosaic statement. It forgets that what they express is not only poetry, but the poetry of intense and impassioned feeling, which naturally embodies itself in the boldest metaphors. The inner sense of the soul, when its deepest affections are moved, infallibly takes metaphors in their true significance (1880, 97–98).

Unarguably, Cowper's hymns as well as Hart's were shaped by their intense anguish, resulting sometimes in their use of strong words to express their deepest emotions. Yet their agonizing experiences led them to pen some of the finest lyrics on the subject of despair and doubt interfused with faith in God. In her article "Faith, Doubt and Despair in William Cowper's Selected Poetry and Prose," Teresa Bela fairly observed, "The hymns he wrote which expressed his hesitations, uncertainties or doubts, and which occasionally may have even approached despair, were ultimately the poems of faith" (2011, 89). This comment applies also to Hart, whose hymns, while expressing doubt, end on a note of hope, or a prayer for God to take his doubt:

> The World opposes from without;
> And Unbelief within.

---

92. Hymn 1, "On the Passion" ("Come, all ye chosen Saints of God"), line 5:2. Hart used the expression "bathed in blood" four times in his corpus of hymns.

93. As in Thomas Cotterill, *A Selection of Psalms and Hymns*, 8th ed. (London: T. Cadell, 1819), 121.

> We fear, we faint, we grieve, we doubt;
> And feel the Load of Sin.
>
> But let not all this terrify.
> Pursue the narrow Path;
> Look to the Lord with steadfast Eye;
> And fight with Hell by Faith.
>
> Tho' we are feeble; Christ is strong,
> His promises are true;
> We shall be conqu'rors all, e're long;
> And more than Conqu'rors too.[94]

Or consider his hymn "Of Sanctification," where he concluded with a prayer for faith:

> These Trials Weaklings suffer here,
> Censure and scorn without;
> And from within (what's worse to bear)
> Despondency and Doubt.
>
> Thy Holy Spir't into us breathe.
> A perfect Saviour prove.
> Lord, give us Faith; and let that Faith
> Work all Thy Will by Love![95]

When Hart sank into deep melancholia he said, I had no "Friend in the World, to whom I could communicate the Burden of my soul" (1767, viii). This was not true of Cowper, for he had John Newton, who often referred to Cowper as "my dear friend."[96] At the request of Newton, in 1767 Cowper moved to Olney in Buckingham where Newton was the curate. For the next twelve years Newton took Cowper under his care.

---

94. Hymn 15, "Tribulation" ("The Souls that would to Jesus press"), stanzas 3, 6–7. See also Cowper's "Vanity of the World" ("God gives his mercies to be spent") in *Olney Hymns*, 70.

95. Hymn 9, "Of Sanctification" ("The Holy Ghost in Scripture saith"), stanzas 10 and 13. See also Cowper's hymn "Jehovah-Rophi" ("Heal us, Emmanuel, here we are"), where he confessed his "faith is feeble," but prayed, "O help my unbelief." Similarly, in his hymn "The Contrite Heart" ("The Lord will happiness divine"), he began with doubt and ended with prayer to God to break and heal his doubt. *Olney Hymns* (1779), 19, 81 (respectively).

96. In fact, in his preface, Newton viewed the *Olney Hymns* "as a monument, to perpetuate the remembrance of an intimate and endeared friendship" (1779, vi).

Newton's deep concern for his friend's health is seen in his diary entry dated three days after Cowper suffered a relapse on January 2, 1773: "I have now devoted myself and time as much as possible to attend on [Mr. Cowper]. We walked today, and probably shall daily."[97] Eventually, the two published a volume of hymns called *Olney Hymns* (1779), which was a reflection of their Calvinistic, evangelical, Anglican commitment. This hymnal contained 348 hymns, of which 67 were by Cowper, the rest by Newton, who also wrote the preface. In this preface, Newton indicated the hymns were "originally composed" for the use of his parish at Olney. Newton scholar Marylynn Rouse noted how "most of the hymns were written for the informal Sunday evening fellowship group in Olney," but some hymns were definitely composed for specific services such as Christmas, New Year, and Easter, held in the church.[98]

Newton was forthright about his hymns being "the fruit and expression of my own experience," and they contained the Calvinistic "doctrines of grace," without which he said, "I could not live comfortably a day or an hour" for they "are essential to my peace." These doctrines, added Newton, are "friendly to holiness" and "have a direct influence in producing and maintaining a gospel conversation [or behavior], and therefore I must not be ashamed of them" (1779, ix–x). Flowing out of his Calvinism and running through his hymnody was the theme of amazing grace, which was a result of his deep sense of unworthiness as a sinner.[99] His hymn titled "Faith's review and expectation," which became well known by its

---

97. John Newton, diary (January 5, 1773) Transcribed for the John Newton Project from Princeton University Library, John Newton Diary, CO199, https://www.johnnewton.org/Groups/252356/The_John_Newton/new_menus/Diaries/1773_1805/1773/Jan_73.asp. On January 22, 1773, Newton again recorded, "My dear friend [Mr Cowper] still walks in darkness. I can hardly conceive that anyone in a state of grace and favour with God, can be in greater distress. And yet no-one walked more closely with him, or was more simply devoted to him in all things. Thus as in the case of Job he shows his right to deal as he wills with his own, he knows how to make up for all, to bring light out of darkness and real good out of seeming evil. When we presume to say, Why hast thou done this? He answers in his word, Be still and know that I am God." Despite Cowper's struggle with doubt and despair, Newton saw him as a child of God.

98. Marylynn Rouse, *Introduction to Olney Hymns*, https://www.johnnewton.org/Groups/227061/The_John_Newton/new_menus/Hymns/Introduction/Introduction.aspx. "The Great House was used both for the Tuesday evening prayer meetings and the Sunday evening informal meetings (until a much later point). Sunday services in the church were in the morning and afternoon." Marylynn Rouse, email message, April 1, 2021.

99. A common pattern found in Newton's hymns is the mention of man's guilt

opening line "Amazing grace! (how sweet the sound)," beautifully encapsulates this theme. It was Newton's practice to write hymns to accompany his sermons, and most likely that hymn was written for the sermon he preached on New Year's Day, January 1, 1773. His text for this sermon and the scripture reference he gave to his hymn are the same—1 Chronicles 17:16–17:

> And David the king came and sat before the LORD, and said, Who am I, O LORD God, and what is mine house, that thou hast brought me hitherto? And yet this was a small thing in thine eyes, O God; for thou hast also spoken of thy servant's house for a great while to come, and hast regarded me according to the estate of a man of high degree, O LORD God.

Newton related to David's unworthiness when David asked in wonder, "Who am I, O LORD God, and what is mine house, that thou hast brought me hitherto?" In his sermon notes, Newton wrote, "This question should be always upon our minds. Who am I? What was I when the Lord began to manifest his purposes of love?" One of the answers he gave was "Blinded by the god of this world." Then he went on,

> We had not so much a desire of deliverance. Instead of desiring the Lord's help, we breathed a spirit of defiance against him. His mercy came to us not only undeserved but undesired. Yea [a] few [of] us but resisted his calls, and when he knocked at the door of our hearts endeavoured to shut him out till he overcame us by the power of his grace.[100]

With these viewpoints, it is no surprise Newton sang,

> Amazing grace! (how sweet the sound)
> That sav'd a wretch like me!
> I once was lost, but now am found,
> Was blind, but now I see.[101]

---

followed by God's grace, a pattern characteristic of Calvinism. See, for example, his first two hymns in *Olney Hymns* (1779), 1–3.
    100. Transcribed by Marylynn Rouse for the John Newton Project from John Newton's sermon notebook, Lambeth Palace Library, MS 2940. https://www.johnnewton.org/Groups/231011/The_John_Newton/new_menus/Amazing_Grace/sermon_notes/sermon_notes.aspx
    101. *Olney Hymns* (1779), 53, stanza 1.

Considering himself a wretch and reflecting on what God had done to him when God saved him caused Newton to exclaim in awe, "Amazing grace!" Writing on September 12, 1776 to his financial supporter John Thornton (1720–1790), Newton talked more about this amazing grace:

> Surely no one could be a greater libertine in principle or practice, more abandoned or more daring than I. But I obtained mercy. I can hardly feel any stronger proof of remaining depravity, than in my having so faint a sense of the Amazing Grace that snatched me from ruin, that pardoned such enormous sins, preserved my life when I stood upon the brink of Eternity, and could only be preserved by miracle, and changed a disposition which seemed so incurably obstinate and given up to horrid wickedness.[102]

The hymn Newton labeled "My name is Jacob," based on Genesis 32:27, resembles the overall theme of "Amazing Grace." In this hymn, Newton personally answered God's question to Jacob, "What is thy name?"

> Dost thou ask me, who I am?
> Ah, my LORD, thou know'st my name!
>
> Thou didst once a wretch behold,
> In rebellion blindly bold;
> Scorn thy grace, thy pow'r defy,
> That poor rebel, LORD, was I.
>
> Once a sinner near despair,
> Sought thy mercy-seat by pray'r;
> Mercy heard and set him free,
> LORD, that mercy came to me.[103]

The historical background for the last verse is evidently the incident Newton had in the Atlantic Ocean when he was still a captain of a slave ship. His ship was struck by a fierce storm in 1748. He was "near despair," but he prayed for mercy and "Mercy heard him and set him free." Having

---

102. Letter to John Thornton, September 12, 1776, Cambridge University, Thornton Papers, Add 7674/1/B19, transcribed by Marylynn Rouse for the John Newton Project. Thornton supported Newton with £200 a year while Newton was "curate of Olney, Buckinghamshire, which he increased when Newton took charge of the affairs of the poet William Cowper." See Edwin Welch (2004).

103. *Olney Hymns* (1779), 13–14, beginning "Nay, I cannot let Thee go," stanzas 2a, 3–4.

never forgotten this event, 48 years later, writing in his journal, the former "infidel and libertine"[104] said, "Oh, it was mercy indeed to save a wretch like me!"[105]

Newton's admiration for Isaac Watts as a hymn writer is recognized, but few are aware that Joseph Hart was also one of Newton's favorite hymn writers. He cited his hymns in his sermons, prayers, and letters.[106] Perhaps the reason Hart became one of Newton's esteemed hymnists was because Newton saw himself in Hart. Like Newton, Hart was once an infidel and libertine saved by God's grace. Without going into details, the description Hart gave to himself during the time when he was a libertine was very shocking yet he said it was "too true": "I committed all Uncleanness with Greediness" (1767, vi). In his thinking, he had obtained "by Christ a Liberty of sinning." Turning "the Grace of God into Lasciviousness," he thought he "even out-went professed Infidels, and shocked the Irreligious

---

104. See the epitaph, which Newton himself wrote for his tombstone at the Churchyard of St Peter and Paul in Olney:

> JOHN NEWTON. Clerk.
> Once an infidel and libertine
> a servant of slaves in Africa was
> by the rich mercy of our
> LORD and SAVIOUR JESUS CHRIST
> preserved, restored, pardoned, and appointed to preach
> the faith which he had long laboured to destroy.

105. Newton's journal, March 21, 1796.

106. In a sermon on Psalm 90:9 preached on Sunday afternoon, December 31, 1769: "Believers will find cause of humilation, but you have an advocate with the Father. Thank him for all that is past, trust him for all that's to come." Cowper & Newton Museum, Newton's Notebook, No. 41. The last sentence was drawn from one of Newton's favorite hymns by Hart, namely, hymn 73, labeled "If there arise among you a Prophet, or a Dreamer of Dreams, &c. Deut. xiii.i, &c." ("No prophet, nor Dreamer of Dreams"). Newton quoted again from this hymn in his prayer on New Year's Eve, December 31, 1772: "O Lord accept my praise for all that is past, enable me to trust thee for all that's to come." The Morgan Library and Museum, New York, MA 731. He was still quoting it on his birthday on August 4, 1789: "Once more I attempt to set up my Ebenezer. I praise thee for all that is past, I desire to trust thee, and to yield myself to thee, for all that is to come." Princeton University Library, John Newton Collection, CO199, 308–9. Then on January 16, 1789 he wrote to William Bull: "Shall I not then praise him for all that is past? Ought I not to trust him for all that is to come?" *One Hundred and Twenty-Nine Letters from the Rev John Newton late Rector of St Mary Woolnoth, London, to the Rev William Bull of Newport Pagnell* (London, 1847), 234. I owe these quotes to Marylynn Rouse.

and Profane with [his] horrid Blasphemies, and monstrous Impieties" (v). Hart continued in this "abominable State" for "nine or ten years" during which he also infected others "with the Poison of [his] Delusions" (v–vi). His autobiographical hymn puts it this way:

> The Road of Death with rash Career
> I ran; and gloried in my Shame:
> Abus'd His Grace; despis'd His Fear;
> And Others taught to do the same.[107]

Later in his hymn 44, labeled "Jabez's Prayer," which is based on 1 Chronicles 4:9–10, Hart exhorted his fellow believers to use their Christian liberty properly and not abuse God's grace and turn it to sin:

> To use this Liberty aright,
> And not the Grace of God abuse,
> We always need his Hand, his Might;
> Lest what he gives us we should lose;
> Spiritual Pride would soon creep in,
> And turn his very Grace to sin.[108]

Similarly, in one of his hymns on Christmas, addressing the unbelievers, he wrote,

> Abusers of Grace,
> Come, cease your Backslidings,
> And once more return;
> Receive the glad Tidings,
> A Saviour is born.[109]

As with Newton, Hart's former libertinism created a profound sense of unworthiness and inexpressible amazement of God's grace in his life. In his writings, Hart referred to himself as "the unworthy author," "the worst of Men," or "the chief of Sinners" saved by "God's free sovereign Grace" (ii). His hymn called "The Prodigal," in which he depicted himself

---

107. Hymn 27, "The Author's own Confession" ("Come hither, ye that fear the Lord"), stanza 3.
108. Hymn 44, "Jabez's Prayer" ("A Saint there was in Days of old").
109. Hymn 13, "Another [hymn on Christ's Nativity]" ("How blest is the Season"), lines 5:4–8.

as the one who "long abus'd [God's] Grace," expresses what he called elsewhere "The Wonders of his [God's] sov'reign Grace":[110]

> Good God, are these thy Ways!
> If Rebels thus are freed,
> And favour'd with peculiar Grace,
> Grace must be free indeed.[111]

In another hymn, reflecting on what God had done for him, Hart burst,

> What an amazing Change was here!
> I look'd for Hell; he brought me Heav'n.[112]

For Hart, God's "free distinguishing Grace is the Bottom on which is fixt the Rest of [his] poor weary tempted soul" (1767, xx). And repeatedly, Hart informed his readers how he wrote his hymns "to make known the inexhaustible Riches of [Christ's] free Grace and long suffering" among sinners (xx). In a sense, his entire hymnody is a doctrinal and experiential exposition of Christ's free and saving grace:

> What wond'rous Grace was this!
> We sinn'd; and Jesus died.
> He wrought the Righteousness,
> And We were justified.[113]

The emphasis on divine grace in Hart's hymnody was perhaps the main reason Newton became enamored with Hart's hymns. Both Hart and Newton were five-point Calvinists (Hindmarsh: 1993, 42). On February 9, 1766, about two years after Newton accepted the curacy at Olney, Newton wrote to his friend Captain Alexander Clunie, "I beg you either to bring me one of Mr. Hart's Hymn Books, or to send it, if you have time, by Mr. S[emple]'s" (1790, 95). Given Newton's high regard for Hart's hymns, it was very possible Newton used his hymns for informal services at Olney. This was the period when hymn singing was becoming

---

110. Supplement hymn 75, "[Another hymn on Baptism]" ("By what amazing Ways"), line 1:3.
111. Hymn 71, "The Prodigal" ("Now for a wond'rous Song"), stanza 7.
112. Hymn 27, "The Author's own Confession" ("Come hither, ye that fear the Lord"), lines 5:1–2.
113. Supplement hymn 7, "[Another hymn for the Lord's Supper]" ("Join ev'ry Tongue to sing"), lines 2:1–4.

widely common, especially among evangelical Anglicans. As Karen Tucker explained,

> Most Evangelical Anglicans valued the liturgy of the Church of England's Book of Common Prayer (1662), and attended—or presided at, if clergy—the church's Lord's Day gatherings or morning and evening prayer. Sunday worship in most parish churches consisted of morning prayer, litany, ante-communion, and sermon; the Lord's Supper might be offered monthly, quarterly, or less. Evangelical Anglicans typically added other occasions for worship outside of church hours, including services with preaching and/or exhortation as well as prayer meetings [...]. Hymn singing was usual at these extra liturgical sessions and in some cases, made an irregular appearance during the church's liturgy—irregular because a standing injunction of Elizabeth I (1559) only permitted hymns prior to or following common prayer; metrical psalmody was the approved liturgical repertoire. Permission for hymn singing in the liturgy proper came in 1820 with the Archbishop of York's approval of Thomas Cotterill's A Selection of Psalms and Hymns (2019, 2:243–44).

Although the singing of hymns rose increasingly in value within the Established Church among evangelicals during Newton's time, not all evangelicals were in favor of this practice. William Romaine (1714–1795), who was regarded by Newton as "the most popular man of the Evangelical party since Mr Whitefield" (Bull: 1870, 328), was one of the outspoken leaders against hymn singing in the church. In 1775, Romaine published *An Essay on Psalmody* "to restore the singing of them [i.e., psalms] in the congregation to their primitive usefulness" (3).

3.2.5 William Romaine: "Most Perfect Hymns": A Return to Psalmody

Romaine was one of the most intellectual and influential evangelical Anglicans of the eighteenth century. His *Essay on Psalmody*, which contains *A Collection out of the book of Psalms suited to every Sunday in the Year*, demonstrated his skill as a Hebrew scholar.[114] The essay was, in Tim Shenton's words, "A defense of the exclusive use of Psalms (in

---

114. Romaine explained the purpose for which he attached this collection of psalms: "That the congregation might have a key to the true sense, and each might know, what particular grace was to be exercised in singing it" (92).

the Sternhold and Hopkins version) in church services" (2004, 275). Understanding psalm singing as "an ordinance of God, and one of the means of grace, instituted for the exercise and for the improvement of grace," Romaine lamented how this ordinance was "so much neglected" (1775; 6, 86). In fact, a "total neglect" of this ordinance even existed in other congregations where "Human compositions are preferred to divine" and where "Man's poetry is exalted above the poetry of the holy Ghost" (110). Romaine's observation shows how widespread hymn singing already was by the end of the third quarter of the eighteenth century. Essentially, the singing of hymns became "so great, and [...] so universal (except in the church of England)" that no one hardly dared to challenge such a practice (112). For Romaine, this hymn explosion was a result of religious decay:

> It was a gradual decay, and went on, till at last there was a general complaint against Sternhold and Hopkins. Their translation was treated, as poor flat stuff. The wits ridiculed it. The prophane blasphemed it. Good men did not defend it. Then it fell into such contempt, that people were ready to receive any thing in its room, which looked rational and was poetical. In this situation the hymn-makers find the church, and they are suffered to thrust out the psalms to make way for their own compositions: of which they have supplied us with a vast variety, collection upon collection, and in use too, new hymns starting up daily—appendix added to appendix—sung in many congregations [...] to such a degree, that the psalms are become quite obsolete (111).

By "new hymns [...] appendix added to appendix" Romaine was probably thinking, for instance, of hymnals such as that by Joseph Hart, who published his first edition of *Hymns* (119 in total) in 1759. In 1760, he resumed writing hymns, resulting in his *Supplement* (82 hymns) and *Appendix* (13 hymns). Romaine knew Hart personally. On July 16, 1874, writing to A.J. Baxter, editor of *The Gospel Advocate*, Thorpe Smith shared a fascinating story behind Hart's hymn called "The Prodigal". He wrote, "I have been told, many years ago, the origin of that hymn arose from the following story—when the late Mr. Romaine was told of Hart's conversion, he replied, *What, that Devil!* Hart hearing of this wrote that hymn" (6:269). The hymn can be taken as Hart's admonition of Romaine's thoughtless remark. Here Romaine is the elder son and Hart is the younger (cf. Wright: 1910, 52):

> The prodigal's return'd,
> Th' Apostate bold and base;
> That all his Father's Counsels spurn'd,
> And long abus'd His Grace.
>
> Ye elder Sons, be still;
> Give no bad Passion vent:
> My Brethren, 'tis our Father's Will,
> And you must be content.
>
> All that He has is yours:
> Rejoice then, not repine.
> That Love that all *your* States secures,
> That love has alter'd *mine*.[115]

Going back to Romaine's essay, as he clarified his position on the issue it shows he was not opposed to hymns when sung outside of the church: "I speak not of private people, or of private singing; but of the church in its public service" (1775, 106). He elucidated, "I blame no body for singing human compositions. I do not think it sinful or unlawful, so the matter be scriptural. My complaint is against preferring men's poems to the good word of God, and preferring them to it in the church" (112). He went on:

> I have no quarrel with Dr. Watts, or any living or dead versifier. I would not wish all their poems burnt. My concern is to see christian congregations shut out divinely inspired psalms, and take in Dr. Watts's flights of fancy; as if the words of a poet were better than the words of a prophet (113).

Showing a firm commitment to the regulative principle, Romaine argued psalm singing "is commanded by divine authority, and commanded as a part of divine worship" (114). Therefore, to neglect it is to neglect God's command. God has given us psalms, or what Romaine called "a divine collection of most perfect hymns" to be sung in the church and "when we use them in humble faith, God will render them the means of exercising, of preserving, and of increasing our holy joy" (94). In later years, Romaine revised his essay and added what other evangelicals considered an extreme claim: "Experience demonstrates, that God does bless

---

115. Hymn 71, "The Prodigal" ("Now for a wond'rous Song"), stanzas 2, 5–6.

the singing of psalms in the church, and does not bless the singing of men's hymns" (1880, 122).

As can be expected, Romaine's criticism of "hymn singing in general and of the Hymnody of the Revival in particular" upset a number of evangelicals both outside and inside the Anglican Church (Benson: 1915, 239). For example, writing from Olney on August 3, 1775, John Newton expressed his disappointment to John Thornton about Romaine's book:

> I have received (I suppose from the Author) a book Mr Romaine has lately published on the subject of Psalmody. I wish he had treated it in a different manner. I do not feel myself hurt, by his censure of modern hymn-makers, but I am afraid it will hurt some weak, well-meaning people, who consider him as little less than infallible, to be told, that whatever comfort they may think they have received from singing hymns in public worship was only imagined. And he has laid himself very open to those who do not love him. He seems to ascribe all the deadness that is complained of in many places where the Gospel is preached (I suppose he chiefly means the London Dissenters) to their not singing Sternhold and Hopkins. Strange that a wise man can advance such paradoxes. This judgement involves not only the Dissenters, and the Lock, but the Tabernacle, Tottenham Court, Everton, Helmsley, and many other places where I should think he must allow the Lord has afforded his blessing. The Curate of Olney and his poor people may be content to be ranked amongst so much good company. I think many of his best friends must wish this book had not appeared. What a mercy is it, that we are not to stand or fall by man's judgement! Some of us here, know that the Lord has comforted us by hymns, which express Scriptural truths, though not confined to the words of David's Psalms. And we know by the effects we are not mistaken. I believe Dr Watts' Hymns have been a singular blessing to the churches, notwithstanding Mr Romaine does not like them.[116]

Also disagreeing with Romaine was the Calvinistic Anglican hymn writer Augustus Toplady, who in the preface to his *Psalms and Hymns for Public and Private Worship* averred, "The singing of hymns is an Ordinance, to which God has repeatedly set the Seal of his own Presence and Power; and which He deigns eminently to bless" (1776, 2). In common with Toplady and other evangelical hymnists of the eighteenth century,

---

116. Cambridge University, Thornton Papers, Ms Add 7826.

Hart also saw hymns as a means of grace and vehicle for spreading God's truths. Hart put it this way in the preface to his *Hymns*:

> All I would humbly wish is; that Jesus of *Nazareth* the mighty God, the Friend of Sinners, would be pleased to make them, in some Measure (weak and mean as they are) instrumental in setting forth his Glory, propagating and enforcing the Truths of his Gospel, chearing the Hearts of his People, and exalting his inestimable Righteousness, upon which alone the unworthy Author desires to rest the whole of his salvation (ii).

With this view of music, Hart could exhort his fellow believers:

> Come, ye Christians, sing the Praises
> Of your condescending God;
> Come, and hymn the holy Jesus,
> Who hath wash'd us in his Blood;[117]

Although Romaine did not promote hymn singing in public worship, he was fond of citing hymns in his preaching (Shenton: 2004, 280). His fellow evangelical preacher Thomas Wills (1740–1802) testified of this in his funeral sermon: "How have I seen his cheeks glow, and his eyes sparkle, when I have heard him repeat in the midst of a sermon from his pulpit those sweet words of one of our hymns, which was, as well it might be, a great favourite with him" (Wills: 1795, 13). The hymn Wills was referring to was the one written by the German hymn writer Nikolaus Zinzendorf, translated by John Wesley into English:

> Jesu, thy blood and righteousness
> My beauty are, my glorious dress;
> 'Midst flaming worlds in these array'd
> With joy shall I lift up my head.[118]

This hymn teaches what Wills called the "glorious doctrine of justification by the righteousness of Christ imputed to the believer" (13). Central to the evangelical faith, this "Doctrine most divine," as Hart styled it, permeated Hart's hymns:

> Imputed Righteousness I own
> A Doctrine most divine;

---

117. Hymn 55, "Another [hymn on Faith and Repentance]," lines 1:1–4.
118. *Hymns and Sacred Poems* (1740), 177, stanza 1, from the German, "Christi Blut und Gerechtigkeit."

> For Jesus to my Heart makes known
> That all His Merit's *Mine*.[119]
>
> Robes of Righteousness imputed,
> White and whole,
> Clothe the Soul,
> Each exactly suited.[120]
>
> Pull his polluted Garments off.
> Here, Soul, here's Raiment rich enough.
> Cloath thee with Righteousness divine,
> Not Creature's Righteousness, but Mine.[121]
>
> "Empty and bare, I come to Thee,
> For righteousness divine.
> O may thy matchless Merits be,
> By *Imputation*, mine!"[122]

As mentioned earlier, this was the "inestimable Righteousness" on which alone Hart rested "the whole of his salvation." According to Wills, "This was the [same] righteousness Mr. Romaine preached constantly; this he received by faith, and by this he found peace with God" (1795, 12–13). So while Hart and Romaine would not see eye to eye on the matter of hymn singing, when it comes to the ground of justification they were in accord.

3.3 Summary

Despite Romaine's "most valiant efforts, he was unable to stop the ever-increasing flow of hymnody that was spilling over from Methodist ranks and affecting every part of the evangelical revival" (Shenton: 2004, 281). Indeed, hymnody became a distinct attribute of early evangelicals on the whole. They were a major factor in the shift from metrical psalms to hymns in English liturgy, both inside and outside the Church of England. Hart contributed to this outbreak of hymnody, and his own hymns can be

---

119. Hymn 90, "For the Kingdom of God is not in Word, but in Power. 1 Cor. iv. 20" ("A Form of Words, tho' e'er so sound"), stanza 5.

120. Hymn 67, "Christ's Righteousness" ("Righteousness to the Believer"), stanza 5.

121. Hymn 104, "Is not this a Brand pluckt out of the Fire? Zech. iii. 2" ("Thus saith the Lord to those that stand"), stanza 2.

122. Hymn 113, "Because thou sayest I am rich, and increased with Goods. Rev. iii. 17" ("What makes mistaken Men afraid"), stanza 9.

taken as an attempt to advance the message of the evangelical movement. If Watts's hymns helped kindle the Evangelical Revival, Hart's hymns continued the revival's fervor. After Watts, Hart became the most renowned eighteenth-century Independent hymnist. Hart, an Independent like Watts, was therefore more akin to Watts in doctrine than to Charles Wesley. But in style Hart was more compatible to Wesley, who showed more enthusiasm than Watts. Comparing Hart to Anne Steele, their sufferings in life shaped them as hymnists who emphasized the twin ideas of resignation to God's sovereign will amid trial and longing for heaven where suffering no longer exists. In spiritual struggles, Hart had more in common with William Cowper than any early evangelical hymn writer. Their intense spiritual agonies led them to produce the unrivaled lyrics on the theme of doubt and despair, intermingled with trust in God. Finally, as with John Newton, Hart's former libertinism created a deep sense of unworthiness and of amazement at divine grace in his life.

CHAPTER 4

The Theology and Spirituality of Joseph Hart

4.1 Introduction

In the preface to *A Collection of Psalms and Hymns, Extracted from various Authors* (1760), Martin Madan (1726–1790) listed some of the theological challenges he and his fellow evangelicals faced in the eighteenth century—deism, Arianism, Socinianism, papism, antinomianism, and formalism (iii–v). According to Augustus Toplady (1740–1778), Joseph Hart guarded his congregation from these erroneous doctrines: "That excellent man, the late Rev. Mr. Joseph Hart, made it his inviolable rule, not to let an Arian, an Arminian, or any unsound preacher, occupy his pulpit, so much as once" (1825, 4:134). Not only did Hart protect his congregation from false teachers, he also refuted their teachings, "contending earnestly for the faith" (Hughes: 1768, 28; cf. Jude 1:3). Indeed, by the time of his death, he gained the reputation as "Valiant for truth," or "a Christian warrior" (R.W.: 1768, 4–5; cf. Hughes: 1768) fighting for God's cause:

> His nervous arm did wield the two-edg'd sword,
> And cut the pillars of their Babel down;
> Arians, Socinians, felt the pow'rful word,
> And Deists, Atheists, sunk beneath his frown.
>
> He th' Antinomian drag'd to public shew,
> His fancy'd robe strip'd off, expos'd to shame;
> To proud perfection gave a deadly blow;
> Her head she bows, nor e'er shall rise again (R.W.: 1768, 4–5).

John Towers (*ca.* 1747–1804), Hart's successor in the ministry, also wrote an elegy of Hart, in which he described his predecessor as a faithful defender of God's truth:

> Should faithful, valiant Hart be quite forgot
> By those who with him had their destined lot;
>
> Whom the predestinating God had fix'd,
> To hear from him the gospel, pure, unmix'd?
> No; let his memory be immortaliz'd;
> Such honoured champions should be highly priz'd.
>
> With other worthies, who for truth were bold,
> In no mean place let Hart's name be enroll'd,
>
> And with the Spirit's sword dealt mighty blows,
> To those who dar'd the truths of God oppose (Hart: 1856, xliii).

Although Hart did not write apologetics, his hymns can be understood as his defense or articulation of evangelical theology and spirituality. As such, his hymns expressed what he believed (theology) and how he behaved (spirituality). As an experimental hymn writer,[1] he stressed how orthodoxy needed to be felt and experienced, not only known intellectually. He sought to apply what he believed and preached, as one of his elegists observed, "In him we virtue's sacred name revere, / He ever practis'd what he others taught" (R.W.: 1768, 6).

This chapter will examine Hart's theology and spirituality as found throughout his hymns, wherein, said Towers, "The doctrines of the gospel are illustrated so practically, the precepts of the word enforced so evangelically, and their effects stated so experimentally" (Hart: 1796, iii). The goal of the study is to provide the reader with the theology and spirituality of Hart. To produce an accurate presentation of his beliefs and practices, they will be studied within the religious context of his day. Peter Rae has identified and very briefly surveyed seven important themes in Hart's hymns: man's wretchedness, God's grace, atonement, Christ's suffering, intimate relationship between believers and the Savior, Holy Spirit, and evangelism (1988, 25–36). In this present study, all these themes, along with others, will be discussed at great length under the four major subjects of Hart's hymns: the Trinity, the Scriptures, salvation, and sanctification—perhaps the four most contested doctrines in the eighteenth century.

---

1. During Hart's time the term "experimental" was used to refer to someone who emphasized the need for Christian religion to be personally experienced and felt.

4.2 The Trinity: "To comprehend the great Three-One"[2]

One of the major threats to the orthodox doctrine of the Trinity in the eighteenth century was Socinianism, which "was perhaps the most notorious heresy in early modern Europe" (Mortimer: 2016, 361). Originating in the sixteenth century, this religious movement was named after the Italian Protestant radical reformer, Faustus Socinus[3] (1539–1604), who was the "principal Founder of a Sect that bears his Name" (Socinus: 1732, vii).[4] Socinus and those who espoused his views argued that "God is only one Person, not three." They embraced Jesus as man but not as God. And they only regarded the Holy Spirit as "the Power and Inspiration of God," not as a distinct divine person. For the Socinians, also known as Unitarians, the doctrine of the Trinity—the existence of one God in three divine persons—was "absurd, and contrary both to Reason and to it self, and therefore not only false, but *impossible*" (Nye: 1687; 3–4, 16, 24). In her article "The Philosophical Legacy of the 16th and 17th Century Socinians: Their Rationality," Marian Hillar noted,

> The doctrines of the Socinians represent a rational reaction to a medieval theology based on submission to the Church's authority. Though they retained Scripture as something *supra rationem*, the Socinians analyzed it rationally and believed that nothing should be accepted *contra rationem* (Hillar: 1998).

The Socinians' belief—that "whatever is contradictory to reason must be rejected"—contributed to the philosophical foundations of the Enlightenment or the Age of Reason, which culminated in the eighteenth century (1998).

Socinianism reached England in the seventeenth century, causing in the Church of England what came to be known as the Trinitarian controversy.[5] The churchman John Biddle (1615–1662), commonly regarded as "the Father of English Unitarianism" (Lloyd: 1899, 169), defended

---

2. Joseph Hart, Hymn 47, "Hymn, and Doxology to the Trinity," line 1:1. Unless otherwise stated, all Hart's hymns are quoted from the 5th ed. (1767).

3. Also spelled as Socin, Socini, Soccini, Sozini, or Sozzini.

4. Although Socinus was considered the founder of Socinianism, it was his uncle Laelius Socinus (1525–1562) who influenced him and laid the foundations for this movement, or was "the first Author of the Principles on which that Scheme is built." But it was Faustus who developed and propagated this heterodox doctrine (xvii, xx).

5. This controversy led to the Salters' Hall debate or the non-subscription controversy

and promoted Socinian doctrines and was almost certainly the one who translated *The Racovian Catechism* into English (printed in Amsterdam in 1652) (Rees: 1818, lxxx). This catechism, originally published in Polish in 1605 was "prepared by the followers of Faustus Socinus and was one of the earliest statements of antitrinitarian belief to surface since the Arian heresy of the fourth century" (Kubright: 2017, 979). For instance, in response to some trinitarian passages, such as Matthew 28:19 and 1 John 5:7, the catechism said, "These quotations onely shew that there is a Father, Sonne, and Holy Spirit, which we not only acknowledge, but constantly assert. [...] But it is evident that these Quotations do not demonstrate the Father, Sonne, and Holy Spirit to be three Persons in one Divine Essence" (20–21). The catechism also stated how the orthodox view of Christ as both God and man was "repugnant not only to sound Reason, but also to the holy Scriptures" (28). "Determined more by Reason than Authority," Biddle made the same case against orthodox Trinitarianism, explaining how it "was not well grounded in Revelation, much less in Reason" (1691, 4–5). Among his antitrinitarian works was A Scripture-Catechism (1654),[6] which Puritan John Owen (1616–1683) refuted in his *"Vindiciae Evangelicae," Or the Mystery of the Gospell Vindicated and Socinianisme Examined* (1655). By the time Biddle died in 1662, "the crisis of the Trinity" (Lim: 2012), which began in the 1640s, subsided. But this crisis resurfaced in the late 1680s when another Anglican clergyman, Stephen Nye (1648–1719), published his *Brief History of the Unitarians, called also Socinians* (1687), wherein he attacked tritheism and contended for Socinianism. According to Sarah Mortimer, "Although few English people agreed with Nye, the late seventeenth century did see the development of alternatives to Athanasian Trinitarianism, and especially of Arianism" (2016, 368). Two notorious supporters of Arian views of this time were William Whiston (1667–1752)

---

among dissenters in 1719. For a study of Socinianism in early modern England, see H. John McLachlan (1951) and Douglas Hedley (2005).

6. Biddle's other works included *A confession of faith touching the Holy Trinity, according to the Scripture* (London, 1648) and *Twelve arguments drawn out of the Scripture,: wherein the commonly received opinion touching the deity of the Holy Spirit, is clearly and fully refuted* ([London], 1647). He also translated some Socinian works such as Samuel Przypkowski's *Vita Fausti Socini Senensis* (1636), translated into English in 1653.

and Samuel Clarke (1675–1729),[7] who both diminished Jesus' deity and thus rejected the traditional doctrine of the Trinity. In defense of orthodox Trinitarianism, Edward Hawarden (1662–1735), a Roman Catholic priest, wrote *An Answer to Dr. Clarke and Mr. Whiston, Concerning the Divinity of the Son and of the Holy Spirit* (1729). The debate on the Trinity continued inside and outside the Established Church, leading up to the formation of Unitarianism as a denomination in the 1770s,[8] of which the Presbyterian minister Joseph Priestley (1733–1804) was the main apologist.[9]

Against this theological backdrop, Joseph Hart wrote his hymns. His hymn entitled "Hymn and Doxology to the Trinity," written around 1758, was therefore to some extent a polemical response to Arian, Socinian, and Unitarian theology:

> To comprehend the great Three-One
> Is more than highest Angels can;
> Or what the Trinity has done
> From Death and Hell to ransom Man.
>
> But all true Christians this may boast
> (A Truth from Nature never learn'd),
> That Father, Son, and Holy Ghost,
> To save our Souls are all concern'd.
>
> The Father's Love in this we find;
> He made His Son our Sacrifice;
> The Son in Love his Life resign'd,
> The Spirit of Love His Blood applies.
>
> Thus we the Trinity can praise
> In Unity, thro' Christ our King;

---

7. For a study of Clarke's nuanced views on the Trinity, consult Thomas C. Pfizenmaier (1997).

8. Andrew James Brown explained, "The group of British churches which collectively came to be known as Unitarian have been characterized by significant and continuous developments in their theological positions, moving from a broadly Arian position at the beginning of the 18th century to a clear Unitarian Christian position by the end of the 19th" (*Canterbury*, n.d.).

9. Joseph Priestly produced several antitrinitarian works, including *Unitarianism Explained and Defended* (London, 1796). For a treatment of his Unitarianism, see J. D. Bowers (2010).

> Our grateful Hearts and Voices raise
> In Faith and Love; while thus we sing.[10]

This hymn strongly affirmed the Athanasian doctrine of the Trinity, in which there is one God who exists in three divine persons: "Father, Son, and Holy Ghost." Hart called this God "the great Three-One," his favorite trinitarian description of God. And for him the Trinity was a mystery, too much even for the "highest angels" to fathom, for it goes above reason and logic. Due to the rise of rationalism, the intellectual environment in which Hart lived maintained that truth should be rational and thus anything inconsistent with reason must be dismissed as unreal. While diverse in belief and practice, eighteenth-century Unitarians rejected the Trinity, because in applying human reason to their interpretation of the Bible, they found this doctrine irrational (cf. Smith: 2021). Hart, who clearly was not rationalistic in his theology, accepted the doctrine not based on reason, but on Scripture. He submitted his mind to God's special revelation, so even if he could not logically comprehend the concept of the Trinity, he still embraced it by faith.[11]

In stanza two of his hymn, Hart declared the Trinity to be a "Truth from Nature never learn'd." Hart must have been thinking of antitrinitarians who argued from natural theology, which "was privileged as never before in the early eighteenth century" (Hindmarsh: 2018, 66). Natural theology insisted that truths "about God [...] can be learned from created things (nature, man, world) by reason alone" (Engen: 2017, 815). The Unitarian Joseph Priestley, whose theism was based on the argument from design, employed this epistemological method to challenge Trinitarianism, when he wrote, "To defend the doctrine of the trinity on the pretense that *three divine persons* make no more than *one God*, is just as absurd as to say that three human persons may make no more than one man [...]. But while the *Father*, the *Son*, and the *Holy Spirit*, separately considered, are each of them maintained to be true and very God [...] they cannot, in common sense, or common arithmetic, make less than three Gods" (Priestley: 1796, 27). To clarify, Priestley did not reject special revelation

---

10. Hymn 47, stanzas 1–4.

11. Although not about the Trinity, Hart's hymn 110, labeled "*But thou shalt know hereafter.* John xiii.7" ("Righteous are the Works of God"), expressed his anti-rationalist sentiment in which he placed faith above reason.

as a source of knowledge about God, which is what the deists essentially did. In fact, in his *Institutes of Natural and Revealed Religion* (1772–1774), Priestley argued for the need of both natural religion and revealed religion to acquire truths about God.[12] However, he claimed "natural religion took primacy over revealed religion" (Thompson: 2018, 322). That is, the truths derived from revelation must correspond to the truth observed from the natural world. Otherwise, these truths should be rejected. Consequently, in reality for Priestley and other Unitarians, the final test for truth was reason rather than revelation. English philosopher John Locke (1632–1704), who admitted the inspiration and infalliblity of Scripture, put it this way:

> Reason must be our last judge and Guide in every Thing. [...] I do not mean, that we must consult reason, and examine whether a proposition revealed from God can be made out by natural principles; and if it cannot, that then we may reject it; but consult it we must, and by it examine whether it be a revelation from God, or no; and if reason finds it to be revealed from God, reason then declares for it, as much as for any other truth, and makes it one of her dictates (1777, 446).

Despite Locke's high view of the Bible, he subjected it to "a rationalistic examination," treating it "like any other book" (Worcester: 1889, 78–79). This rationalistic approach led him into a denial of Trinitarianism. As Elwood Worcester observed, "He considered that the subsistence of three Persons in one Substance is neither explicitly revealed by Scripture nor discoverable by human reason" (16). For this reason, Locke was often accused of being a Socinian. For instance, Calvinisitic Anglican clergyman John Edwards (1637–1716) charged him with Socinianism in his *Some thoughts concerning the several causes and occasions of atheism, especially in the present age with some brief reflections on Socinianism, and on a late book entitled, The reasonableness of Christianity as delivered in the Scriptures* (1695). The late book Edwards was reffering to

---

12. Priestley wrote, "Above all things, be careful to improve and make use of the *reason* which God has given you, to be the guide of your lives, to check the extravagance of your passions, and to assist you in acquiring that *knowledge*, without which your rational powers will be of no advantage to you." Then he added, "Value the Scriptures, as a treasury of divine knowledge, consisting of books which are eminently calculated to inspire you with just sentiments, and prompt you to right conduct; and consider them also as the only proper *authority in matters of faith*" (1794, ii–iv).

was by Locke.[13] Published earlier in the same year and produced at the height of a Trinitarian controversy, this work did not include the doctrine of the Trinity. Edwards took Locke's omission to be an indication that for Locke the doctrine was not essential to the Christian religion. Edwards replied by insisting that this doctrine was a fundamental "part of the *Evangelical Faith*":

> This Gentleman [i.e., Locke] forgot, or rather wilfully omitted a plain and obvious passage in one of the Evangelists, [...] *Mat.* 28. 19. From which it is plain, that all Proselites to Christianity, all that are adult Members of the Christian Church, must be *taught*, as well as baptized, into the Faith of the *Holy Trinity*, Father, Son, and Holy Ghost. And if they must be *taught* this Doctrine [...] then it is certain that they must *believe* it, for this Teaching is in order to Belief. [...] You see it is part of the *Evangelical Faith*, and such as is necessary, absolutely necessary, to make one a Member of the Christian Church, to believe a Trinity in Unity in the Godhead (Edwards: 105–7).

Although Locke did embrace some of the principles of Socinianism,[14] he nevertheless would not accept the label of being a Socinian, and promptly replied to Edwards with *A Vindication of The Reasonableness of Christianity, &c. from Mr. Edwards's Reflections* (1695). Here Locke protested that his exposition of biblical passages along lines similar to the Socinians did not make him a Socinian. He wrote, "I know not but it may be true, that the *Antitrinitarians and Racovians* understand those places as I do: But 'tis more than I know that they do so. I took not my sense of those Texts from those Writers, but from the Scripture it self, giving Light to its own meaning" (22). The two continued to debate. The following year, Edwards replied to Locke with his *Socinianism Unmask'd* (1696), which Locke controverted with his *Second Vindication of the Reasonableness of Christianity* (1697). What is noteworthy here, however, is the way Locke claimed his doctrine of God was not derived from Socinian writers but from the Bible. Yet, while he saw the Scripture as an authoritative source of truth, his rationalistic interpretation of it dissuaded him from

---

13. *The Reasonableness of Christianity, as Delivered in the Scriptures* (London: 1695).

14. Diego Lucci argued how Locke "actually held a non-Trinitarian Christology comprising both Socinian and Arian elements." *John Locke's Christianity* (Cambridge University Press, 2021), 141.

accepting Trinitarian doctrine. Hence, at the end, human reason rather than Scripture was the dictator of truth in Locke's eyes.

For Hart, in contrast to Locke and Priestley, the ultimate source of truth was divine revelation, not human reason. And as an experimental hymnist, he placed more stress on personal experience than on human logic for the confirmation of truth. In other words, he believed the triunity of God even if he could not comprehend it, since it was a mystery. Yet he knew it was true, not only because the Bible said so but because he felt it. That is, he had an experimental knowledge of the Trinity. Hart's hymn 6, one of his hymns on the Holy Spirit, illustrates his experimentalism:

> Thou [Holy Spirit], with the Father and the Son
> Art that mysterious Three-in-One,
> God blest for evermore:
> Whom, tho' we cannot comprehend,
> Feeling thou art the Sinner's Friend,
> We love thee, and adore.[15]

Charles Wesley wrote a similar stanza in one of his hymns of the Trinity:

> Beyond our utmost thought,
> And reason's proudest flight,
> We comprehend him not,
> Nor grasp the infinite,
> But worship in the Mystic Three
> One God to all eternity.[16]

Commenting on Wesley, Bruce Hindmarsh said,

Charles, like his brother [John], rejoiced in what some have called the moderate Enlightenment, marveling at the order of the natural world revealed by experimental science as confirmation of the truths of revelation. Yet he believed that divine revelation went far beyond what natural reason could infer from natural phenomena (Hindmarsh: 2018, 141).

Hindmarsh's comment applies to other early evangelicals like Hart who pressed for the supremacy of divine revelation over human reason in

---

15. Hymn 6, "Another [To the Holy Ghost]" ("Descend from Heav'n, celestial Dove"), stanza 6.
16. *Hymns on the Trinity* (Bristol: Pine, 1767), 124.

their affirmation of truth. "As the 18th century drew to a close," explained Andrew Brown,

> the new emotionalism in orthodox Christian worship, typified by Methodist and Evangelical hymns, caused a number of Unitarians to reflect critically upon their own, rather dry, rational expressions of faith. Anna Letitia Barbauld [b. 1743...] was among those who began to feel that a too philosophical and abstract understanding of God had failed to engage the affections and that, "mere intellectual inquisitiveness in religion would reduce ardour to frigid and inconclusive speculation" (*Canterbury*: n.d.).

The next three subsections will deal with Hart's views of each of the persons of the Trinity with regard to what is known in modern terms as ontological and economic Trinity. In what follows, the reader will see how Hart understood the three persons to be ontologically equal yet economically distinct. Walter Lloyd said,

> The Unitarians arrived at and declared a positive principle of worship and belief, it was simply this—'That worship must be offered to the Father only as God.' Whatever differences of opinion there may have been and may be still amongst Unitarians this is the great religious principle which unites them; and this at once differentiates them from all classes of Trinitarians. [...] The primary difference between Trinitarians and Unitarians is in their worship" (1899, 153).

While Unitarians worshiped only the Father as God, trinitarians like Joseph Hart worshiped each of the three persons of the Trinity, a form of worship the Unitarians considered "as *idolatry*, as much as the worship of the virgin Mary, or any other saints in the Popish calendar" (Priestley: 1796, 9). Hart's trinitarian theology of worship is clearly seen in his seven doxologies:

> No. 1 O Praise the Lord, ye heav'nly Host:
> The same on Earth be done.
> Praise Father, Son, and Holy Ghost,
> The great, the good Three-One.

> No. 2 To the great Godhead, Father, Son,
> And Holy Spirit, Three in One,
> Be Glory, Praise, and Honour giv'n,
> By all on Earth, and all in Heav'n.

> No. 5 Glory to th' Eternal be.
> Three in One, and One in Three,
> God that pitied Sinners lost,
> Father, Son, and Holy Ghost;

For Hart, therefore, each person of the Triune God must be equally worshiped, since each of them is on par ontologically.

In the context of the rise of antitrinitarianism, Hart expounded a classical creedal understanding of the doctrine of the Trinity, but more than that, an experimental understanding of the doctrine was foundational for Hart's belief. And since one's belief informs and influences one's practice, Hart's trinitarian theology created in him a trinitarian spirituality of worship that adores the three persons of the Trinity.

4.2.1 God the Father

Focusing now more specifically on Hart's theology of the first person of the Trinity, Hart like the Unitarians, saw the Father as God but unlike them, Hart did not see only the Father as God, for he also acknowledged the deity of Jesus and the Holy Spirit. He also noted how each of the three persons has a distinct role in redemptive work:

> Thus God Three-One to Sinners lost
> Salvation *sends, procures,* and *seals.*[17]

According to Hart, the Father, out of his love for us, sent his Son for our salvation; the Son through his death procured our salvation;[18] and the Holy Spirit sealed our salvation. Hart's description of the Father's role as the sender of the Son is a recurrent theme in his hymnody:

---

17. Hymn 47, "Hymn, and Doxology to the Trinity" ("To comprehend the great Three-One"), lines 6:3–4. See also supplement hymn 3, where Hart says,

> The Father gives the Son;
> The Son his Flesh and Blood:
> The Spir't applies, and Faith puts on,
> The Righteousness of God.

18. See hymn 119, "The Lord thy God brought it to me. Gen. xxvii. 20" ("And now the work is done"), lines 4:3–6:

> To Father, and to Son,
> And to the Holy Ghost.
> Eternal life's the Gift of God:
> The Lamb procur'd it by His blood.

> What Creatures beside
> Are favour'd like Us!
> Forgiven, supplied,
> And banquetted thus,
> By God our good Father;
> Who gave us his Son;
> And sent Him to gather
> His Children in One?[19]
>
> The Father dearly loves the Son,
> And rates his Merits high.
> For no mean Cause he sent him down
> To suffer, grieve, and die.[20]

In his hymn on the Trinity, he wrote:

> Glory to God the Father be;
> Because he sent his Son to die.
>
> The Father's Love in this we find;
> He made His Son our Sacrifice.[21]

1 John 4:10 was almost certainly the scriptural background for these lines. Perhaps drawing from passages such as Luke 11:13; John 14:26, 15:26; and Acts 2:33, Hart viewed the Father as the sender not only of the Son but of the Holy Spirit as well:

> His Spirit from above
> Our Father sends us down:
> And looks with everlasting Love,
> On all that love the Son.[22]
>
> Give each some Token, Lord, for good;
> And send the Spirit down,
> To feed us with celestial Food,
> The Body of Thy Son.

---

19. Supplement hymn 20, "[For the Lord's Supper]," stanza 1.
20. Hymn 76, "The inestimable Benefits of Christ's Death, inferred from the Excellency of his Person," part 1 ("The Things on Earth which Men esteem"), stanza 4.
21. Hymn 47, "Hymn, and Doxology to the Trinity" ("To comprehend the great Three-One"), lines 5:1–2, 3:1–2.
22. Supplement hymn 19, "[For the Lord's Supper]" ("The God that first us chose"), stanza 6.

> Let ev'ry Tongue the Father own;
> Who, when we all were lost,
> To seek and save us sent the Son;
> And gives the Holy Ghost.[23]

One of Hart's parting hymns summarizes well the repeated theme in his hymns regarding God the Father as the sender of both his Son and Spirit:

> Father, 'ere we hence depart,
> Send thy good Spirit down,
> To reside in ev'ry Heart,
> And bless the Seed that's sown.
> Fountain of eternal love,
> Thou freely gav'st thy Son to die:
> Send thy Spirit from above,
> To quicken and apply.[24]

4.2.2 God the Son

Since antitrinitarians recognized the deity of the Father, there was really not much disputation about the first person of the Trinity among Church of England clergy and Nonconformists such as Baptists, Independents, and Presbyterians (many of whom became Unitarian in the later eighteenth century). Much of the controversial ink was spilled over the area of Christology. While both Arians and Socinians denied the eternal generation of the Son, they differed in their views of his existence. For Arians, the Son of God was

> [...] generated or created some time before the World, and in process of time, for great and necessary cause, became incarnate in our Nature [...]. But the *Socinians* deny, that the Son our Lord Christ had any Existence before he was born of Blessed *Mary*, being conceived in her by the holy Spirit of God (Nye: 1687, 33).[25]

Hart, on the other hand, affirmed the Son's eternality:

---

23. Supplement hymn 4, "[For the Lord's Supper]" ("Father of Heav'n, almighty King"), stanzas 3 and 5. See also supplement hymn 21 ("Once more we come before our God").
24. Supplement hymn 82, "[At Dismission]".
25. For an examination of Arianism in England, see J. Hay Colligan (1915).

> Christ is th' eternal *Rock*,
> On which his Church is built;[26]
>
> Hail, thou mighty Saviour! blest
> Before the world began
> In th' eternal Father's Breast,
> Hail, Son of God and Man![27]

For Hart, there was never a time when the Son of God did not exist. The Son has always been "In the eternal Father's breast," emphasizing the doctrine of eternal Sonship and refuting adoptionism. Not only did Hart affirm the Son's co-eternality with the Father, he also asserted Christ's dual natures—fully divine and fully human. His hymn "Christ very God and man," a title he probably borrowed from the Nicene Creed, reveals Christ's deity and humanity:

> A Man there is, a real Man,
> With Wounds still gaping wide,
> (From which, rich Streams of Blood once ran)
> In hands, and Feet, and Side.
>
> This wond'rous Man, of whom we tell,
> Is true Almighty God.[28]

The adjectives "very," "true," and even "Almighty" before "God" stress Hart's conviction in Jesus being of one substance with the Father, a doctrine the Arians, Socinians, and Unitarians tried to disprove.[29] For example, the Presbyterian minister Samuel Bourn the Younger (d. 1754), who was an avowed Arian, wrote,

> For my Part, I hold Jesus Christ to be God, or a God [...] But I can't bring myself to believe in his *Supreme Deity*, because I believe in the same supreme Deity of God the Father; and it appears to me a plain contradiction to say that there are two Persons or Beings who are both of

---

26. Supplement hymn 27, "Characters and Offices of Christ," lines 1:1–2.
27. Supplement hymn 8, "[For the Lord's Supper]" ("Hail, thou Bridegroom bruis'd to Death!"), lines 2:1–4.
28. Hymn 7, lines 1:1–4, 3:1–2.
29. Alan P.F. Sell noted, "As we delve more deeply into eighteenth century Christology we shall find that as the century proceeds a bolder Unitarianism begins to replace the somewhat milder Socinianism and the inherently unstable Arianism of earlier decades" (2011, 33).

'em *Supreme* or *most High God*; and I never yet had Faith eno' to believe two contradictory Propositions (Bourn: 1739, 48).

Attacking such a form of subordinationism, Hart stressed how Jesus is true and very God, co-equal and co-essential with God the Father. Hart equally underscored Christ's humanity—Jesus is "a real Man," who "partook of human Clay."[30] This statement ruled out both Docetism and Apollinarianism. In one of his hymns on Christ's nativity, Hart described Jesus as "our Infant-God."[31] In Hart's mind when Jesus became man, he remained God. Thus, oftentimes Hart referred to Jesus as "incarnate God," underscoring the God-man nature of Christ:

> To worship an Incarnate God,
> And know He sav'd us by His Blood?[32]

Because Jesus is an incarnate God, Hart thought it proper to render worship to Christ:

> Glory, and eternal laud
> Be to our incarnate God.[33]

On the other hand, with his Arian views, the Nonconformist minister Richard Price (1723–1791) "did not think that Christ was a proper object of worship" (Sell: 2011, 30).

In his hymn labeled "Jesus our All," Hart not only praised Jesus for who he is but also for what he has done in the gospel:

> Jesus is the chiefest Good;
> He hath sav'd us by his Blood.
> Let us value nought but Him;
> Nothing else deserves Esteem.
>
> Jesus therefore let us own.
> Jesus we'll exalt alone.
> Jesus has our Sins forgiv'n.
> Jesu's Blood has bought us Heav'n.[34]

---

30. Hymn 14, "Another" [hymn on Christ's Nativity]" ("Let us all with grateful Praises"), line 1:4.
31. Hymn 12, "Christ's Nativity" ("Come, ye Redeemed of the Lord"), line 2:4.
32. Hymn 44, "Jabez's Prayer. I Chron. iv. 9, 10" ("A Saint there was in Days of old"), lines 4:5–6. The term "incarnate God" appears seven times in Hart's hymnody.
33. Hymn 39, "The Sinner's Hope" ("Come, ye humble Sinner-Train"), lines 1:7–8.
34. Hymn 11, "Jesus our All," stanzas 1 and 4.

At first glance, the lines "Nothing else deserves esteem" and "Jesus we'll exalt alone" seem to suggest Christians should only worship Jesus and not the Father and the Holy Spirit. But when properly understood in their context, these lines simply reiterate the *solus Christus* of the Protestant Reformation, especially highlighting the importance of Christ's atoning blood,[35] what David Bebbington calls "crucicentrism" and what he considers one of the earmarks of early evangelicalism (1989, 14–17). To emphasize the centrality of the cross of Christ in Christianity, the Apostle Paul made a similar remark: "For I determined not to know any thing among you, save Jesus Christ, and him crucified" (1 Cor 2:2). Obviously, Paul was not implying the Corinthian church should not know the other persons of the Trinity. Likewise, when Hart said in the above hymn "Let us value nought but" Jesus, he was expressing the inestimable value of Christ's atoning blood, without which no sinner could be saved. As Hart wrote, "Ev'ry Grace and ev'ry Favour / Come to Us thro' Jesu's Blood."[36]

One of the errors of Socinianism was its so-called "example theory of the atonement," which denied the necessity of Christ's death for the forgiveness of sin. For Socinus, "it was perfectly legitimate to forgive sin without demanding satisfaction and God, just like any absolute ruler, could pardon offenses as he saw fit" without the need for penal substitution. Socinus further argued how "the innocent Christ had not been punished in our place" (Mortimer: 2016, 363). In other words, his death was not vicarious but meant to inspire people. Hence, Socinus rejected the orthodox Reformed view of satisfaction.[37] Later Unitarians adopted this Socinian theory of atonement. For instance, Priestley, who was

---

35. In hymn 103, "[Son, be of good Chear; thy Sins be forgiven thee. Mat. ix. 2.]," stanza 1, Hart declared,

> Blessed are they whose Guilt is gone;
> Whose Sins are wash'd away with Blood;
> Whose hope is fixt on Christ alone;
> Whom Christ hath reconcil'd to God.

36. Hymn 17, "Christ the Believer's All" ("Lamb of God, we fall before thee"), lines 1:7–8.

37. See Socinus, *De Jesu Christo Servatore* (1578), which, according to Alan W. Gomes, was the "most important Socinian work against the doctrine of satisfaction" and taught salvation can be obtained by imitating Christ (1993, 209–10).

considered by John Wesley to be "one of the most dangerous enemies of Christianity" (1931, 265), wrote,

> Another doctrine highly injurious to God, and which cannot have any favourable effect on those who propose to imitate him, and what in a great measure flowed from the doctrine of the trinity, is that of *atonement*, which supposes that God cannot forgive sins without satisfaction being made to his offended justice by the death of Christ; when the uniform and plain language of Scripture represents him as forgiving sins freely, and requiring no satisfaction whatever, besides the repentance and reformation of the sinner (1796, 30–31).

When Hart penned his hymn 40, headed "The World by Wisdom knew not God. I Cor. i. 21," he must have had the Socinian view of atonement in sight:

> When the blessed Jesus died,
> God was clearly justified:
> Sin to pardon without Blood
> Never in his Nature stood.[38]

Hart's message is straightforward: it is never in God's just and holy nature to pardon sin without Christ's death, which is what satisfied God's justice:

> On the Cross thy Body broken
> Cancels ev'ry penal Tie.
> Tempted Souls, produce this Token
> All Demands to satisfy.[39]
>
> Vengeance, when the Saviour died,
> Quitted the believer;
> Justice cried, "I'm satisfied
> Now henceforth for ever."[40]

In short, Christ's blood is necessary for the atonement of sin: "That precious Blood atones all Sin."[41] Hart's scriptural basis for this teaching is

---

38. Hymn 40 ("O Ye Sons of Men, be wise"), stanza 4.
39. Hymn 56, "[Faith and Repentance]," part 2 ("Great High-Priest, we view stooping"), lines 2:1–4.
40. Hymn 18, "Lord, if thou wilt, thou canst make me clean. Matt. viii.2" ("Oh! the Pangs by Christians felt"), lines 5:1–4.
41. Supplement hymn 71, "His Mercy endureth for ever. Psal. cxxxvi" ("God's mercy is for ever sure"), line 3:1.

most likely Hebrews 9:22, "without shedding of blood is no remission." Then Hart continued,

> Think not that he will, or may
> Pardon any other Way.[42]

Again, Hart made it emphatically clear—God cannot forgive sin in any other way apart from Christ's atoning blood, with which Jesus "sav'd us from the Wrath of God; / And paid our Ransom."[43] In some other places, the hymn-writer said,

> Nothing but thy Blood, O Jesus,
> Can relieve us from our Smart;
> Nothing else from Guilt release us;
> Nothing else can melt the Heart.[44]

> Whoe'er believes aright,
> In Christ's atoning Blood,
> Of all his Guilt's acquitted quite;
> And may draw near to God.[45]

> The Blood of Jesus surely saves
> The sinful Soul from Death.[46]

In a sense, Socinians and Unitarians disapproved the orthodox teaching on Christ's satisfaction because while they appealed to Scripture, they found it irrational for God to demand satisfaction before he could pardon sin. For Hart, however, the whole subject of atonement remains a mystery beyond human reason though it is true and to be embraced:

> Much we talk of Jesu's Blood.
> But how little's understood!
> Of his Suff'rings so intense
> Angels have no perfect Sense.
> Who can rightly comprehend
> Their Beginning, or their End!

---

42. Hymn 10, "The World by Wisdom knew not God. I Cor. 1.21" ("O Ye Sons of Men, be wise"), lines 5:3–4.

43. Supplement hymn 7, "[For the Lord's Supper]" ("Join ev'ry Tongue to sing"), lines 1:5b–6a.

44. Hymn 54, "Faith and Repentance" ("Jesus is our God and Saviour"), lines 3:1–4.

45. Hymn 53, "Faith is the Victory," stanza 1.

46. Supplement hymn 75, "[Baptism]" ("By what amazing Ways"), lines 4:3–4.

> 'Tis to God, and God alone,
> That their Weight is fully known.[47]

4.2.3 God the Holy Ghost

Returning to Hart's hymn on the Trinity, he attributed to the Holy Spirit the application of Christ's blood to sinners:

> The Father's Love in this we find;
> He made his Son our Sacrifice.
> The Son in Love his Life resign'd.
> The Spir't of Love his Blood applies.[48]

Unless the Spirit applies the blood, it will do sinners no good. This truth shows the Spirit's indispensability in sinners' salvation:

> Sinners, I read, are justified
> By Faith in Jesu's Blood:
> But, when to *Me* that Blood's applied,
> 'Tis then it does me Good.[49]

Hart therefore exhorts his singers to pray,

> Extend thy Mercy, gracious God.
> Thy quick'ning Spir't vouchsafe to send;
> Apply the reconciling Blood;[50]

Hart's emphasis on the Holy Spirit's role in salvation and sanctification was not uncommon among early evangelicals. As Thomas Kidd observed,

> Many eighteenth-century evangelicals focused heavily on the work of the Spirit. Outpourings of the Spirit generated revivals, but the Spirit also regenerated sinners, giving them new life in Christ. Moreover, the Spirit comforted and guided individual believers, offering them the assurance and joy of salvation, and strength through trials (2014, 36; cf. 2007, xix).

---

47. Hymn 41, "Behold and see, if there be any Sorrow like unto my Sorrow. Lam. i. 12," stanza 1.
48. Hymn 47, "Hymn and Doxology to the Trinity" ("To comprehend the great Three-One"), stanza 3.
49. Hymn 90, "For the Kingdom of God is not in Word, but in Power. I Cor. iv. 20" ("A Form of Words, tho' e'er so sound"), stanza 3.
50. Supplement hymn 30, "Desertion" ("Deep in a cold, a joyless Cell"), lines 3:1–3.

For this reason, Kidd felt pneumatology should be added to Bebbington's quadrilateral as another descriptor of early evangelicals. While this quadrilateral, he explained,

> Accurately reflects four distinctive emphases of evangelical faith, it does not account for the enormous weight that evangelicals such as Whitefield put on the Holy Spirit's ministry. Along with conversion, the experience of the Holy Spirit's presence and power was what struck Whitefield and other evangelicals as the most novel aspect of their new-born lives (2014, 36).

Likewise, Timothy Larsen argued, "An emphasis on the work of the Spirit has always been a distinguishing mark of evangelical Christian life, not least in the first generation of Wesley and Whitefield" (2007, 10). A study of Hart's pneumatology strengthens the claim of both Kidd and Larsen.

The Socinians denied both the deity and personhood of the Holy Spirit. As their catechism taught, "The Holy Spirit is no where in the Scripture expresly called God; and though in some places the things of God are attributed to him, yet doth it not thereupon follow, that he is either God, or a person of the Deity" (*Recovian Catechisme*: 1652, 20). In *Twelve arguments drawn out of the Scripture, wherein the commonly received opinion touching the deity of the Holy Spirit, is clearly and fully refuted* (1647), John Biddle rejected the Spirit's divinity while maintaining the Spirit's personhood.[51] This shows not all antitrinitarians were Socinian.

In contrast to Socinians and other antitrinitarians, Hart understood the Holy Spirit as a divine person, distinct from the other two persons of the Trinity:

> Blest Spir't of Truth, eternal God,
> Thou meek and lowly Dove,[52]

Here the word "eternal," modifying God, denotes how the Spirit is co-eternal and co-equal with the Father and the Son, and not "inferiour to God," as Biddle averred (1647, 13–14). In his hymn called "Whitsunday," Hart further displayed the Spirit's co-equality with the Father and the Son:

---

51. As mentioned earlier, for the Socinians the Spirit "is only the Power and Inspiration of God." See Nye (1687), 16.
52. Hymn 5, "[To the Holy Ghost]" lines 1:1–2.

> When the blest Day of Pentecost
> Was fully come; the Holy Ghost
> Descended from above,
> Sent by the Father and the Son,
> (The Sender and the Sent are one)[53]

Hart saw the Spirit as coming from both the Father and the Son, indicating his support of the addition of *filioque* (and from the Son) to the original Nicene Creed in the East-West controversy on the procession of the Holy Spirit. Whereas Christians in the East insisted that the Spirit proceeded from the Father alone, Christians in the West maintained that the Spirit proceeded from both the Father and the Son. In Hart's own words, the Spirit was "Sent by the Father and the Son." Then he added, "The Sender and the Sent are one," underscoring the Spirit's co-equality with the Father and the Son, both of whom sent him. In another stanza, Hart addressed the Spirit as "thou Almighty Paraclete" "Thy Pow'r, thy Godhead, still the same."[54] Hart applied this same term "Almighty" to both the Father and the Son, pointing out again how the three are co-equal in power.[55]

Perhaps because it was on Pentecost Sunday (May 29, 1757) that Hart experienced conversion, the theme of Holy Spirit became dominant in his hymnody (Rae: 1988, 35). Three of his early hymns, numbers 4, 5, and 6, are all on the Spirit. For him one of the roles of the Spirit is to convict sinners of their sin and to bring them to Christ, who alone can cleanse them from all their sins by his blood. As Hart wrote,

> To understand these Terms aright,
> This grand Distinction should be known;
> Tho' all are Sinners in God's Sight,
> There are but few so in *their own*.
> To such as these our Lord was sent:
> *They're* only Sinners, who repent.
>
> What Comfort can a Saviour bring
> To those who never felt their woe?
> A Sinner is a sacred Thing;
> The Holy Ghost has made him so.

---

53. Hymn 45, "Whitsunday," lines 1:1–5.
54. Hymn 45, "Whitsunday," lines 6:1, 5.
55. See also hymn 7, "Christ very God and Man" ("A Man there is, a real Man"), and supplement hymn 4, "[For the Lord's Supper]" ("Father of Heav'n, almighty King").

> New Life from Him we must receive,
> Before for Sin we rightly grieve.[56]

The point Hart was making here is this: while all are sinners, not every sinner will see their sin and their need to repent. Only those whom the Spirit has convicted of their sin will feel their misery and grieve and come to Christ for mercy. So to be "A sinner is a sacred thing," said Hart. That is, to know our sin and feel its burden is a blessing from the Spirit, who has made us aware of our sin. Charles Spurgeon (1834–1892) said,

> I always love that phrase of Hart's—"A sinner is a sacred thing, / The Holy Ghost hath made him so". […] I love to see one who feels himself to be a real sinner; not the one who says, just by way of compliment, that he is a sinner; not the one who can read the Ten Commandments all through, and say that he has not broken any of them; but the real sinner, the downright guilty man, the man who is a thorough sinner, and knows it, that is the man to whom I like to preach the gospel (Spurgeon/Harrold: 1898, 334).

In another hymn, Hart further underscored the Holy Spirit's convicting work:

> Th' Holy Ghost will make the Soul
> Feel its sad Condition;
> For the Sick, and not the Whole,
> Need the good Physician.[57]

When writing this stanza, Hart was probably thinking of Mark 2:17, where Jesus said, "They that are whole have no need of the physician, but they that are sick…" Again, for Hart, unless the Spirit exposes the true nature of our soul, we will not see our need to come to Jesus, "the good Physician," for the healing of our soul. People may hear Scripture proclaimed to them, telling them how they have offended God, but the mere hearing of God's Word, unaccompanied by the convicting power of the Spirit, cannot change their hearts. The Spirit must first "wound" or convict them, before they can be healed:

---

56. Hymn 38, "This is a faithful Saying, and worthy of all Acceptation, that Christ Jesus came into the World to save Sinners. I Tim. i.15" ("When Adam by Transgression fell"), stanzas 4–5.

57. Hymn 89, "These are they which came out of great Tribulation; and have washed their Robes, and made them white, in the Blood of the Lamb. Rev. vii.14" ("Brethren, those who come to Bliss"), stanza 4.

> A form of Words, tho' e'er so sound,
> Can never save a Soul.
> The Holy Ghost must give the Wound:
> And make the Wounded whole.[58]

Notably, here Hart attributed the healing of the wounded souls to the Spirit's work, when in the New Testament such work is commonly attributed to Jesus (Matt. 9:22; 15:28; Mark 6:56; John 5:9). Nonetheless, Hart was aware of the way the Spirit heals the "fest'ring Sores of Sin [...] with Balm from Jesu's Wounds."[59] Indeed, "Great are the Graces he [the Spirit] confers, / But all in Jesus' name."[60] To put it another way, all the blessings sinners receive from the Spirit come to them through Jesus. After all, for Hart, the Spirit's ultimate work is to "Direct us to the bleeding Wounds / Of our Incarnate God" Jesus Christ.[61]

The Spirit not only convicts sinners of their sin, but positively he also reveals to them God's "secret love" of the gospel, secret to those whose eyes remain spiritually blind:

> Come, Holy Spirit, come;
> Let thy bright Beams arise,
> Dispel the darkness from our Minds;
> And open all our Eyes.
>
> Convince us of our Sin;
> Then lead to Jesu's Blood:
> And to our wond'ring View reveal
> The secret love of God.[62]
>
> Glory to God the Holy Ghost,
> Who to our Hearts this Love reveals.[63]

---

58. Hymn 90, "For the Kingdom of God is not in Word, but in Power. I Cor. iv.20," stanza 1.
59. Hymn 5, "[To the Holy Ghost]" ("Blest Spir't of Truth, eternal God"), lines 6:3–4.
60. Hymn 116, "For he shall not speak of Himself. John xvi.13" ("Whatever prompts the Soul to Pride"), lines 4:1–2.
61. Hymn 6, "[To the Holy Ghost]" ("Descend from Heav'n, celestial Dove"), lines 2:5–6.
62. Hymn 4, "To the Holy Ghost," stanzas 1 and 4.
63. Hymn 47, "Hymn, and Doxology to the Trinity" ("To comprehend the great Three-One"), lines 6:1–2.

The idea of the Spirit as the one who unveils the gospel love to sinners was important to Hart, since he once thought he was too sinful to be an object of divine love. But once the Spirit dispelled the darkness from his mind and opened his eyes, he began to see and understand it:

> For Love of Me the Son of God
> Drain'd ev'ry Drop of vital Blood.
>
> O love, of unexampled Kind!
> That leaves all Thought so far behind:
> Where Length, and Breadth, and Depth, and Height,
> Are lost to my astonish'd Sight.[64]
>
> Dearly are we bought; for God
> Bought us with his own Heart's Blood.
> Boundless Depths of Love divine!
> Jesus, what a Love was Thine!
> Tho' the wonders thou hast done
> Are, as yet, so little known;[65]

Hart recognized an element of mystery in God's saving love—even after the Spirit had opened his eyes to it, because it is boundless, he confessed how little he understood it: "Oh, what Wonders Love has done! / But how little understood!"[66] For Hart, no one can fully comprehend "The Wonders of redeeming Love!"[67] Nevertheless, this truth did not keep him from praying to the Spirit:

> Descend, celestial Dove,
> Give us that best of Blessings, Love,[68]
>
> Shew us the Father's boundless Love,
> And Merits of the Son.[69]

Another important ministry of the Spirit pertains to Christian life. He

---

64. Hymn 1, "On the Passion," part 2 ("And why, dear Saviour, tell me why"), lines 10:1–2, 9:1–4.
65. Hymn 41, "Behold and see, if there be any Sorrow like unto my Sorrow. Lam. i.12" ("Much we talk of Jesu's Blood"), lines 4:1–6.
66. Hymn 75, "Jesus oft-times resorted thither, with his Disciples. John xviii.2" ("Jesus, while he dwelt below"), lines 12:1–2.
67. Hymn 21 ("How wond'rous are the Works of God").
68. Hymn 50, "Charity never faileth. I Cor. xiii.8" ("Faith in the bleeding Lamb"), lines 9:1, 3.
69. Hymn 5, "[To the Holy Ghost]" ("Blest Spir't of Truth eternal God"), lines 7:3–4.

comforts "the heavy Heart" pressed by "sin and sorrow."[70] Hart pleaded with the Spirit to "Breathe Comfort, where Distress abounds."[71] He again prayed, "Chear our desponding Hearts, / Thou heav'nly Paraclete."[72] Thrice in his hymnody he addressed the Spirit as Paraclete,[73] which is derived from John 14:16, where the Greek word παράκλητον (from which the term "Paraclete" comes) is translated as "Comforter" in the King James Version, the version Hart used.

Hart also saw the Spirit as one who sanctifies believers, strengthening their faith, cleansing their hearts, and securing their salvation:

> Revive our drooping Faith;
> Our Doubts and Fears remove;
> And kindle in our Breasts the Flames
> Of never-dying Love.
>
> 'Tis thine to cleanse the Heart,
> To sanctify the Soul,
> To pour fresh Life on ev'ry Part,
> And new create the Whole.[74]
>
> We laud thy Name, blest Spir't of Truth,
> Who dost Salvation seal,
> Incline the heart, unclose the Mouth,
> And sanctify the Will.[75]

Part of the sanctifying work of the Spirit is to apply Christ's word to believers[76] and bear witness to his word[77] for the purpose of assur-

---

70. Hymn 5, lines 2:1–2.
71. Hymn 5, line 6:1.
72. Hymn 4, "To the Holy Ghost" ("Come, Holy Spirit, come"), 2:1–2.
73. See hymns 4, 6, and 45, which are all about the Spirit.
74. Hymn 4, "To the Holy Ghost" ("Come, Holy Spirit, come"), stanzas 3 and 6.
75. Doxology 7.
76. Hymn 94, "I am the Way, and the Truth, and the Life. John xiv. 6" ("I am, saith Christ, the Way"), stanza 4:

> If what those Words aver,
> The Holy Ghost apply;
> The simplest Christian shall not *err*,
> Nor be *deceiv'd*, nor *die*.

77. Hymn 90, "For the Kingdom of God is not in Word, but in Power. I Cor. iv. 20" ("A Form of Words, tho' e'er so sound"), stanza 8:

ing Christians of their status in Christ.[78] Thus the Spirit operates in the believers by Christ's Word. And for Hart, Jesus and his Word are "both the same," exhibiting Hart's high view of the Scriptures.

4.3 The Scriptures: "Thou [Jesus] and thy Word are both the same"[79]

In his tract, *An Account of the Growth of Deism in England* (1696), William Stephens (d. 1718), a Church of England clergyman, related how deism, which for him was "a denial of all reveal'd Religion," crept into England (1696, 4). He also distinguished two kinds of deism: "some who pretend themselves Deists, are Men of loose and sensual lives," who "ridicule the reality of all *Miracles* and Revelation." For Stephens, though, these people are "meer Sceptics, and practical Atheists, rather than real Deists." "But there are others," explained Stephens, "who, although they have not a due regard to Revelation, are Men of Sobriety and Probity" (5). Nonetheless, whether liberal or self-proclaimed Christian deists, they all essentially rejected the Bible as God's divine revelation and as a source of religion. This is how they differed from Arians, Socinians, and Unitarians, who, while rationalistic in theology, still somewhat appealed to the sufficiency of Scripture for answers about God. Deists, on the other hand, ruled out special revelation as divine authority for religious belief. They created a philosophically religious system based highly on human reason to understand God and his relation to his creation. John Toland (d. 1722), who has been called "the most important deist thinker of the eighteenth century" (Lucci: 2008, 14), said, "We hold that Reason is the only Foundation of all Certitude; and nothing reveal'd, whether as to its Manner or Existence, is more exempted from its Disquisitions, than the ordinary Phenomena of

---

      Thus Christians glorify the Lord.
      His Spirit joins with ours,
      In bearing Witness to his Word,
      With all it's saving Pow'rs.

78. Hymn 18, "Lord, if thou wilt, thou canst make me clean. Matt. viii. 2" ("Oh! the Pangs by Christians felt"), lines 5.5–8:

      "It is *finish'd*," said the Lord,
      In His dying Minute;
      Holy Ghost, repeat that Word;
      Full salvation's in it.

79. Supplement hymn 62, "Christ is holy" ("Jesus, Lord of Life and Peace"), line 1:6.

Nature" (Toland: 1696, 6).[80] Likewise, Matthew Tindal (d. 1733), whose *Christianity as old as the Creation* (1730) was often regarded as "the Deists' Bible" (Lalor: 2006, 111), argued, "true religion or Christianity has no serious need of divine revelation since humans are equipped to discover it themselves, and if some purported revelation is found not to be so, it is rejected from being part of the true faith" (Marco: 2017, 137).

In sharp contrast to the deists, convinced that the Bible is God's inspired revelation, early evangelicals maintained that "all spiritual truth is to be found in" the Bible (Bebbington: 1989, 12). Standing in the tradition of Reformed Protestants, they believed in this Holy Book as the primary means by which God reveals himself to his creation. Their unwavering commitment to Scripture, which Bebbington styled as "biblicism," became one of the defining features of early evangelicalism (12–14). Hart wrote a hymn devoted to the subject of the Bible, simply entitled "The Scriptures," wherein he clearly showed his evangelical view of Scripture. The hymn begins with a question,

> Say, Christian; wouldst thou thrive,
> In Knowledge of thy Lord?[81]

Then Hart answered,

> Against no Scripture ever strive;
> But tremble at his Word.[82]

Hart's basic message here is this: contrary to the deistic teaching, anyone who wants to know God must know him by means of his Word. More specifically, Christians who desire to grow in their knowledge of God must not obstinately resist or revolt against the authority of Scripture but "tremble at his Word," or as Hart says in the second stanza, must "Revere the sacred Page." "To injure any Part" of this sacred Book "Betrays, with blind and feeble Rage, / A hard and haughty Heart." In short, in Hart's mind, those who insult or revile God's Word only prove themselves to be unbelievers.[83] The second stanza thus indirectly challenges those deists

---

80. For a study of Toland and deism, see Robert E. Sullivan (1982).
81. Appendix hymn 8, "The Scriptures," lines 1:1–2.
82. Appendix hymn 8, "The Scriptures," lines 1:3–4.
83. Some "laugh at the story of *Baalam*'s Ass, and *Samson*'s Locks." See Stephens (1696), 5.

who consider themselves Christians but openly reject the Bible as God's divine revelation. The hymn goes on to affirm the infallibility of Scripture:

> If ought there dark appear,
> Bewail thy Want of Sight:
> No imperfection can be there:
> For all God's words are right.[84]

Since God's Word is perfect, if its reader finds therein something "dark" or seemingly contradictory, the problem does not lie with the Bible but with the reader's spiritual ability to understand. In that case, Hart exhorted the reader to mourn his need of spiritual eyes to perceive the Scriptures: "Bewail thy Want of Sight." Hart was, of course, aware of how God alone, in particular the Holy Spirit, can "Dispel the Darkness from our Minds; / And open all our Eyes."[85] Consequently, the third stanza implicitly admonishes the reader to pray to God for illumination, without which no one can understand his Word. Therefore, elsewhere Hart prayed, this time, to Jesus: "The Word of Truth, from thy blest Mouth: / O, make it clearly known!"[86]

Returning to the third stanza of Hart's hymn on Scripture, the line "For all God's words are right" is emphatic, for it attacks those rational dissenters[87] who picked and chose from the Bible what they thought to be right. They approved parts of the Scriptures they deemed consistent with their natural religion and thus rejected anything supernatural, such as Christ's virgin birth and other miracles. Soame Jenyns (b. 1704), who might have been the first one to use the term "rational dissenters," put it this way: rational dissenters have "arbitrarily expunged out of their Bibles every thing, which appears to them contradictory to reason, that is, to their own reason, or in other words, every thing which they cannot understand, are displeased to see those tenets explained, which they

---

84. Appendix hymn 8, "The Scriptures," stanza 3.
85. Hymn 4, "To the Holy Ghost" ("Come, Holy Spirit, come"), lines 1:3–4.
86. Supplement hymn 11, "[For the Lord's Supper]" ("Lord, send thy Spirit down"), lines 2:3–4.
87. "When the phrase 'rational dissenters' first began to be used in the early 1760s, it most often denoted, at least when used by those sympathetic to its aims, a group of Presbyterian divines advocating a species of practical and rational religion, in opposition to the evangelical doctrine of the rival bodies of dissent" (Mills: 2009, 12).

have thought proper to reject" (Jenyns: 1761, xvi).[88] For Hart, however, "all God's words," including those which seem contradictory to human reason, "are right." Simon Mills's observation is therefore unrefuted that rational dissent emerged "largely in reaction to the rise of evangelical Calvinism among the Congregationalist and Baptist congregations comprising the orthodox wing of Protestant dissent" (2009, 12).[89]

In the fourth stanza, Hart made a bold but orthodox claim,

> The Scriptures and the Lord
> Bear one tremendous Name:
> The written, and th' Incarnate Word
> In all Things are the same.[90]

In Hart's thinking, to declare "The written, and th' Incarnate Word / In all Things are the same" means just as "Jesus is the Truth" so is the Bible.[91] This appellation "the Truth" is the "one tremendous Name" which both Jesus and his Word bear. In his other hymn, entitled "Christ is holy," Hart proclaimed, "Sweet and terrible's thy Word: / Thou and thy Word are both the same."[92] That is, the Bible is as holy or divine as Jesus is. After all, the written Word is the very Word of Christ, proceeding out of his own mouth, as Hart indicated in stanza five of his hymn on Scripture,

> The two-edg'd Sword that's in His Mouth,
> Shall all proud Reas'ners slay.[93]

Undoubtedly the scriptural background for this stanza is Hebrews 4:12, "For the word of God is quick, and powerful, and sharper than any twoedged sword..." With this description given to Christ's Word, it then has the power to destroy "all proud Reas'ners," which might have generally referred to theistic rationalists, or those deists who considered

---

88. This edition has an additional preface where the phrase "rational dissenters" might have appeared for the first time in literature. See Mills (2009), 12.
89. Mills, "Joseph Priestley and the Intellectual Culture of Rational Dissent, 1752–1796," 12.
90. Appendix hymn 8, "The Scriptures," stanza 4.
91. See the first two lines of stanza 5, "For Jesus is the Truth, / As well as Life and Way."
92. Supplement hymn 62, "Christ is holy" ("Jesus, Lord of Life and Peace"), lines 1:5–6.
93. Appendix hymn 8, "The Scriptures," lines 5:3–4.

themselves Christians like Tindal.[94] In the next stanza Hart challenged these arrogant reasoners:

> Why dost thou call Him Lord;
> And what He says resist?
> The soul that stumbles at the Word,
> Offended is at Christ.[95]

For Hart, to call Jesus Lord and resist his Word at the same time is a contradiction. And since Jesus and his Word "are both the same," to attack his Word is to attack him. The hymn ends by comparing man's thoughts and God's Word, and calling for submission to the Bible:

> The Thoughts of Man are Lies.
> The Word of God is true.
> To bow to *That* is to be wise:
> Then hear, and fear, and Do.[96]

Because God's Word is true, it deserves full trust on man's part.[97] As Hart wrote elsewhere, "Believe thy God: believe his Word, / His Spirit, and his Son."[98] Here Hart showed how the Bible is as trustworthy as the three persons of the Trinity, indicating his high regard for Scripture.

Since one's doctrine affects one's life, Hart's high view of God's Word resulted in his Word-centered spirituality. He strove to live by and rest his soul on this Holy Word:

> 'Tis by Thy Word we live,
> And not by Bread alone.[99]

---

94. Henry C. Thiessen states, "During the course of history there have appeared three types of rationalism: atheistic, pantheistic, and theistic. Atheistic rationalism appeared first in the early Greek philosophers. [...] Pantheistic rationalism is represented in Anaxagoras and the Stoics, and theistic rationalism appeared first in the form of English and German Deism in the eighteenth century" (1979, 17).
95. Appendix hymn 8, "The Scriptures," stanza 6.
96. Appendix hymn 8, "The Scriptures," stanza 7.
97. See also hymn 48, "Heaven and Earth shall pass away, but my Words shall not pass away. Matt. xxiv. 35" ("The Moon and Stars shall lose their Light").
98. Supplement hymn 2, "[For the Lord's Supper]" ("This is the Day the Lord has made"), lines 5:1–2.
99. Supplement hymn 11, "[For the Lord's Supper]" ("Lord, send thy Spirit down"), lines 2:1–2.

> We rest our Souls on Jesu's Word,
> And give the Glory to the Lord.[100]

It is worth mentioning, too, that Hart revered the Bible because herein God reveals the way of salvation to sinners.[101]

4.4 Salvation: "the peculiar doctrines of the gospel"

In a funeral sermon for Hart, his brother-in-law John Hughes (d. 1773) spoke of Hart's "undaunted courage in stoutly defending, with all his might, the peculiar doctrines of the gospel" (1768, 28). By "the peculiar doctrines of the gospel," Hughes was undoubtedly thinking of the Calvinistic doctrines of the gospel. Indeed, as will become clear in this study, Hart's soteriology was Reformed in essence.

4.4.1 "So dead, so lost"[102]

Believing man is by nature dead, incapable to save himself from sin, Hart wrote,

> Needy, and naked, and unclean,
> Empty of Good, and full of Ill,
> A lifeless Lump of loathsome Sin,
> Without the Pow'r to act or will![103]

This stanza clearly teaches total depravity, a doctrine which had already appeared in Hart's pre-conversion work, *The Unreasonableness of Religion*, wherein his defense of the doctrine was shaded by his antinomianism.[104] Peter Rae has remarked, "Hart's view of man is that in his unregenerate state, he is without beauty and there is nothing that could

---

100. Hymn 80, "Thou hast guided them in thy Strength unto thy holy Habitation. Exod. xv. 13." ("Mistaken Men may bawl"), lines 3:5–6.
101. Hymn 9, "Of Sanctification" ("The Holy Ghost in Scripture saith").
102. Hymn 10, "The enlightened Sinner" ("My God, when I reflect"), line 6:4.
103. Hymn 111, "Blessed be ye Poor. Luke vi. 20" ("Lord, when I hear thy Children talk"), stanza 3.
104. In that tract Hart wrote, "When I was in my natural state, it was impossible for me to move one step towards heaven; no, not so much as to implore the divine assistance aright; but was utterly *dead in trespasses and sins* [Eph 2:1]; and as incapable of exerting the least power, or motion towards any spiritual good, as a dead carcass is of performing any action of natural life" (1741, 6). But again, here Hart argued for total depravity from an antinomian perspective. This was not the case when he defended the doctrine in his hymns.

possibly attract the divine mercy, except by grace" (1988, 26). Hart's teaching on total depravity is further seen in his hymns with his use of the following phrases:

> *All my powers are deprav'd,*
> *Blind, perverse, and filthy.*[105]

> On one so foul, so base, so blind,
> So dead, so lost, as I?[106]

In his natural condition man cannot "stand still, and see the salvation of the LORD" (Ex. 14:13).[107] Indeed, man is so dead that he "never move[s]," said Hart, "For who can move, that's *dead*?"[108] Hence, Hart prayed,

> Lord, let thy Spirit prompt us when
> To go, and when to stay.
>
> Give Pow'r and Will; and then command;
> And we will follow Thee:
> And when we're frighten'd, bid us stand,
> And thy Salvation see.[109]

The request to "Give Pow'r and Will" stresses the deficiency by which man has no inherent ability or desire to respond to God's command to stand and come to him for salvation. Therefore, unless God gives man power and will, he cannot and will not respond to the gospel call. To put it concisely, for Hart, unless God quickens the dead, they remain lifeless. And Hart specifically attributed this work of regeneration to the Holy Spirit, "Who to the Dead [can] Life impart."[110] In one of his hymns on the

---

105. Hymn 24, "A Dialogue between a Believer and his Soul" ("Come, my Soul, and let us try"), lines 6:5–6.
106. Hymn 10, "The enlightened Sinner" ("My God, when I reflect"), lines 6:3–4.
107. Hart's hymn 30 is a reflection on this verse and is labeled after it, "Stand still, and see the Salvation of the Lord. Exod. xiv. 13" ("Oh! what a narrow, narrow path").
108. Hymn 30, line 4:4.
109. Hymn 30, lines 9:1–2, 10:1–4.
110. Hymn 5, "[To the Holy Ghost]" ("Blest Spir't of Truth, eternal God"), line 2:3. See also hymn 45, "Whitsunday" ("When the blest Day of Pentecost"), lines 5:4–6:

> What? Has the Holy Ghost forgot
> To quicken Souls that Christ has bought,
> And lets them lifeless lie?

Elsewhere Hart credited Jesus for the work of regeneration; see hymn 25, "A Dialogue

Spirit, Hart prayed, "Breathe on these Bones so dry and dead."[111] When Hart wrote this line, he must have been reflecting on Ezekiel 37, particularly verse 9, where God asked Ezekiel to pray to the Spirit to "breathe upon these slain [that is, the spiritually dead Israelites], that they may live." Here, again Hart showed how God alone can give spiritual life to dead sinners.[112]

Yet, contrary to the hyper-Calvinistic mindset, Hart did not think the doctrine of total inability frees man from his moral duty to respond to the gospel call. Despite his total inability, man is responsible to believe and repent.[113] In his study of hyper-Calvinism in the long eighteenth century, Paul Helm has observed how

> the Hyper-Calvinist and the Arminian agree together on the claim that obligation implies ability. The Arminian thus holds that a person has an obligation to believe in Christ only because he has ability to exercise faith, and the Hyper-Calvinist holds that a person ought not to be commanded to believe in Christ because he does not have ability to do so (Helm: 2018, 132).[114]

Hart maintained, however, that while man has no natural ability to believe, he remains under obligation to believe. Thus, with no hesitation Hart called sinners to come to Jesus by faith,[115] for unless they believe, they will not be saved:

---

between a Believer and his Soul": "Soul. *But I'm cold, I'm dark, I'm dead.* / Bel[iever]. Jesus will revive thee." The word "revive" here has the sense of restoring a dead person to life.

111. Hymn 6, "[To the Holy Ghost]" ("Descend from Heav'n, celestial Dove"), line 2:1.

112. Likewise, the Calvinists argued, "As in Adam the whole human race, created in the image of God, has with Adam fallen into sin and thus become so corrupt that all men are conceived and born in sin and thus are by nature children of wrath, lying dead in their trespasses so that there is within them no more power to convert themselves truly unto God and to believe in Christ than a corpse has power to raise itself from the dead." See the Counter Remonstrance (1611), art. 1.

113. Alverey Jackson concluded, "But if this argument, which is made use of, with so much confident assurance, against faith in Christ being a duty, be true and conclusive; then the whole undertaking of Christ, his sinless obedience, painful sufferings, invaluable sacrifice, and precious atonement, as for us, is nothing but an idle dream, and a meer empty noise of words" (1752, 55).

114. Wayman, Brine, and Gill were examples of those hyper-Calvinists who believed man is not under duty to believe in Christ, when hearing the preaching of the gospel.

115. See his well-known evangelistic hymn 100, "Come, and welcome, to Jesus Christ" ("Come, ye sinners, poor and wretched").

> Ev'ry one, without Exemption,
> That believes,
> Now receives
> Absolute redemption.[116]
>
> The Sinner that truly believes,
> And trusts in his crucified God,
> His Justification receives,
> Redemption in full thro' his Blood:[117]

These stanzas display lucidly Hart's doctrine of justification by faith alone,[118] which is different from eternal justification, which taught how the imputation of Christ's righteousness to the elect takes place from eternity before they even believe. For instance, in *A Defence of the Doctrine of Eternal Justification* (1732), the hyper-Calvinistic Baptist John Brine (1703–1765) wrote,

> Justification, as it is an act in God [...] ought not to be considered as the birth of time, but is eternal, because all his immanent acts are so. [...] If there is a personal election from eternity, there also may be a personal Justification from eternity, because the latter requires our existence no more than the former (1732, 37–38).[119]

Disagreeing with such a view, Hart believed a sinner is justified at the time he first believes: "The sinner that truly believes, [...] His Justification receives."[120] In short, not until a sinner believes in Christ does he receive the blessing of justification.[121] This is because Hart understood

---

116. Hymn 67, "Christ's Righteousness" ("Righteousness to the Believer"), stanza 4.
117. Hymn 88, "Saving Faith," lines 1:1–4.
118. See also supplement hymn 2, "[For the Lord's Supper]" ("This is the Day the Lord has made").
119. Likewise, John Gill argued, "As God's will to elect, is the election of his people, so his will to justify them, is the justification of them; as it is an immanent act in God, it is an act of his grace towards them, is wholly without them, entirely resides in the divine mind, and lies in his estimating, accounting, and constituting them righteous, through the righteousness of his Son; and, as such, did not first commence in time, but from eternity" (1796, 1:298).
120. Hymn 88, "Saving Faith," lines 1:1, 3.
121. Here Hart agreed with the Westminster Confession of Faith (1646), "God did, from all eternity, decree to justify all the elect (Gal 3:8; 1 Pet 1:2, 19–20; Rom 8:30), and Christ did, in the fulness of time, die for their sins, and rise again for their justification (Gal 4:4; 1 Tim 2:6; Rom 4:25): nevertheless, they are not justified, until the Holy Spirit

faith as an instrument by which Christ's righteousness is imputed to sinners,[122] and on account of this divine righteousness they are declared righteous before God:

> Sinners, I read, are justified
> By Faith in Jesu's Blood:[123]
>
> Robes of Righteousness imputed,
> White and whole,
> Cloath the Soul,
> Each exactly suited.[124]
>
> Unrighteous are they all, when tried:
> But God himself declares,
> In Jesus they are justified;
> *His Righteousness* is Theirs.[125]

Nevertheless, to emphasize God's sovereign grace in salvation, Hart taught faith is God's gift, given to sinners so they may believe and be saved:

> Faith in Jesus can repel
> The Darts of Sin and Death.
> *Faith* gives Vict'ry over Hell:
> But who can give us *Faith*?"
> To believe's the Gift of God.[126]

Likewise, Hart saw repentance as a gift from God, and for him faith and repentance are two sides of the same coin and are thus inseparable and necessary for salvation. As Hart explained in one of his hymns on faith and repentance,

---

doth, in due time, actually apply Christ unto them (Col 1:21–22; Gal 2:16; Titus 3:4–7)" (Chap. XI, par. 4).

122. Hart called the imputation of Christ's righteousness "A Doctrine most divine." See hymn 90, "For the Kingdom of God is not in Word, but in Power. I Cor. iv. 20" ("A Form of Words, tho' e'er so sound").

123. Hymn 90, lines 3:1–2.

124. Hymn 67, "Christ's Righteousness" ("Righteousness to the Believer"), stanza 5.

125. Hymn 77, "Who of God is made unto us Wisdom, and Righteousness, and Sanctification, and Redemption. I Cor. i. 30" ("Believers own but they are blind"), stanza 2.

126. Hymn 64, "In the Lord have I Righteousness and Strength. Isa. xlv. 24," lines 1:1–4, 2:5.

> Hear the Terms that never vary;
> "To repent, and to believe."
> Both of these are necessary:
> Both from Jesus we receive.
> Would-be Christian, duly ponder
> These in thine impartial Mind:
> And let no Man put asunder
> What the Lord has wisely join'd.[127]

4.4.2 "Had not thy Choice prevented mine, / I ne'er hadchosen *Thee*"[128]

Opposing the traditional Reformed view of election, Jacobus Arminius (1560–1609) and his supporters, called the Remonstrants, argued,

> God, by an eternal and unchangeable decree [...] before laying the foundation of the world, determined, out of the human race [...] to save those [...] who through the grace of the Holy Spirit, would believe on His [...] Son, and who would persevere in that very faith.[129]

Such was also the view of John Wesley and his subsequent followers, the Methodists, who understood election as conditional on what sinners will decide to do. If they believe, they will be chosen; if they do not, they will be condemned. Thus, in this context, ultimately God's election in eternity past depends on his foreknowledge of man's decision in eternity future.[130] For Hart, however, the doctrine of election—whereby

---

127. Hymn 55, "[Faith and Repentance]" ("Come, ye Christians, sing the Praises"), stanza 3.

128. Hymn 113, "Because thou sayest, I am rich, and increased with Goods. Rev. iii. 17" ("What makes mistaken Men afraid"), lines 7:3–4.

129. The Remonstrance (1610), art. 1. This confession was based on Arminius's *Declaration of Sentiments* (written in 1608).

130. On one occasion Wesley explained why he rejected the doctrine of unconditional election: "I do not believe, (what is only preterition, or reprobation in other words,) any such *absolute election*, as implies that all but the *absolutely elect* shall inevitably be damned." In Wesley's mind unconditional election, or what he called "absolute election" (God's predestination of some to salvation) logically leads to preterition or reprobation (God's decision to pass over others or his predestination of others to eternal damnation), which he regarded as inconsistent with God's character. As Wesley said, "I believe no decree of *reprobation*. I do not believe the Father of spirits even 'Consign'd one unborn soul to hell, Or damn'd him from his mother's womb.' I believe no decree of *preterition*, which is only reprobation whitewashed. I do not believe God even sent one man into the

"Long before our Birth, / Nay, before Jehovah laid / The Foundations of the Earth, / We were chosen in our Head"[131]—is solely based on God's sovereign grace and irrespective of any foreseen human action or decision. Hart put it this way:

> What makes mistaken Men afraid
> Of sov'reign Grace to preach?
> The Reason is (if Truth be said,)
> Because they are so *rich*.
>
> Why so offensive in their Eyes,
> Doth God's Election seem?
> Because they think themselves so wise,
> That they have chosen *Him*.
>
> His language is; "Let *me*, my God,
> On sov'reign Grace rely;
> And own 'tis free, because bestowed,
> On one so vile as I."
>
> "Election! 'Tis a Word divine:
> For, Lord, I plainly see,
> Had not thy Choice prevented mine,
> I ne'er had chosen *Thee*."[132]

Doubtlessly Hart was addressing Arminians who,[133] according to him, were afraid "Of sov'reign Grace to preach" and who also found the Reformed doctrine of election "so offensive in their Eyes [...] Because they think themselves so wise, / That they have chosen *Him*." For the

---

world, to whom he had decreed, never to give that grace, whereby alone he could escape damnation" (1827, 479).

131. Hymn 42, "Election" ("Brethren, would you know your stay?"), lines 1:5–8.

132. Hymn 113 "Because thou sayest I am rich, and increased with Goods. Rev. iii. 17." Stanzas 1, 2, 6, 7. Revelation 3:17 says, "Because thou sayest, I am rich, and increased with goods, and have need of nothing; and knowest not that thou art wretched, and miserable, and poor, and blind, and naked." In this stanza, Hart compared the Arminians to the Laodiceans, who thought they needed nothing because they were rich enough. In the same manner, these Arminians did not want to preach God's sovereign grace because they thought they were "so rich" (in a spiritual sense) that they did not need such grace.

133. In his *The Unreasonableness of Religion* (1741), Hart already defended the doctrine of election against Arminians, more specifically against Wesley. But he did so from an antinomian viewpoint. Such was not the context when he wrote hymn 113 to contend for election.

Arminians, God had chosen them because God foresaw that they would choose him. Hart thought the opposite: he chose God because God had chosen him first. Therefore, his choosing of God was a response to God's "electing grace."[134] What Hart believed was consistent with the Calvinists' position, which is,

> God in his election has not looked to the faith or conversion of his elect, nor to the right use of his gifts, as the grounds of election; but that on the contrary He in his eternal and immutable counsel has purposed and decreed [...] to save those who He according to his good pleasure has chosen to salvation.[135]

Hyper-Calvinists, it should be mentioned, saw a theological reason in the doctrine of election for preachers not to freely and indiscriminately offer the gospel to all sinners. In their minds, "Because the electing purposes of God were known only to God himself, such free offers might produce presumption on the part of the non-elects" (Shaw: 2013, 134). This mentality had its origin with the Congregationalist minister Joseph Hussey, who wrote *God's Operations of Grace but No Offers of His Grace* (1707), wherein he strongly argued that "only the elect are to be invited to accept the grace of God" because God's grace is only given to the elect. "Therefore," Hussey reasoned, "to offer the gifts of God's grace to everybody in preaching is wrong for they are only intended for the elect" (Toon: 2011, 80). Similarly, John Gill, who was often associated with hyper-Calvinism,

> asserted that in making invitations of salvation to the unconverted, the minister derogates God's glory and electing initiative, making the cruel presumption that any of his hearers could respond, when, in fact, there were some who were not elect and eternally justified, and therefore not granted the gift of saving faith (Grant: 2013, 44).

Gill explained, "How irrational it is, for ministers to stand offering Christ, and salvation by him to man, when, on the one hand, they have neither power nor right to give; and, on the other hand, the persons they offer to, have neither power nor will to receive?" (1773, 146).[136] In his

---

134. Hymn 60, "Election" ("Mighty Enemies without"). Hart wrote a couple of hymns on the subject of election, showing how this doctrine was important to him.
135. The Counter Remonstrance (1611), art. 3.
136. Gill made a distinction between preaching Christ and offering Christ. For him,

discourse on predestination, Gill stated pointedly, "That there are universal offers of grace and salvation made to all men, I utterly deny; nay. [...] Let the patrons of universal offers defend themselves from this objection; I have nothing to do with it; till it is proved there are such universal offers" (1752, 29). One of the staunch patrons of the universal free offer of the gospel was Andrew Fuller, who wrote *The Gospel of Christ Worthy of All Acceptation* (1785),[137] in which he argued that preachers have the responsibility to offer the gospel to all sinners and call them to believe in Jesus and repent of their sins, and those who hear the gospel have the duty to respond to the gospel call by faith and in repentance.

Hart would have completely agreed with Fuller in this issue. Hart's conversionist approach in preaching is seen when he addressed the unconverted in his sermon on Matthew 2:2 and pleaded with them earnestly to come to Christ for mercy:

> I shall address myself to the unconverted. [...] remember, you are a subject either in the kingdom of God, or of the devil. [...] But I would turn my thoughts another way, and would to God that every one who hears me this day, might be of the number of those, who with an importunate desire of finding Christ the Savior, to be their King, ask, for that purpose, where is he that is born King of the Jews? for we would gladly have him to reign over and in us, and rejoice in it. To such I answer, he is now in the midst of his people Israel, in his holy city Jerusalem, and he stands there, with open hands, to receive all that are willing to come to God by him: for all must submit to his here or hereafter. If you will not be subjects of his mercy now, you must be subjects of his wrath hereafter—there is no medium (1814, 26–28).

---

ministers are to preach or proclaim Christ to all but not to offer him with the condition that if sinners believe, they will be saved. "The ministers of the gospel are sent to preach the gospel to every creature; that is, not to offer, but to preach Christ, and salvation by him; to publish peace and pardon as things already obtained by him. The ministers are [...] criers or heralds; their business is [...] to proclaim aloud, to publish facts, to declare things that are done, and not to offer them to be done on conditions; as when a peace is concluded and finished, the herald's business, and in which he is employed, is to proclaim the peace, and not to offer it; of this nature is the gospel" (146–47).

137. This work was written in 1781 but was not published until 1785. The first edition's subtitle was *The Obligations of Men Fully to Credit, and Cordially to Approve, Whatever God Makes Known, Wherein is Considered the Nature of Faith in Christ, and the Duty of Those where the Gospel Comes in that Matter*. Its second edition appeared in 1801 with a more concise title: *The Gospel Worthy of All Acceptation: The Duty of Sinners to Believe in Jesus Christ*.

Since Hart's hymns "so exactly describe" his preaching, said John Towers, his hymns would look like his sermons (Hart: 1799, iii). Thus, as his hymns invited sinners indiscriminately to come to Christ for salvation, so did his sermons. In fact, what Hart proclaimed in the above sermon—"he stands there, with open hands, to receive all that are willing to come to God by him"—echoes what Hart said in his hymn 100, "Come, and welcome, to Jesus Christ," one of the finest invitation hymns:

> Come, ye Sinners, poor and wretched,
> Weak and wounded, sick and sore.
> Jesus ready stands to save you,
> Full of Pity join'd with Pow'r.
> He is able, he is able, he is able;
> He is willing: doubt no more.
>
> Ho! ye needy; come, and welcome;
> God's free Bounty glorify.
> True Belief, and true Repentance,
> Ev'ry Grace that brings us nigh,
> Without Money, without Money, without Money,
> Come to Jesus Christ, and buy![138]

And to those who might think they are too sinful to come to Christ, here was Hart's reply:

> This Fountain, tho' rich,
> From Charge is quite clear;
> The poorer the Wretch
> The welcomer here.
> Come needy, come guilty,
> Come loathsome and bare;
> You can't come too filthy—
> Come just as you are.[139]

---

138. Hymn 100, stanzas 1–2.
139. Hymn 86, "In that Day there shall be a Fountain opened to the House of David, and to the Inhabitants of Jerusalem, for Sin, and for Uncleanness. Zech. xiii. 1" ("The Fountain of Christ"), stanza 7.

4.4.3 "The Lamb that died for *Me*"[140]

Particular redemption or definite atonement logically follows the doctrine of election. If God has not chosen all to be saved from eternity past, it logically follows that Jesus did not die for all but only for the elect; and thus, his death is limited or definite. While the doctrine of atonement was central to all evangelicals, they were not all on the same page when it comes to the extent of Christ's atonement. For example, as a practical consequence of his rejection of the doctrine of election and reprobation, John Wesley argued that Jesus died for all, although only those who believe will be saved. Writing against the doctrine of predestination, he said, "How will you reconcile Reprobation with the following Scriptures,[141] which declare that Christ came to save all Men, that he died for all, that he atoned for all, even for those that finally perish?" "Here you see," Wesley added, "not only that Christ died for all Men, but likewise the End of his Dying for them." That is, Christ Jesus "gave himself a ransom for all" (1 Tim. 2:6) (1755, 16). In one of his polemical hymns against Calvinism, Charles expressed his brother John's position this way:

> Help us thy mercy to extol,
> Immense, unfathom'd, unconfin'd;
> To praise the Lamb who *died for all*,
> The *general Saviour of mankind*.
>
> A *world* he suffer'd to redeem;
> For *all* he hath th' atonement made:
> For those that *will not come* to him
> The ransom of his life was paid.[142]

In another hymn called "The Horrible Decree," which refers to the Reformed doctrine of limited atonement, Charles emphatically concluded:

> In Death will I proclaim
> That All *may* hear thy Call,
> And clap my Hands amidst the Flame,
> And Shout—He Died For All."[143]

---

140. Supplement hymn 17, "[For the Lord's Supper]" ("That doleful Night before his Death"), line 2:8.

141. Citing Matt 18:11; John 1:29, 3:17, 12:47; Rom 14:15; 1 Cor 8:11; 2 Cor 5:15.

142. *Hymns on God's Everlasting Love; To Which is Added the Cry of a Reprobate and the Horrible Decree* (Bristol, 1741), 3–4 ("Father, whose everlasting love"), stanzas 2, 8.

143. *Hymns on God's Everlasting Love* (1741), 33–36 ("Ah! gentle gracious Dove"), lines 15:5–8.

This view of atonement was aligned with the Arminian belief as expressed in the Remonstrance (1610)—that "Jesus Christ, Savior of the world, has died for each and every man, and through His death on the cross has merited reconciliation and forgiveness of sins for all."[144]

In *The Unreasonableness of Religion* (1741), a response to Wesley's *Free Grace* (1739), Hart challenged Wesley's doctrine of universal redemption, showing the doctrine's inconsistency:

> He begins by telling us in a confused manner of the Freeness of God's Love, or Grace. *That it is Free in All and for All.* [...] And yet Many, who are loved with this Free Love of God, shall, in his own Opinion, be never the better for it; but Perish with it Everlastingly. For he has no where said, that he Believes, all Men shall be saved; but seems to grant in several Parts of his Sermon that many shall fall short of Heaven, tho' loved by God, with this Free Love, or Grace, he is so much Exalting" (19).

In contrast to Wesley, Hart held to the Calvinist view in which Jesus died only for those whom God has chosen from eternity past.[145] While Hart offered the gospel to all—"This Fountain, unseal'd, / Stands open for all, / That long to be heal'd, / The Great and the Small"[146]—he never declared Jesus died for all. Yet, he would not find a problem in saying, "Jesus died for sinners' sake!"[147] or "The Son of God and man has died, / Sinners as black as Hell to save."[148] He said of himself, "*For Me*, he died, *for Me*," or "The Lamb that died for *Me*."[149] And if he ever said, "Jesus died for you," it was addressed to his fellow believers,

---

144. The Remonstrance (1610), art. 2.

145. Or in the words of the Counter Remonstrance (1611), art. 4: "He has first of all presented and given to them his only-begotten Son Jesus Christ, whom He delivered up to the death of the cross in order to save his elect, so that, although the suffering of Christ as that of the only-begotten and unique Son of God is sufficient unto the atonement of the sins of all men, nevertheless the same, according to the counsel and decree of God, has its efficacy unto reconciliation and forgiveness of sins only in the elect and true believer."

146. Hymn 86, "In that Day there shall be a Fountain opened to the House of David, and to the Inhabitants of Jerusalem, for Sin, and for Uncleanness. Zech. xiii. 1" ("The Fountain of Christ"), lines 6:1–4.

147. Hymn 41, "Behold, and see, if there be any Sorrow like unto my Sorrow. Lam. i. 12" ("Much we talk of Jesu's Blood"), line 4:8.

148. Hymn 115, "Who was delivered for our Offences, and was raised again for our Justification. Rom. iv. 25" ("Jesus, when on the bloody Tree"), lines 5:1–2.

149. Supplement hymn 17, "[For the Lord's Supper]" ("That doleful Night before his Death"), lines 1:8, 2:8.

> The dying Saviour left
> These Tokens of his Love:
> Which seem to say, "While this ye do,
> Remember Him that died for You."[150]

Nevertheless, despite their disagreement regarding the extent of the atonement, both the Wesley brothers and Hart strongly agreed about the necessity of Christ's atoning death, without which there would be no forgiveness and redemption. In this way, they all stood together against the Socinian doctrine of the atonement.

4.4.4 "Salvation's of God, / Th' Effect of free grace"[151]

Both Calvinists[152] and Arminians[153] recognized the necessity of God's grace in salvation. However, for the Arminians, God's grace (what they called "prevenient" grace), can be resisted. The Remonstrants explained it this way: "As for the rest, what pertains to the manner of operation of this grace—that it is not irresistible, since indeed it is written about many that 'they resisted the Holy Spirit,' Acts 7:[51] and several other places."[154] In his study of the doctrine of prevenient grace in the theology of Jacobus Arminius, Abner F. Hernandez Fernandez summarized how for Arminius,

> prevenient grace monergistically operates in the human heart to restore its freedom of will. That is, it gives the person power to understand the Gospel and accept the work of Christ in its favor. In this way, Arminius

---

150. Supplement hymn 16, "[For the Lord's Supper]" ("When Jesus underetook"), lines 3–6. This hymn would have been sung during the communion service of Hart's congregation.

151. Supplement hymn 20, "[For the Lord's Supper]" ("What Creatures beside"), lines 2:1–2. This doctrine is also known as "effectual grace."

152. For the Calvinists, "Without the regenerating grace of the Holy Spirit, they are neither able nor willing to return to God, to reform the depravity of their nature, or to dispose themselves to reformation." See the Canons of Dort (1618-19), III/IV heads, art. 3; cf. the Counter Remonstrance (1611), art. 5.

153. For the Arminians, "This grace is the beginning, the increase, and completion of every good thing; to be sure even that the regenerate person himself is not even able to think, will, or accomplish good, nor resist any temptation to evil apart from or preceding that prevenient, moving, accompanying, and cooperating grace, so that all good works and actions which are able to be conceived must be ascribed to the grace of God in Christ." See the Remonstrance (1610), art. 4.

154. The Remonstrance (1610), art. 4.

understood that the initial working of prevenient grace occurs in an unavoidable manner in human beings. God renews and heals human infirmities and gives them a completely freed will. Once humans enjoy their freed will, they have a measure of a restored spiritual capacity to respond to God and receive the gift of faith. In this way, Arminius also understood that prevenient grace is resistible. The freed will of humans not only has the capacity to accept, but because the corruption of sin is still present in the human heart, it has the capacity to reject the offer of salvation (2017, 270).[155]

John Wesley, who has been called along with Arminius "artisans of prevenient grace" (Shelton: 2014, 99), adopted the concept of such grace. While acknowledging the total depravity of man, Wesley said, "No man living is entirely destitute of what is vulgarly called *natural conscience*. But this is not natural; it is more properly termed, *preventing grace*. Every man has a greater or less measure of this, which waiteth not for the call of man" (1829, 2:285). In Wesley's mind, the word "preventing" means "going before" or "preceding." Preventing grace, thus, comes before salvation or predisposes a sinner to faith and repentance.[156] Like the Calvinists, Wesley affirmed man's natural incapability of believing in Christ for salvation. But as Wesley explained,

> this is no excuse for those who continue in sin, and lay the blame upon their Maker, by saying, It is God only that must quicken us; for we cannot quicken our own souls. For allowing that all the souls of men are dead in sin by *nature*, this excuses none, seeing there is no man that is in a state of mere nature [...] that is wholly void of the grace of God [...]. So that no man sins because he has not grace, but because he does not use the grace which he hath (284–85).

---

155. This Arminian doctrine of resistible grace was rebutted by the Calvinists in their Counter Remonstrance (1611), art. 5, and the Canons of Dort (1618–19), III/IV heads.

156. Wesley wrote, "Salvation begins with what is usually termed, (and very properly) *preventing grace*; including the first wish to please God, the first dawn of light concerning his will, and the first slight, transient conviction of having sinned against him. All these imply some tendency toward life, some degree of salvation, the beginning of a deliverance from a blind, unfeeling heart, quite insensible of God and the things of God. Salvation is carried on by *convincing grace*, usually in scripture termed *repentance*; which brings a larger measure of self-knowledge, and a farther deliverance from the heart of stone. Afterwards we experience the proper Christian salvation; whereby, *through grace, we are saved by faith*" (1829, 2:282).

God unilaterally gives every sinner "a greater or less measure of" preventing or prevenient grace, which enables them to choose to believe and be saved. But since this kind of grace is resistible, man can either use this grace for his spiritual good or reject it. In Wesley's mind, therefore, it is ultimately up to man's decision if he wants to be saved. Hence, Wesley could reconcile his teachings on total depravity, *sola gratia* (salvation is by God's grace alone), and *sola fide* (but man has the responsibility as well as the given ability to believe) (Cox: 1969, 147–48).

Hart, however, understood salvation as the "effect of God's free grace." In this case, grace is irresistible, for it efficaciously saves those on whom this grace was bestowed from eternity past:

> Salvation's of God,
> Th' Effect of free grace,
> Upon us bestowed,
> Before the world was;[157]

Previously, Hart said to God with regard to the doctrine of election, "Had not thy Choice prevented mine, / I ne'er had chosen *Thee*."[158] This is the only time Hart used the term "prevented," which in this context means "to act before" so as to incline a person toward God. Thus, what Hart is saying is this: Were it not because of God's electing grace, which caused Hart to choose God, he would not have chosen God. So ultimately Hart saw his choosing of God as the cause and effect of God's sovereign grace. Elsewhere Hart said,

> Those who are call'd by Grace divine,
> Believe, but not alone:
> Repentance to their Faith they join;
> And so go safely on.[159]

In short, those who are sovereignly called by divine grace will inevitably believe in God and repent of their sins,[160] because this grace is

---

157. Supplement hymn 20, "[For the Lord's Supper]" ("What Creatures beside"), lines 2:1–4.

158. Hymn 113, "Because thou sayest, I am rich, and increased with Goods. Rev. iii. 17" ("What makes mistaken Men afraid"), lines 7:3–4.

159. Supplement hymn 59, "Repentance" ("What various Ways do Men invent"), stanza 5.

160. And for Hart, they will believe because they have been granted the gift of faith and repentance: "True Belief, and true Repentance / Are thy Gifts, thou God of

efficacious and irresistible, always accomplishing what it intends to: "The Work of Grace in all it's Parts, / Accomplish in the Soul."[161] Here, of course, Hart followed the view of John Calvin, who said,

> Grace is not offered to us in such a way that afterwards we have the option either to submit or to resist. [...] I say that it is not given merely to aid our weakness by its support as though anything depended on us apart from it. But I demonstrate that it is entirely the work of grace and a benefit conferred by it that our heart is changed from a stony one to one of flesh, that our will is made new, and that we, created anew in heart and mind, at length will what we ought to will (1996, 174).

For Calvin and Hart, God's saving grace does not simply create a possibility for man to believe but actually causes him to believe so as to be saved. It not only enables the human will to choose to believe but also overcomes the human power to resist what grace intends to accomplish.

4.4.5 *"God's Elect can never fail"*[162]

In their 1621 confession, written in response to the Canons of Dort (1618–19), the Remonstrants gave their more mature and clearer position on the issue of perseverance, teaching how a true believer can fall away from grace:

> [W]e believe that it is entirely possible, if not rarely done, that they fall back little by little and until they completely lack their prior faith and charity. And having abandoned the way of righteousness, they revert to their worldly impurity which they had truly left [...] and are again entangled in lusts of the flesh which they had formerly, truly fled. And thus totally and at length also they are finally torn from the grace of God unless they seriously repent in time.[163]

Later, John Wesley adopted this Arminian teaching. In his *Serious Thoughts Upon the Perseverance of the Saints* (1751), he asked, "Can any of

---

Grace." Hymn 56, "[Faith and Repentance]" part 2 ("Great High-Priest, we view stooping"), lines 3:7–8.

161. Hymn 9, "Of Sanctification" ("The Holy Ghost in Scripture saith"), lines 12:3–4.
162. Hymn 42, "Election" ("Brethren, would you know your Stay?"), line 2:8.
163. *The Arminian Confession of 1621*, trans. and ed. Mark A. Ellis (Eugene, OR: Pickwick Publications, 2005), chap. 11, sec. 7. The original title is "The Confession or Declaration of the Pastors which in the Belgian Federation are Called the Remonstrants, on the Principle Articles of the Christian Religion."

these [saints] fall away? By *falling away* we mean, not barely falling into Sin. This, it is granted, they may. But can they fall totally? Can any of these so fall from God, as to perish everlastingly?" (4). Wesley's answer was yes, and the rest of his work was an explication of his stance. If the same question was put to Hart, he would have emphatically answered no. In fact, he wrote an entire hymn called "Perseverance" to defend the Reformed doctrine of the perseverance of the saints. The hymn opens with this stanza:

> The Sinner that, by precious Faith,
> Has felt his Sins forgiv'n,
> Is, from that Moment, pass'd from Death,
> And seal'd an Heir of Heav'n.[164]

As mentioned previously, Hart attributed the work of sealing to the Holy Spirit: "We laud thy Name, blest Spirit of Truth, / Who dost Salvation seal."[165] This concept is drawn from Ephesians 4:30, "And grieve not the holy Spirit of God, whereby ye are sealed unto the day of redemption." Elsewhere Hart wrote, "Christians are sealed by the Holy Ghost to the Day of Redemption: And to this Seal they trust their eternal Welfare" (1767, xviii). The word "seal" here carries the idea of security or preservation. For Hart, believers are sealed by the Spirit so as to be preserved. Their salvation is secured by none other than the Spirit. They are "Redeem'd from Hell, and seal'd for heav'n."[166] The hymn on perseverance goes on:

> Tho' thousand Snares enclose his Feet,
> Not one shall hold him fast,
> Whatever Dangers he may meet,
> He shall get safe at last.
>
> Not as the World the Saviour gives.
> He is no fickle Friend:
> Whom once He loves, He never leaves;
> But loves him to the End.[167]

Here Hart was probably reflecting on Romans 8:35–39, wherein Christians

---

164. Hymn 37, "Perseverance," stanza 1.
165. Doxology 7 ("We laud thy Name, Almighty Lord"), lines 1:5–6.
166. Hymn 44, "Jabez's Prayer. I Chron. iv. 9, 10." ("A Saint there was in Days of old"), line 4:4.
167. Hymn 37, "Perseverance," stanzas 2–3.

are assured that nothing can separate them from the love of Christ. Hart finds such love as a basis for believers' perseverance:

> For *Perseverance* Strength I've none:
> But would on this depend;
> *That Jesus, having lov'd his own,*
> *He lov'd them to the End.*[168]

Christians do not find security in their own strength to persevere but in Christ's preserving love. They cannot fall away from grace because although they are weak, Jesus loves them to the end. Yes, like lambs, they are vulnerable to their enemy, but their great shepherd will keep them eternally safe from the devil:

> Remember one Thing:
> (Oh! may it sink deep)
> Our Shepherd and King
> Cares much for his Sheep;
>
> But Lambs are preserv'd,
> Tho' helpless in Kind;
> When Lions are starv'd,
> *They* Nourishment find.
> Their Shepherd upholds them,
> When faint, in his Arms;
> And feeds them, and folds them;
> And guards them from Harms.[169]

Remarkably, in another hymn, Hart equally saw both God's electing grace and everlasting love as the unshakable foundation for believers' eternal security:

> But we build upon a Base
> That nothing can remove,
> When we trust electing Grace
> And everlasting Love.
> Vict'ry over all our Foes
>
> Christ has purchased with His blood:

---

168. Hymn 113, "Because thou sayest, I am rich, and increased with Goods. Rev. iii. 17" ("What makes mistaken Men afraid"), stanza 8.

169. Hymn 81, "The young Lions do lack, and suffer Hunger" ("Ye Lambs of Christ's Fold"), lines 2:1–4, 5:1–8.

> Perseverance he bestows
> On ev'ry Child of God.[170]

The last two lines of this stanza show how, for Hart, perseverance is a divine gift given to every believer. Perseverance is as much a gift as faith and repentance.[171] The elect will believe and be saved and repent and be forgiven because they are granted the gift of faith and repentance. In the same manner, the elect will also persevere because they are given the gift of perseverance. Hart goes on to say the elect will persevere because it is God's sure promise:

> To Perseverance I agree:
> The Thing to me is clear;
> Because the Lord has promised Me,
> That I shall persevere.[172]

In one of his hymns on election, Hart again grounded the believers' perseverance in God's election:

> God's Election is the Ground
> Of our Hope to persevere,
> On this Rock your Building found:
> And preserve your Title clear.
> *Infidels* may laugh;
> *Pharisees* gainsay, or rail;
> Here's your Tenure, (keep it safe)
> *God's Elect can never fail.*[173]

The last line of this stanza well summarizes Hart's standpoint on the matter: "*God's elect can never fail!*" Therefore, in contrast to the Arminians, Hart understood the perseverance of the saints as a blessing of election. The elect will believe and Jesus will ensure, "Not one, that on Me shall believe, / Shall ever be finally lost."[174]

---

170. Hymn 60, "Election" ("Mighty Enemies without"), stanza 4.
171. For faith and repentance, see hymn 56 "[Faith and Repentance]" part 2 ("Great High-Priest, we view stooping"), and supplement hymn 60, "[Repentance]" ("Repentence is a Gift bestow'd").
172. Hymn 90, "For the Kingdom of God is not in Word, but in Power. I Cor. iv. 20" ("A Form of Words, tho' e'er so sound"), stanza 4.
173. Hymn 42, "Election" ("Brethren, would you know your Stay?"), stanza 2.
174. Hymn 73, "If there arise among you a Prophet, or a Dreamer of Dreams. &c. Deut. xiii. 1, &c" ("No Prophet, nor Dreamer of Dreams"), lines 6:7–8.

In his hymns, Hart resonated with Calvinistic soteriology, which was seen in the Thirty-nine Articles of Religion (1563), later found in the Counter Remonstrance (1611), and articulated in the Canons of Dort (1618–19).[175] These canons, also called "the Five Articles against the Remonstrants", consisted of doctrinal propositions adopted by the Synod of Dort in 1618–19 against the Remonstrance (1610) or "the Five Articles of the Remonstrants": conditional election based on foreseen faith, universal atonement, partial depravity of man, resistible grace, and the possibility of falling from grace.[176] The Synod's counteraction to these five articles came to be known in modern times as the "Five Points of Calvinism," or the acronym TULIP: total depravity, unconditional election, limited atonement, irresistible grace, and perseverance of the saints.[177] J. Todd Billings, however, found TULIP problematic, as it "does not provide accurate summary" of the Canons of Dort (2011, 10). J.I. Packer also noted,

> The very act of setting out Calvinistic soteriology in the form of five distinct points (a number due, as we saw, merely to the fact that there were five Arminian points for the Synod of Dort to answer) tends to obscure the organic character of Calvinistic thought on this subject (Owen: 1959, 6).

Regardless, Hart embraced all these five points, which according to Packer, "present Calvinistic soteriology in a negative and polemical form" (5). These doctrines of grace shaped Hart's spirituality, exalting God's free and sovereign grace.

4.5 Sanctification: "a daily Increase in all true Grace and Godliness"[178]

Lest others abuse the doctrine of sovereign grace, and being aware of the danger of libertinism, Hart stressed the need of good works, devoting

---

175. For a historical and theological background of the Canons of Dort (1618–19), consult Beeke/Klauber (2020) and Goudriaan/Lieburg (2011).

176. See the Remonstrance (1610) in *Reformed Confessions of the 16th and 17th Centuries in English Translation*, vol. 4 (Grand Rapids, MI: Reformation Heritage Books, 2014), 41–44.

177. See Steele/Thomas (1963). This book popularized the five points of Calvinism, which first appeared in Boettner (1932).

178. Hart (1767), xiv.

three hymns to the subject.[179] True believers will be sanctified by the Holy Spirit,[180] whereby it is impossible for them not to produce good works.

According to Hart, he published his hymns "not only in the same *Order*, but almost in the same *Manner* in which they were first written" (1767, i). It is thus important to note how his hymn 8, "Salvation by Christ alone" is followed by hymn 9, "Of Sanctification." For Hart then, the dogma logically following the doctrine of salvation is sanctification, which pertains to the believer's daily growth in holiness. Hart believed unless God saves us, we cannot produce good works:

> Experience likewise tells us this;
> Before the Saviour's Blood
> Has wash'd us clean, and made our Peace,
> We can do nothing good.[181]

Hart therefore saw good works not as a means of salvation but as a manifestation of salvation. This means, for Hart, true spirituality flows out of a saved soul. So the kind of spirituality he promoted in his hymns is neither antinomian nor legalistic but biblical. In fact, in his hymn on sanctification, stanzas four and five, he addressed these two dangers (antinomianism and legalism), which Satan uses to "cheat the human mind":

> But here, my Friends, the Danger lies;
> Errors of diff'rent Kind
> Will still creep in; which Dev'ls devise
> To cheat the human Mind.
>
> "I want no Work within, (says one)
> "'Tis all in Christ the Head."
> Thus, careless he goes blindly on,
> And trusts a Faith that's dead.

Here Hart is talking about those antinomians who say, "I want no Work within," since it is all Christ's work. Antinomianism's "root lies in a false view of the atonement; its view of the imputation of Christ's righteousness implies that he performs for men the obedience which they ought

---

179. See supplement hymns 56–58, which he simply labeled "Good Works."
180. Hart also attributed the work of sanctification to Christ: "But Christ has Holiness enough / To *sanctify* us all." See hymn 77, "Who of God is made unto us Wisdom, and Righteousness, and Sanctification, and Redemption. I. Cor. i. 30" ("Believers own they are but blind"), lines 3:3–4.
181. Hymn 9, "Of Sanctification" ("The Holy Ghost in Scripture saith"), stanza 3.

to perform, and therefore that God, in justice, can demand nothing further from man" (McClintock/Strong: 1896, 264–65).[182] In the eighteenth century, antinomianism was linked to high-Calvinists, who, out of their desire to guard the doctrine of justification by faith alone from a works-based salvation, ended up minimizing the need of good works in sanctification. One may recall, such was Hart's attitude when he wrote *The Unreasonableness of Religion* (1741) against the Arminian John Wesley. In a sense, antinomianism was an overreaction to Arminianism, which tended to overemphasize human responsibility over sovereign grace in salvation.

In the eighteenth century, one of the strongest critics of antinomianism was Wesley, who defined it as, "The doctrine which makes void the law through faith." It teaches, Wesley continued, "A believer is not obliged to use the ordinances of God, or to do good works" and "a Preacher ought not to exhort to good works; not unbelievers, because it is harmful; not believers, because it is needless."[183] In the previous century, Richard Baxter (1615–1691) described antinomianism as follows: "It boasts in the doctrine of the perseverance of the saints, while it believes in no saint but one, that is Jesus, and neglects to persevere" (1830, 1:678).

Siding with Baxter and Wesley on the issue, Hart depicted an antinomian as someone who "trusts a Faith that's dead." In another place, he described an antinomian as a "dead Professor" of faith:

> The dead Professor counts
> Good Works as legal Ties.
> His Faith to Action seldom mounts;
> On Doctrine he relies.[184]

---

182. The editors have cited Tobias Crisp (1600–1643), who was often linked to antinomianism, and taught, "Christ's righteousness is so imputed to the elect, that they, ceasing to be sinners, are as righteous as he was, and all that he was. An elect person is not in a condemned state while an unbeliever; and should he happen to die before God calls him to believe, he would not be lost. Repentance and confession of sin are not necessary to forgiveness." One of the notorious objectors of antinomianism in the seventeenth century was Richard Baxter, who wrote *The Scripture Gospel defended, and Christ, grace, and free justification vindicated against the libertines* [...] *in two books: the first, a breviate of fifty controversies about justification* [...]*: the second upon the sudden reviving of antinomianism* [...] *and the re-printing of Dr. Crisp's sermons with additions* (London: 1690).

183. "Minutes of Some Late Conversations between the Rev. Mr. Wesleys and Others. Conversation I. Monday, June 25th, 1744," in John Wesley (1830), 8:278.

184. Supplement hymn 58, "[Good Works]" ("Vain Man, to boast forbear"), stanza 5.

In this stanza, Hart must have been thinking of James 2:17: "Even so faith, if it hath not works, is dead, being alone." For Hart, saving faith bears good works and is thus not alone. Where "there is true Faith," he insisted, "there will be Obedience and the fear of God" (xvii).[185] A true believer longs "to grow; and desire at the same time a daily Increase in all true Grace and Godliness" (xiv). For that reason, anyone who claims to be a believer and does not bring forth the fruit of righteousness has a dead faith:[186]

> Faith implanted from above,
> Will prove a fertile Root;
> Whence will spring a Tree of Love,
> Producing precious Fruit.[187]

In one of his hymns on good works, Hart wrote, "The righteous Man does Righteousness; / And true Faith works by Love."[188] Markedly, Hart highlighted love as one of the fruits of saving faith. Since "a true Christian is as vitally united to Christ, as my Hand or Foot to my Body," said Hart, he who is connected by faith to "Our wonderful Lover,"[189] will inevitably produce love. This means, for Hart, Christian piety ultimately emanates from Jesus Christ, who is the source of all godly virtues, so that without Jesus it is impossible for one to have true spirituality: "Thou art that green, that fruitful Tree; / From Thee our fruit is found."[190] In another hymn on good works, Hart rebuked those who claim to have living faith but bear no fruit:

> In vain Men talk of living Faith,
> When all their Works exhibit Death,
> When they indulge some sinful View
> In all they say, and all they do.
>
> The true Believer fears the Lord;
> Obeys his Precepts, keeps his Word;

---

185. Hart penned three hymns on the fear of the Lord. See supplement hymns 23–25.
186. "The Faith is vain such Men profess; / It comes not from above." See supplement hymn 57, "[Good Works]" ("When filthy Passions or unjust"), lines 3:1–2.
187. Hymn 23, "Cleaving to Christ" ("Brethren, let us praise our Lord"), lines 2:1–4.
188. Supplement hymn 57, "[Good Works]" ("When filthy Passions or unjust"), lines 3:3–4.
189. Hymn 13, "[Christ's Nativity]" ("How blest is the Season"), line 2:3.
190. Supplement hymn 57, lines 6:3–4.

> Commits his Works to God alone;
> And seeks *His* will before his own.
>
> A barren Tree, that bears no Fruit,
> Brings no great Glory to its Root;
> When on the Boughs rich Fruit we see,
> 'Tis then we cry, "A goodly tree!"[191]

Returning to his hymn on sanctification (No. 9, stanza 6), the other danger Hart addressed was legalism:

> "'Tis dangerous, (another cries)
> To trust to Faith alone:
> Christ's Righteousness will not suffice,
> Except I add my own."

If antinomianism encourages a believer to have faith without works in sanctification, legalism sways an unbeliever to have faith plus works for salvation. In another hymn, Hart compared the former to "Dead Sloth" and the latter to "Pharisaic Pride."[192] The former promotes a piety marked by spiritual sluggishness, whereas the latter promotes a piety marked by spiritual pride like that of the Pharisees in the Bible. Both systems, for Hart, are "the two Engines of Satan, with which he grinds the Church in all Ages, as betwixt the upper and the nether Milstone" (xiv). Hart's spirituality stands between these "Two dang'rous Gulphs." Before his conversion, he stood first in the gulf of legalism and then in the gulf of antinomianism, so he knew personally how dangerous these two systems were. And even after his conversion, he admitted these "two hideous Monsters" continued to trouble his soul:

> The Space between them [i.e., "Pharisaic Zeal, and Antinomian Security"] is much narrower and harder to find, than most Men imagine. It is a path which Vulture's Eye hath not seen; and none can shew it us but the Holy Ghost. Here, let no one trust the Directions of his own Heart, or of any other Man; lest by being warned to shun the One, he be dashed against the Other. The Distinction is too fine for Man to discern. Therefore, let the Christian ask Direction of his God. These two hideous Monsters continually worry and perplex my Soul. [...] Inward Corruptions and spiritual Wickedness continually harass and perplex

---

191. Supplement hymn 56, "Good Works," stanzas 1–3.
192. Hymn 26, "The Narrow Way" ("Wide is the Gate of Death"), line 4:3.

my Soul, and often make me cry out, "O wretched Man that I am; who shall deliver me from the Body of this Death" (1767, xviii).

Nevertheless, Hart saw his spiritual struggle as a mark of saving grace in his life. Whereas a dead soul does not struggle, a born-again soul will struggle and yet it cannot fall back again. As Hart said to his nephew,

> I am glad the Lord has so far wrought on your soul as to make you concerned for its everlasting state; and I sincerely wish you may hold out to the End and be saved. As to your Fears of falling back again, they are no signs that you will fall, but rather the contrary; for none depart from God while they have any fears of departing from him. You do well to hear the Gospel at all opportunities as the means appointed for the God of souls; but always endeavour to look thro' all means to the God of Grace, and depend on his strength and not your own [...].[193]

It is noteworthy how Hart counseled his struggling nephew to "always endeavour to look thro' all means to the God of Grace." For Hart, God uses the means of grace to empower the believer's spiritual life. So sanctification lies in the regular pursuit of these means, which antinomianism neglects to observe. Yet, Hart warned, "All Duties, Means, Ordinances, &c are [...] only rich, when they are enriched with the Blood of the Lamb, in Comparison of which, all Things else are but Chaff and Husks." To rephrase it, the practice of the means of grace of an unsaved soul can lead to legalism. The means of grace or spiritual disciplines are not saving but sanctifying. And while it is the Spirit who sanctifies us, we have the duty to observe the means that the Spirit ordinarily uses to sanctify us:

> Never did Men by Faith divine
> To Selfishness or Sloth incline.
> The Christian works with all his Pow'r:
> And grieves that he can work no more.[194]

Believers must work hard to pursue holiness, exercising the spiritual disciplines which God is pleased to use for their sanctification. One of the means highlighted in Hart's hymns is prayer, which he called "the Privilege and Delight of a Christian—That God grants not the Requests

---

193. Letter from Joseph Hart to his nephew, December 29, 1767. See Appendix 2.
194. Supplement hymn 56, "Good Works" ("In vain Men talk of living Faith"), stanza 4.

of his People, because they pray, but they pray, because he designs to answer their Petitions" (1767, xv). Hart viewed prayer as a mark of a true Christian—"That a prayerless Spirit, is not the Spirit of Christ; but that Prayer to a Christian, is as necessary and as natural as Food to a natural Man" (xvii). His teaching on prayer is further fleshed out in his hymn entitled "Praying without ceasing":

> Pray'r was appointed to convey
> The Blessings God designs to give.[195]

Prayer supports the weak soul:

> 'Tis Pray'r supports the Soul that's weak;
> Tho' Thought be broken, Language lame.
> Pray; if thou canst, or canst not, speak:
> But pray with Faith in Jesu's Name.[196]

God also uses baptism and the Lord's Supper to strengthen the believer's faith. Hart wrote three hymns on the former and twenty hymns on the latter. As for baptism, it illustrates the gospel in a special way and thus helps believers better understand what Jesus has done for them:

> By what amazing Ways
> The Lord vouchsafes t' explain
> The Wonders of His sov'reign Grace
> Towards the Sons of Men!
>
> He shews us first, how foul
> Our Nature's made by sin.
> Then teaches the believing Soul
> The Way to make it clean.
>
> Our Baptism first declares
> What Need we've all to cleanse.
> Then shews that Christ to all God's Heirs
> Can Purity dispense.
>
> Water no Man denies:
> But, Brethren, rest not there;
> 'Tis Faith in Christ that justifies,
> And makes the Conscience clear.[197]

---

195. Appendix hymn 12, "Pray without ceasing. I Thess. v.17," lines 1:1–2.
196. Appendix hymn 12, "Pray without ceasing. I Thess. v.17," stanza 5.
197. Supplement hymn 75, "[Baptism]," stanzas 1–4.

The paedobaptist Hart clarified how baptism cannot save but only signifies what the Spirit has done for believers in the gospel. It is a sign, pointing to the effects of God's sovereign grace:

> Baptiz'd into his Death,
> We rise to Life divine.
> The Holy Spirit works the Faith'
> And Water is the Sign.[198]

Hart also understood the Lord's Supper as a sign: "Thy suff'rings, Lord, each sacred Sign / To our Remembrance brings."[199] That is, each element of the Lord's Supper—the bread and the wine—is a sign, representing Christ's death. Communion service therefore is a special occasion whereby believers remember and celebrate what Jesus has done for them on the cross:

> Thus assembling, we, by Faith,
> Till he come, shew forth his Death.
> Of his Body, Bread's the sign;
> And we drink his Blood in Wine.
>
> Bread thus broken, aptly shews
> How his Body God did bruise.
> When the Grape's rich Blood we see,
> Lord! we then remember Thee.
>
> Saints on Earth, with Saints above,
> Celebrate his dying Love,[200]

But, for Hart, the Lord's Supper is not just a sign or symbol of Christ's death; it is also a meal provided by Christ for the spiritual sustenance of his people:

> I eat the Bread, and drink the Wine:
> But oh! my Soul wants more than Sign.
> I faint; unless I feed on Thee,
> And drink thy Blood as shed for *Me*.[201]

---

198. Supplement hymn 75, "[Baptism]," stanza 6.
199. Supplement hymn 17, "[For the Lord's Supper]" ("That doleful Night before his Death"), lines 2:1–2.
200. Supplement hymn 18, "[For the Lord's Supper]" ("Jesus, once for Sinners slain"), lines 4:1–6:2.
201. Supplement hymn 12, "[For the Lord's Supper]" ("Pity a helpless Sinner, Lord"), stanza 3.

In this ordinance, Jesus freely offers himself as spiritual food to be received by faith. He feeds his sheep with his flesh and blood and his sheep feed on him:

> Oh, How good our gracious God is!
> What rich Feasts does he provide!
> Bread and Wine to feed our Bodies:
> But much more is signified.
> All his Sheep (amazing Wonder!)
> Feeds he with his Flesh and Blood.[202]

So, for Hart, the Lord's Supper serves as a means of grace to nourish the believer's soul. On this account, repeatedly and earnestly he pleaded with his fellow believers to "Come, sit at Table with your Lord; / And eat celestial Food."[203] And to those who hesitate to come because of their unworthiness and doubt, his reply was the following:

> This is the Day the Lord has made.
> Rejoice, my Friends, to see
> His royal Table richly spread
> For such vile Worms as We.
>
> Welcome, poor Sinner, welcome here.
> Leave all thy Cares behind.
> Dismiss thy Doubt, cast off thy Fear,
> Give Reas'nings to the Wind.
>
> Come, eat his Flesh, and drink his Blood.[204]

4.6 Summary

The doctrines on the Trinity, the Scriptures, salvation, and sanctification found in Hart's hymns were not novel; they simply echoed the views of the orthodox reformers. Hart affirmed the Athanasian doctrine of the Trinity and rejected Arianism, Socinianism, and Unitarianism. In contrast to the Socinian view of the atonement, he embraced the Reformed view of the penal substitution, which saw the necessity of Christ's death for the forgiveness of sin. Unlike the deists, he highly upheld the Bible

---

202. Supplement hymn 13, "[For the Lord's Supper]," lines 1:1–6.
203. Supplement hymn 1, "For the Lord's Supper" ("The King of Heav'n a Feast has made"), lines 2:3–4.
204. Supplement hymn 2, "[For the Lord's Supper]," lines 1:1–4, 4:1–4, 6:1.

as infallible divine revelation and as a source of our knowledge of God. Religious truth, for him, is tested ultimately not by what the mind thinks (reason) but by what God says in his Word (revelation). In the pursuit of religion, reason must submit to the authority of the Scriptures.

Furthermore, Hart differed from rational dissenters, who gave more emphasis on human reason in their interpretation of Scripture, and from other dissenters who tried to harmonize rationalism and evangelicalism. Instead, he tended to place more emphasis on experience than on reason for the validation of truth, yet even subjective experience must submit to God's objective revelation. Nonetheless, Hart believed orthodoxy needed to be felt, not known only intellectually. His experimentalism was a reaction not only to rationalism but also to dry orthodoxy as seen among hyper-Calvinists and Unitarians of his day. He also recognized some elements of mystery in religion, such as the Trinity, which goes beyond human reason and is to be received as truth by faith without question.

Against hyper-Calvinism and Arminianism, he defended the Reformed doctrines of God's grace. In fact, as he claimed, the main intent for which he wrote his hymns was to proclaim "the Riches of his free Grace" (1767, "To the Reader"). His hymnody was his experimental presentation of these doctrines. And since what one believes affects how one behaves, Hart's theology produced a Reformed evangelical spirituality in him, a form of piety that is neither legalistic nor antinomian. He believed such spirituality, freed from legalism, flows from a soul saved by grace alone, and which, unhindered by the taint of antinomianism, strives for daily increase in holiness through the means of grace. His hymns, therefore, can be seen as his contribution to the spread of the Reformed faith and piety in the evangelical movement.

CHAPTER 5

Conclusion and Prospect

The Independent minister John Towers (d. 1804), who later became pastor to Joseph Hart's widow at Barbican Chapel, rhetorically asked in his elegy of Hart: "Should faithful, valiant Hart be quite forgot?" To which he forcefully replied: "No; let his memory be immortaliz'd" (Hart: 1856, xliii). The present study demonstrates why Hart, whose name has gone into near anonymity, deserves to be remembered. In the words of his brother-in-law John Hughes (d. 1773), Hart has "a right to be remembered of you all" (1768, vi, 28–29). Or as Peter Rae averred, "Because he is not regarded by historians as a major figure in the 18th century revival, that does not mean that his memory should be left unsung" (1988, 21). Indeed, Hart has a right to be remembered if only for his hymn "Come, Ye Sinners, Poor and Wretched," one of the most enduring hymns written on invitation. After its publication in 1759, it appeared in nearly every major collection of evangelical hymns in the eighteenth and nineteenth centuries.[1] It was often quoted in sermons by Charles Spurgeon (1834–1892) to urge sinners to come to Christ for salvation.[2] Starting in the earliest part of the nineteenth century, it became a favorite hymn of American revivalists for their camp meetings. Commenting on this hymn, Philip P. Bliss (1838–1876) said, "It is one of the old-fashioned, camp-meeting 'Spirituals,' and well deserves

---

1. To name a few, Richard Conyers, *A Collection of Psalms and Hymns* (1767); Augustus Toplady, *Psalms and Hymns* (1776); John Rippon, *Selection of Hymns* (1787); *Canterbury Hymnal* (1863); Charles Spurgeon, *Our Own Hymn-Book* (1866); *Baptist Praise Book* (1871).

2. See Spurgeon, "Out of the Depths" (no. 2353), a sermon intended for reading on Lord's Day, March 25, 1894, delivered on Thursday evening, January 26, 1888; and "Salvation to the Uttermost" (no. 84) delivered on Sabbath Evening, June 8, 1856.

a place among 'Gospel Songs'" (1874, 111). Still in use today,[3] this hymn has immortalized Hart's memory.

After he was converted in 1757, Hart carried forward the message and work of the Evangelical Revival by preaching the gospel, "always insisting upon a life and conversation becoming the Gospel" (Hughes: 1768, 28) by helping orphans, and most considerably, by producing hymns centered on the cross of Christ. In his funeral sermon for Hart, Hughes summed up Hart's ministry by saying Hart was "made an instrument in the hands of God for several years, to bring out of the magazine of Jesus Christ, cloaths for the naked, food for the hungry, physic for the sick, and a sharp rod for the hypocrite and impenitently wicked" (vi). Hart's ministry proved him to be a true evangelical, in alignment with David Bebbington's four defining features of early evangelicalism: conversionism, activism, biblicism, and crucicentrism (1989, 14–17).

Through careful manuscript and genealogical research, a more accurate biography of Hart has emerged, especially compared to what was presented in Thomas Wright's *The Life of Joseph Hart* (1910) and in John A. Kingham's *A Prodigal Made A Blessing: The Life and Hymns of Joseph Hart* (2015). Significantly, we now know the maiden name of Hart's second wife was not Hughes but Lamb, and he was a widower when he married her. We also know Hart had another important ministry, as a guardian to orphans. This indicates how Hart fits into and illustrates the characteristic pattern of early evangelicals, who sought to address the social crisis in eighteenth-century England. Unfortunately, other than what is found in *An Elegy on the Death of the Rev. Mr. Joseph Hart* (ca. 1768) by R.W., there is no other information about this ministry. Nevertheless, this newly discovered aspect of Hart's ministry gives us a more comprehensive portrait of Hart than has been previously available. Moreover, with our examination of Hart's letter to William Shrubsole (1729–1797), we not only see his connection to the Independent congregation in Sheerness, pastored by Shrubsole, but also to the Independent congregation in Chatham, whose pulpit George Whitefield (1714–1770) frequently supplied. Whitefield wrote in his Journal, August 6, 1739, "I preached at Chatham, to nearly 10,000 people. I never observed more decency and order in any

---

3. For instance, the hymn appears in the *Trinity Psalter Hymnal* (2018), a hymnbook produced jointly by the Orthodox Presbyterian Church and the United Reformed Churches in North America.

place at my preaching, than at that" (Timpson: 1859, 323). As Hart's letter expressed his intent to preach for these two churches, it reveals how popular Hart was as a preacher during his time.

In addition, this new portrait of Hart as a hymn writer does not support the insensitive characterization of his hymns as being possessed "of an ultra-Calvinistic tone," as James Rigg maintained.[4] While his hymns exalt the doctrine of sovereign grace, they also emphasize the universal call and free offer of the gospel and the duty of the unregenerate to repent and believe. Whereas an "ultra-Calvinist objects to revival because Christ is freely offered to sinners. Ultra Calvinism keeps scowling watch at the gate of mercy, lest sinners, hearing a rumour that the gospel is for every creature, should make too free of entrance" (Macpherson: 1875, 305). It is also not accurate to label the hymn writer Hart as a "high-Calvinist" (Hindmarsh: 2005, 245), as the epithet does not precisely represent his hymns.

Contrary to what Lawrence Dodson believed, Hart was not a Particular Baptist but an Independent. Hart wasn't the author of *A Discourse Upon Justification* (1740), which was in fact authored by Anne Dutton (1692–1765), a Calvinistic Baptist.

Hart's theological-spiritual journey raises important questions about his view of soteriology and how his descriptions of finding salvation accord with the beliefs of his contempories or with the interpretive beliefs of later scholars. For example, as early as 1733, he believed he was a Christian, except he later admitted to being a legalist, thinking his morality could earn him salvation. During Hart's time, such moralism was widespread within the Church of England. Then about 1740 he adopted an antinomian perspective, as may be seen in his book *The Unreasonableness of Religion* (1741). Herein, writing against the Arminian John Wesley, Hart tended to emphasize God's sovereignty at the expense of human responsibility in the context of salvation and sanctification, a tendency typical of a hyper-Calvinist, and an overreaction to Arminianism, which tends to stress man's responsibility more than God's sovereignty.

In about 1752, he left antinomianism and underwent, first, a mere outward reform (*ca.*1752–1756), followed by intense spiritual despondency,

---

4. When John S. Andrews revised Rigg's original entry (1891) on Hart for the new Oxford DNB (2004), he changed the statement to say, "Most of the hymns are strongly Calvinist."

which lasted until what he called his "reconversion" experience on Pentecost Sunday, May 29, 1757. This raises the question: what did Hart mean by reconversion? He was probably thinking his original conversion happened around 1740, after he left legalism:

> After some Weeks passed in this gloomy, dreadful State, the Lord was pleased to comfort me a little, by enabling me to appropriate, in some measure, the Merits of the Saviour to my own Soul. This Comfort increased for some Time. And my Understanding was also wonderfully illuminated in reading the holy Scriptures, so that I could see Christ in many Passages where before I little imagined to find him; and was encouraged to hope I had an interest in his Merits, and the Benefits by him procured to his People (iv–v).

But then shortly after this experience, Hart slid into antinomianism:

> In this blessed State my Continuance was but short: For, rushing impetuously into Notions beyond my Experience, I hasted to make myself a Christian by mere doctrine, adopting other Men's Opinions before I had tried them; and set up for a great Light in Religion, disregarding the internal Work of Grace begun in my Soul by the Holy Ghost. This *Liberty*, assumed by myself, and not given by Christ, soon grew to *Libertinism* [...]. In this abominable State I continued, a loose Backslider, an audacious Apostate, a bold-faced Rebel, for nine or ten Years (v).

Interestingly, during his period of antinomianism (*ca.* 1740–1751), he considered himself to be a "loose Backslider," who disregarded "the internal Work of Grace begun in [his] Soul by the Holy Ghost." Such a statement seems to belong to a converted person. But perhaps because his backsliding was so deep and long, Hart felt he was not really converted during this time. In his autobiographical hymn, he recounted his backsliding this way:

> The Lord, from whom I long backslid,
> First check'd me with some gentle Stings:
> Turn'd on me, look'd, and softly chid;
> And bid me hope for greater Things.[5]

---

5. Hymn 27, "The Author's own Confession" ("Come hither, ye that fear the Lord"), stanza 9.

In light of his long and deep fall, when he experienced "sweet Peace in my Soul" on Pentecost Sunday (May 29) of 1757 after hearing a sermon on Revelation 3:10 at the Moravian Chapel (1767, xi–xii), it probably felt for him a second experience of conversion. Puritan scholar Joel Beeke, who is not aware of any Puritan who used the term "reconversion," stated, "Thomas Goodwin may come the closest to the idea. He at times, when speaking of full assurance of faith, says that the joy received from this is so great that it is almost like a second conversion."[6] But since Hart himself hesitatingly described his Pentecost experience as his reconversion (1767, xiii), most likely what he questioningly called reconversion was actually his true conversion. Such was the understanding of his close friend Andrew Kinsman, who delivered an oration at Hart's interment. Addressing the vast crowd at the committal, Kinsman declared,

> Let me exhort you, not to sorrow as those without hope, *For if ye believe that Jesus died and rose again, even so them also that sleep in Jesus, will God bring with him*, 1 Thess. iv. 14. and among them our departed brother; who after his remarkable conversion, or what he himself calls *his re-conversion to God*, you well know, not only preached free grace, but are witnesses he lived free grace, and adorned it by an exemplary life and conversation (Hughes: 1768, 40).

Kinsman's assessment is the view commonly held in Hart research regarding Hart's date of conversion, and this is the view adopted in the present study. The way Hart described it, he experienced a sudden but felt spiritual change:

> The Alteration I then felt in my Soul, was as sudden and palpable, as that which is experienced by a Person staggering, and almost sinking under a Burden, when it is immediately taken from his Shoulders. Tears ran in Streams from my Eyes for a considerable while, and I was so swallowed up in Joy and Thankfulness, that I hardly knew where I was (1767, xii).

---

6. Joel R. Beeke, email message to me, October 25, 2021. In my email correspondence with D. Bruce Hindmarsh (October 24, 2021) and David W. Bebbington (October 25, 2021), two specialists in the history of early evangelicalism, they both indicated how they could not recall any other evangelical (besides Hart) who employed the term "reconversion." Thus, it appears the term was unusual among early evangelicals. For additional study of evangelical conversion, see Hindmarsh (2005) and Bebbington (2021).

In Hart's mind, a true conversion is not simply a change from one belief to another but a change of soul from death to life, felt and experienced by faith in Christ: "That mere Doctrine, tho' ever so sound, will not alter the Heart; consequently that to turn from one Set of Tenets to another, is not Christian conversion" (xvi). To illustrate his point, Hart went on:

> As much as *Lazarus* coming out of his Grave, and feeling himself restored to Life, differed from those who only saw the Miracle, or believed the Fact when told them; so great is the Difference between a Soul's real coming out of himself, and Having the Righteousness of Christ imputed to him by the precious Faith of God's Elect, and a Man's bare Believing the Doctrine of imputed Righteousness because he sees it contained in Scripture, or assenting to the Truth of it when proposed to his Understanding by Others (xvi–xvii).

So, for Hart, evangelical conversion involves not only believing the gospel doctrine, but also feeling and experiencing it. This view became standard among the evangelicals of the eighteenth century.

Robert W. Oliver, on the other hand, thought Hart's conversion occurred in the week before Resurrection Sunday of 1757, which fell on April 10 (2000, 7). Regardless, after this turning point in his life, the evidence of his conversion in the evangelical sense started to take shape. He started to write evangelical hymns and published his first edition in 1759. The following year, despite having no formal theological training, he began preaching "the gospel, pure, unmix'd" (1856, xliii). Eventually, he became pastor of Jewin Street Independent Chapel, where he diligently served until his death in 1768. He "labored hard when on earth," said Kinsman, "for the conversion of souls" (Hughes: 1768, 39). Also, following the example of Whitefield, Hart devotedly took care of orphans. His life was marked by physical suffering and intense spiritual struggle, yet he remained faithful in his profession until his last breath. "Hart lived," said Towers, "to praise the God who him redeem'd" (1856, xliii).

In light of the above discussion about Hart's conversion, two years afterward he wrote in his spiritual autobiography:

> That the Dealings of God with his People, tho' similar in the general, are nevertheless so various, that there is no chalking out the Paths of one Child of God by those of another; no laying down regular Plans of Christian Conversion, Christian Experience, Christian Usefulness, or Christian Conversation (xvi).

One wonders if this statement suggests that toward the end of his life, Hart changed his view on morphology of conversion found in *The Unreasonableness of Religion* (1741), especially considering the big gap between the writing of this tract and his spiritual experience in 1757. This is a good topic to explore for further studies. One might also investigate how much of his doctrine of conversion was shaped by his early hyper-Calvinism and antinomianism. Lastly, further studies might explore whether his reconversion experience could be alternatively seen as an expression of assurance of faith.

In relation to Hart's contributions to eighteenth-century English hymnody, we have seen how Hart's hymnbook added to the surge of materials being produced by more recognizable names (Isaac Watts, Charles Wesley, etc.). Hart and these other early evangelical hymn writers supplied significant resources for the shift from metrical psalms to hymns in English liturgy, both outside and inside the Church of England.

This flowering of hymnody contradicts Brian Wibberley's assertion that "it was not until the Oxford Movement originated, that hymnody began to be fostered within the Establishment" (1934, 131) and supports Robin Leaver's claim that "the transition from metrical psalmody to hymnody was affected not so much by the ideals of nineteenth-century Tractarians as by the practice of eighteenth-century Evangelicals, who were innovative with regard to the liturgical use of hymns" (McCart: 1998, vii). Congregational hymn-singing should therefore be added to David Bebbington's quadrilateral as one of the distinct attributes of early evangelicalism on the whole. We say "on the whole" because the evangelical Anglican William Romaine (1714–1795) argued for the exclusive use of metrical psalms in public worship and thought God had no blessing for the singing of hymns in the church. Admittedly, this was also not characteristic of most Scottish evangelicalism in the eighteenth century.[7]

Not only did Hart's hymnody contribute to this hymn explosion in the eighteenth century, but quite specifically his writing of hymns became

---

7. Though not covered in this present study, it should be noted, too, that during the eighteenth century only the metrical Psalms were used almost everywhere in Scotland, though in some congregations of the Church of Scotland the authorized collection of biblical paraphrases was also in use, and the Relief Church allowed for use of hymns alongside Psalms. Of course, at that time, there were few congregations anywhere in Scotland which were not Presbyterian, and of those only the Relief Church was customarily using hymns alongside Psalms.

a major aspect of his life endeavor to spread the beliefs and convictions of the evangelical movement. Hart saw his hymns not only as a liturgical tool but as a vehicle through which he could propagate what he believed was true religion.

Hart's hymns are important expressions of theology, covering his views on the Trinity, the Scriptures, and salvation. His theological convictions on these doctrines clearly separated him from what William Shrubsole styled as "three well known troublers of Christianity": the Arians, Socinians, and Deists (1810, 383). His orthodox position on the Trinity, high regard for the authority of Scriptures, and sound teaching on salvation certified his evangelicalism. And Hart's emphasis on the Holy Spirit supports the assertion of both Thomas Kidd (2014, 36) and Timothy Larsen (2007, 10) that pneumatology should be added to Bebbington's quadrilateral as another signifier of early evangelicals—thus making Hart a six-point evangelical, all things considered. Hart's Calvinistic soteriology distinguished him from Arminian evangelicals like John Wesley. Theologically, Hart became known as "a general of the Lord's host [...] who fought his master's battles valiantly, against those gigantic errors, which daily wound and grieve the church of Christ" (Hughes: 1768, vi). Accordingly, his hymns were not only a didactic tool for spreading Calvinistic evangelical theology, but a polemical response to unorthodoxy.

Since, for Hart, doctrine and devotion are inseparable, we have also considered his spirituality. And key to understanding his piety was his experimentalism, which was what attracted many to his hymns. For instance, William Gadsby (1773–1844) included several of Hart's hymns in *A Selection of Hymns for Public Worship* (1838) because in his estimation Joseph Hart and John Berridge (1716–1793) were "the sweetest and greatest experimental" hymnwriters who "left any hymns on record" (1838, 4).[8] Although the term "experimental" never appeared in any of Hart's hymns, they were "experimental and comfortable hymns," said Hughes, and "have been a means of refreshing and strengthening the souls of many" (1768, vi–vii).

Hart's experimentalism was his response to the "dry doctrine" of his day, a doctrine only in the head and not felt in heart. He depicted himself as having once had such a doctrine in the head and not felt in the

---

8. For an analysis of Gadsby's experimentalism, see Deborah A. Ruhl (2014), 14–22.

heart at the time when he fell into antinomianism: "For, rushing impetuously into Notions beyond my Experience, I hasted to make myself a Christian by mere doctrine, adopting other Men's Opinions before I had tried them" (1767, v). Notice how as an antinomian, Hart had embraced others' opinions before trying or testing them first. Such is not the case with experimentalism, which first puts a certain belief to the test to see if it is true or not before espousing it. Correspondingly, Hart believed the ultimate test for truth is not human reason but God's special revelation. Thence, Hart's experimentalism was opposed to rationalism, which uses reason as the final measure for truth.

Additionally, Hart's experimentalism contributed to his defense of orthodox theology against heterodox religious sects such as the Socinians and Deists. For instance, he embraced the doctrine of the Trinity not only because the Bible teaches it but also because of his experimental knowledge of it, even if it is contrary to human logic. In his spiritual autobiography, Hart mentioned what he termed "experimental Evidence":

> His free, distinguishing Grace is the Bottom on which is fixt the Rest of my poor weary tempted Soul. On this I ground my Hope, oftentimes when unsupported by any other Evidence, save only by the Spirit of Adoption received from him. He hath chosen me out from everlasting, in whom to make known the inexhaustible Riches of His free Grace and long Suffering. Tho' I am a Stranger to Others, and a Wonder to Myself, yet I know Him, or rather, am known of him. Tho' poor in myself, I am rich enough in Him. When my dry, empty, barren Soul is parched with Thirst, he kindly bids me come to him, and drink my Fill at the Fountain-head. In a word, he empowers me to say, with experimental Evidence, *Where Sin abounded, Grace did much more abound*. Amen and Amen (xx).

Hart's point was simple: he believed the doctrine of free grace to be true because he personally experienced it. In other words, the evidence he had for this belief to be true was an observance of divine revelation confirmed by his own experience of it. This is a critical aspect of Hart's experimentalism. Again, observe how he—when he was yet an antinomian—had embraced doctrines without experiencing them, making himself "a Christian by mere doctrine." This is not the case with experimentalism, which emphasizes the need for doctrine to be experienced and felt. Such an emphasis is indicated in Hart's post-conversion statement:

> I am daily more and more convinced, that the Promises of God, to *his People*, are absolute; and desire to build my Hopes on the free electing Love of God in Christ Jesus to my Soul, before the World began; which, I can experimentally and feelingly say, he hath delivered me from the *lowest Hell* (xix).

Here Hart's adverbs "experimentally" and "feelingly" are keys to his worldview: He could say experimentally (i.e., as a result of his religious experience of God's electing grace) and feelingly (i.e., from his personal experience of the effects of this doctrine of election) that God had delivered him from hell based on God's promises. And for Hart, Christians feel the effects of divine doctrines through faith, as is seen in his prayer to the Holy Spirit, "Pray, thou for Us; that we thro' Faith / May feel th' Effects of Jesu's Death."[9]

For Hart, experimentalism is the experiencing and feeling of God's truths through faith in Christ. One must not only know and believe the gospel but feel it. So Hart wrote, "That the Sinner, which is drawn to Christ, is not he that has *learnt* that he is a Sinner by Head-Knowledge, but that feels himself such by Heart-Contrition" (1767, xvii). Elsewhere Hart said, "True religion's more than notion; / Something must be known and felt."[10] That is, true or experimental religion does not just appeal to the intellect but to the heart as well; it unifies the head and the heart—a view shared by other evangelicals of the eighteenth century.

Hart's theology informed and influenced his spirituality, while his spirituality gave life to his theology. Taking that into consideration, it is not a surprise to hear Kinsman say of Hart, he "not only preached free grace, but [...] he lived free grace, and adorned it by an exemplary life and conversation" (Hughes: 1768, 40). Similarly, Hart did not only "preach the glory of a life of faith," but lived this kind of life even if at times his faith was "like a bruised reed" because of his spiritual affliction (27, 30). Yet, according to his brother-in-law, God "so ordained it, that it was a means of making him through the super-abundant grace of God, experimentally wise and humble" (20–21).

---

9. Hymn 6, "[To the Holy Ghost]" ("Descend from Heav'n, celestial Dove"), lines 5:4–5.

10. Hymn 56, "[Faith and Repentance]" Part 1 ("Let us ask th' important Question"), lines 1:7–8.

Conclusion and Prospect

In his last will and testament, written on May 17, 1768, eight days before his death, the afflicted Hart expressed his full assurance of faith with these words:

> I, Joseph Hart of the Strand, in the parish of Saint Martin in the Fields, in the County of Middlesex, Gentleman, being sick and weak in Body but of sound Mind, Memory, and understanding, do make this my Last will and Testament in manner following (that is to say): I Commit my Soul to Almighty God in good and Firm Hope that he will save it from Perdition in and through the Sole Merits of his dear Son, in whom I have believed and do still believe that through him I shall receive the Full Remission of all my Sins.[11]

---

11. Last Will and Testament of Joseph Hart, May 17, 1768. For a full transcription, see Appendix 4.

Afterword

Solomon said, "It is the glory of God to conceal a thing: but the honour of kings is to search out a matter" (Prov. 25:2). There is something kingly about historical studies that uncover lost information about influential but neglected figures. We are indebted to the research of Brian Najapfour for filling in gaps and correcting errors about the life and ministry of Joseph Hart.

The picture that emerges about Hart is one of a quintessential British evangelical of the eighteenth century. Hart's story brings together the striking combinations of evangelicalism: orthodox in beliefs and experimental in piety, evangelistic in preaching Christ crucified and compassionate in caring for the poor, renouncing legalism to flee to the righteousness of Christ alone and eschewing antinomianism to follow Christ in obedience to God's commandments, doctrinal in all his devotion and doxological in all his theology.

Perhaps the most striking combination in Hart's experiential orthodoxy is one that divided evangelicalism, even Whitefield and the Wesleys—namely, the combination of sovereign grace and the free offer of the gospel. Hart believed that the only prevenient grace (following Augustine contra Arminius) was that which springs from unconditional election and resulted in conversion:

> Had not thy Choice prevented mine,
> I ne'er had chosen Thee.

This eternally decreed grace touches the sinner at the time of God's appointing in the effectual calling that produces saving faith and repentance unto life.

> Those who are call'd by Grace divine,
> Believe, but not alone:
> Repentance to their Faith they join;
> And so go safely on.

However, Hart did not draw the conclusion, so injurious to the church and its mission, that preachers cannot offer Christ to all who hear them. Rather, he insisted on the biblical view of the gospel call and even addressed that call to the unconverted in his hymns:

> Come, ye Sinners, poor and wretched,
> Weak and wounded, sick and sore.
> Jesus ready stands to save you,
> Full of Pity join'd with Pow'r.

This welding of sovereign grace and the free offer of the gospel, though appearing to some as a paradox, was essential to Hart's evangelical biblical piety. Without such a balance of doctrines, evangelicals have historically found it difficult to avoid sliding into either legalism on the one hand or antinomianism on the other—both of which are closely related forms of rationalism. Hart's embraced election and evangelism as non-identical twins born of the same divine love. This made his piety fervently doxological, so that he lived unto God and preached and wrote "to the praise of the glory of his grace" (Eph. 1:6).

—Joel R. Beeke

APPENDICES

APPENDIX 1

Letter from Joseph Hart to William Shrubsole, 10 June 1766[1]

10 June 66
To Mr. Will Shrubsole[2]
Quarterman, at Sheerness Kent

London Tuesday 10th June 1766

Dear sir,

As I intend (the Lord permitting) to visit the Chatham Brethren next Lord's Day Se'nnight,[3] I intend likewise to reach you the Monday following (viz. 23d Inst.)[4] and Preach Monday and Tuesday Evenings and Administer the Lord's Supper on one of the Days, as shall be judged most convenient, and so take my Leave of you on the Wednesday Morning. If this be [agre]eable and your Pulpit vacant for me at those times, let me know by a Line from you as soon as you can; and withal acquaint me whither I must go; for if Mr. Bishop has left his Cabbins, I shall not know where to find him.

Give my kind Love to the Brethren; and exhort them to join with you in Prayer to the Lord for a Blessing on my Visit. And may the Lord bless you all, confirm strengthen [e]stablish and unite you in Truth and Love, so wisheth

Your Friend and Servant for the Lord's sake

Jos. Hart

---

1. University of Manchester, John Rylands Library, Thomas Raffles Collection, MS 370, No. 58.
2. William Shrubsole, 1729–1797.
3. Seven-night (a week from now).
4. Namely, the 23rd of this month.

APPENDIX 2

Letter from Joseph Hart to His Nephew 29 Dec. 1767[2]

London Tuesday 29th Dec. 1767

Dear Nephew,

I am glad the Lord has so far wrought on your soul as to make you concerned for its everlasting state; and I sincerely wish you may hold out to the End and be saved. As to your Fears of falling back again, they are no signs that you will fall, but rather the contrary; for none depart from God while they have any fears of departing from him. You do well to hear the Gospel at all opportunities as the means appointed for the God of souls; but always endeavour to look thro' all means to the God of Grace, and depend on his strength and not your own. When you are comforted, bless God for the Encouragement, and when it is otherwise trust in the Name of the Lord and stay upon the God of your salvation. Remember, the Lord will cast out none that come unto Him, tho' they come ever so poor and helpless. The alteration of your Frames from warm to cold, from lively to dead, is what all Christians experience, and therefore let not that make you cast off your Confidence; remember, we are made partakers of Christ if we hold fast our Profession to the End. The just live by Faith; but if any Man draw back, my Soul shall have no pleasure in him. Fear not, be of good Courage; wait on the Lord, and He shall bring it to pass. When you are weak, then you will be strong if you look out of your self to Christ Jesus, whose Strength is made perfect in Weakness. Be often in secret Prayer. And remember, the Trial is, not what frames of mind you may be in, but whether you endure to the End. The Lord strengthen settle and stablish you. If I can be of any Service to you, write as often as you please. Our love to you and yours, from Your loving Brother,

Joseph Hart

P.S. Your brother Joe never comes nigh me nor his aunt.

---

1. Reprinted in *Memorial to Mr. Joseph Hart* (1877) and Thomas Wright, *Joseph Hart* (1910).

APPENDIX 3

Marriage Bond and Allegation of Joseph Hart to Mary Lamb, 27 December 1752[1]

December 27th 1752

Appeared personally Joseph Hart of the parish of Saint Dunstan in the West London Widower and Alledged that he intends to intermarry with Mary Lamb of the same parish aged twenty five years a Spinster.

Tho Pearson for
Mast Mr Sronley

And that he knoweth of no lawfull Let or Impediment by reason of any Precontract, consanguinity, Affinity, or any other lawfull means whatsoever to hinder the said intended marriage Of the truth of which he made Oath and prayed a Licence to solemnize the said marriage in the Parish Church of St. Gregory & St. Benedict Pauls Wharf or St. Antholins London or at Audley Street Chapel in the County of Midd[lesex].

Sworn before me
Robert Chapman Sunogals[?]

Present M Holman
J Hart

Marriage Record of Joseph Hart and Mary Lamb, 28 December 1752[2]

Marriages in 1752

Hart & Lamb

Joseph Hart of St. Dunstan in the West Lon[don] W[idower] & Mary Lamb of the same Par[ish] Sp[inster] — 28 Dec — 1752

---

1. Marriage Bonds and Allegations. MS 10091/92. London Metropolitan Archives, England. Accessed via Ancestry.com.

2. Church of England Parish Registers, 1538–1812. P69/BEN3/A/003/MS05718/003. London Metropolitan Archives, England. Accessed via Ancestry.com.

Marriage Bond of Joseph Hart to Mary Lamb, 27 December 1752[3]

Know all Men by these Presents, That We *Joseph Hart of the parish of Saint Dunstan in the West London Gent[leman]*—

are hereby become bound unto the Right Reverend Father in God *Thomas*—by Divine Permission, Lord Bishop of London in the Sum of Two Hundred Pounds of good lawful Money of Great Britain, to be paid to him the said Right Reverend Father in God, or his lawful Attorney, Executors, Successors, or Assigns: For the good and faithful Payment of which sum we do bind ourselves, and both of us, jointly and severally, for the Whole, our Heirs, Executors, and Administrators, firmly by these Presents. Sealed with our Seals, Dated the *twenty seventh* Day of *December* in the Year of our Lord *1752*—

The Condition of this Obligation is such, That if hereafter there shall not appear any lawful Let or Impediment, by Reason of any Pre-Contract, Consanguinity, Affinity, or any other lawful Means whatsoever but that *the above bounden Joseph Hart Widower and Mary Lamb Spinster*—may lawfully solemnize Marriage together, and in the same afterwards lawfully remain and continue for Man and Wife, according to the Laws in that Behalf provided: And moreover, if there be not at this present Time any Action, Suit, Plaint, Quarrel, or Demand, moved or depending before any Judge Ecclesiastical of Temporal, for or concerning any such lawful Impediment between the said Parties: Nor that either of them be of any better Estate or Degree, than to Judge at granting of the License is suggested.

And lastly, if the same Marriage shall be openly solemnized in the Church, in the License specified, between the Hours appointed in the Constitutions Ecclesiastical confirmed, and according to the Form of the Book of Common Prayer, now by Law established, and do save harmless, and keep indemnified, the above mentioned Reverend Father in God, his Chancellor and Surrogates, and all other his Officers and Ministers whatsoever, by reason of the Premises, then this Obligation to be void, or else to remain in full Force and Virtue.

Sealed and Delivered,
in the Presence of

Tho. Pearson

J Hart

---

3. Marriage Bonds and Allegations. DL/A/D/24/MS10091E/65. London Metropolitan Archives, England. Accessed via Ancestry.com.

APPENDIX 4

Last Will and Testament of Joseph Hart, 17 May 1768 (proved 30 May 1768)[2]

In the Name of God Amen

I Joseph Hart of the Strand in the parish of Saint Martin in the Fields in the County of Middlesex Gentleman being sick and weak in Body but of sound Mind Memory and understanding do make this my Last will and Testament in manner following (that is to say) I Commit my Soul to Almighty God in good and Firm Hope that he will save it from Perdition in and through the Sole Merits of his dear Son in whom I have believed and do still believe that through him I shall receive the Full Remission of all my Sins. My Body I resign to the Earth from whence it was taken and I desire it may be Interred without the least pomp in a plain frugal and Sober manner and in respect to my worldly Estate wherewith it hath pleased God to bestow upon me I give devise and bequeath the same as follows (viz.) First I do hereby charge all my Real and personal Estate with the payment of all my just debts. Secondly I give and devise unto my dear wife Mary Hart All that Messuage or Building heretofore called or known by the Name of the Cockpit and now or late by the Name of a Meeting House and all those two Messuages or Tenements and being heretofore in the tenure or occupation and Joseph Ard and the other of John Miller and now or late in the Tenure or occupation of Thomas Atwood and William Hale and all that other Messuage or Tenement (heretofore called or described as part of a Messuage or Tenement and in the Tenure of Elizabeth Cawne or her assigns) late in the Tenure or occupation of [...] Cole and now or late in the Tenure or occupation of John Porter and also all that piece or imite of ground or garden imi Lying behind or near adjoining to the said last Mentioned Messuage or Tenement and also in Cockpit Yard in Jewin Street heretofore in the Tenure or occupation of [...] Phillips widow and now or late in the Tenure or occupation of Benjamin Davis all which said premises are Scituate Lying and being in or near Jewin Street in the parish of

---

1. Prerogative Court of Canterbury and Related Probate Jurisdictions: Will Registers (PROB 11), the National Archives, Kew, England. Accessible via Ancestry.com.

St. Botolph without Aldersgate in the City of London together with all and Singular the appmt. to the same respectively belonging and which were lately purchased by me of Mary Dandridge and James Dandridge To hold to the said Mary Hart her Heirs and assigns for ever and all the Rest residue and remainder of me Real and personal Estate and Effects of what nature or kind soever or wheresoever I give devise and bequeath the same unto my said dear wife Mary Hart to and for her sole only and separate use and behoof for ever and I do hereby nominate and appoint the said Mary Hart sole Executrix of this my Last Will and Testament hereby revoking all Former will and wills by me heretofore made. In witness whereof I have here unto set my hand and seal this seventeenth day of May in the year of our Lord one thousand seven hundred and Sixty Eight Joseph Hart. Signed sealed published and declared by the above named Joseph Hart as and for his Last Will and Testament in the presence of us who in his presence and at his request and in the presence of each other subscribed our Names as witnesses hereto. J Ford. Tho[mas] Justy[?]. Sam Gawler. Clements Inn.

This Will was proved at London on the thirtieth day of May in the year of our Lord one thousand seven hundred and Sixty Eight before the worshipfull Andrew Coltee Ducarel Doctor of Laws and Surrogate of the Right worshipfull George Lorey[?] also Doctor of Laws Master Keeper or Commissary of the prerogative Court of Canterbury Lawfully Constituted by the oath of Mary Hart widow the Relick of the deceased and Sole Executrix named in the said will to whom administration was granted of all and singular the goods Chattels and Credits of the said deceased she having been First sworn duly to administer.

APPENDIX 5

Last Will and Testament of Mary Lamb (proved 18 March 1790)[2]

[This includes her original will of 26 Feb. 1784, an addendum of 8 Jan. 1787 after the death of daughter Mary, another addendum 27 Jan. 1790, and the finalization of the will 18 Mar. 1790 after the death of the elder Mary.]

Mary Hart

In the Name of God Amen

I Mary Hart of the parish of St Sepulchre London & widow of Joseph Hart late of the parish of St. Martin in the Fields in the county of Middlesex Gentleman deceased / hoping for Eternal Life only through the meritorious death and righteousness of Jesus Christ the Almighty God / do make this my last will and Testament as follows (that is to say) I give and devise all that Brick Building commonly called a Meeting House and now used for the publick worship of God situate on the South Side of Jewin Street in the parish of St. Botolph Aldersgate London with the ground whereon the same stands and all and evry of in Appurtenances unto my worthy Friends the Reverend John Towers of Red Lion street in the parish of St James Clerkenwall in the County of Middlesex Clerk John Ford of the Old Jewry London Corner of Physick and William Abington now or late of Beaufort Buildings in the Strand in the said County of Middlesex Gentleman and their Heirs and assigns for and during the natural Life of my son Thomas Hart Your Trust that they the said John Towers John Ford and William Abington and their heirs and assigns do and shall receive and take up the Rents and profits of the said Building or Meeting House Ground and premisses and pay the same unto my said son Thomas Hart or otherwise permit and suffer him to receive and enjoy the same Rents and Profits during his natural Life for his own use and Benefit and also Your Trust to preserve and support the [renting?] out Remainders herein after limitted of the same Premises from being defeased or destroyed and for that purpose to make Entries and bring Actions as Occasion shall require and immediately [?] and after the decease of my said Son Thomas Hart I give and devise all the said Building or Meeting House Ground and

Premisses unto the first Son of the Body of the said Thomas Hart lawfully issuing and the Heirs Male of the Body of such first Son lawfully issuing and for want of such Issue I give and devise the same unto the second third fourth and fifth and all and evry other Son and Sons of the said Thomas Hart lawfully issuing [–lly] successively and in remainder one after another and the Heirs Male of their several and respective Body and Bodies lawfully issuing the elder of such Sons and the Heirs Male of his Body being always preferred and to take before the Younger of such Sons and the heirs Male of his and their Body and Bodies and for want of such Issue Make of the Sons of the said Thomas Hart I give and devise the said Building Meeting House Ground and Premisses unto my Son Benjamin Hart his Heirs and Assigns for ever But I hereby declare that my Will and Meaning is that the before mentioned devise of the said Meeting House Ground and Premisses in Trust for my said Son Thomas Hart during his life and after to his Sons shall be upon this condition that he my said Son Thomas Hart shall and do Release assign and transfer all his Part and share and shares Right Title Interest Claim and Demand (if any he hath or shall have) of in to or out of all and evry or any Sum or Sums of Money or Bank or other Annuities now in the Hands or standing in the Names of the said John Ford [...] Justis and the said William Abington or of any of them or of any other person or persons In Trust for me of in Trust for me and any or my children and of in to or out of my personal Estate in any Right or on any account whatsoever unto my Son and Daughters Benjamin Hart Mary Hart and Mercy Hart and in case my said Son Thomas Hart shall refuse so to do for the space of one Year [?] after reasonable request and tender of such Release or Assignment made to him for that purpose then I give the said Meeting House Ground and Premisses unto my said Son Benjamin Hart his Heirs and Assigns for ever also I give to my said Son Benjamin Hart five Silver Table Spoons and two Silver Salt cellars and shovels also I give unto my Daughter Mary Hart the copy of the Volume of Hymns which was written and published by my said late Husband Joseph Hart and the Right of Printing and binding the same also I give to my said Daughter Mary Hart my Watch and Diamond Hoop Ring and I give all my other Rings unto my Daughter Mercy Hart also I give all my wearing apparel Linnen Household Furniture China and Books and the rest of my Plate unto my said Daughters to be equally divided between them by and according to the direction of my executors and I give and bequeath all the Monies and Bank Annuities and other Annuities in the Hands or Standing in the Names of the said John Ford [...] Justis and William Abington or of any of them or any other person In Trust as aforesaid and all the rest and residue of my personal Estate and Effects of every kind whatsoever unto my said Son and Daughters Benjamin Hart Mary Hart and Mercy Hart to be equally divided between them the share of my Daughter Mercy Hart to be paid to her at her age of twenty-five years or sooner if my Executors or the Survivor of them shall think it proper and my will is that my Executors or the Survivor of them may lay out any part of the share of my said Daughter Mercy for her maintenance and Education or for any purpose which they or he shall think will be for her advantage and I request the favour of my said I Mr John Towers Dr John Ford and Mr William Abington to attempt the trouble of being my Executors and I hereby appoint them and my Son Benjamin Hart Executors of this my will and I hereby revoke all other wills by me made and declare this only to be my last will and Testament In witness whereof I have hereunto set my Hand and seal this twenty sixth day of February in the year of our Lord one Thousand seven hundred and eighty four *Mary Hart*

Signed sealed Published and Declared by the said Testatrix Mary Hart as and for her last Will and Testament in the presence of us who in her presence and at her request have hereunto subscribed our Names as witnesses James Atchison, George Hale} of Cow Lane | Tallow Chandler Shoemaker

Frs. Shadd of Clerkenwell Atty—

Whereas I Mary Hart late of the parish of St Sepulchre London but now of Princes Street Barbican London widow have made my last will and Testament bearing date the twenty sixth day of February one thousand seven hundred and eighty four Now I do make this codicil thereto which I desire may be considered and taken as a part of my said will and I do hereby give to my daughter Mercy Hart a copy of the volume of hymns which was written and published by my late husband Joseph Hart and the Right of Printing and binding the same also I give my watch and all my Rings and Plate (except what I have by my said will specifically bequeathed to my Son Benjamin Hart) also all of my Household Goods and Furniture wearing Apparel Linnen China and Books and all Moneys owing to me at the time of my decease for Hymn Books unto my said Daughter Mercy Hart and whereas by my said will I have given all Moneys Bank Annuities and other Annuities in the hands or standing in the Names of Doctor John Ford Mr [...] Justis and Mr William Abington or of any of them or of any other person In Trust for me or my children as in my said will is mentioned and all the rest and residue of my Estate and Effects unto my Daughter Mary Hart since deceased Now I do hereby give and bequeath all the said Moneys Bank Annuities and other Annuities and all the Rest and Residue of my personal Estate and Effects of any kind whatsoever unto my said Son and Daughter Benjamin and Mercy Hart to be equally divided between them the Share of my said Daughter Mercy to be paid to her at her age of twenty five years or the same or any part thereof to be soon & paid to her or applied or disposed of for her benefit if my Executors or the Survivors or Survivor of them shall think fit and except only so far as I have hereby altered my said will I do hereby confirm the same In Witness whereof I have hereunto set my Hand and Seal this Eighth Day of January one Thousand seven hundred and Eighty seven Mary Hart (LS) Signed and Sealed by the said Testament Mart Hart as and for a codicil to her will in the presence of us Mary Falkener, Edward Falkener, Frs. Shadd.

Whereas I Mary Hart late of the Parish of St Sepulchre London but now of Chiswill Street in the Parish of St Luke in the county of Middlesex widow have made my last will and Testament bearing date the twenty sixth day of February one Thousand seven hundred and eighty four and have thereby given and devised all that Brick Building commonly called a Meeting House scituate on the South side of Jewin Street London unto my worthy Friends the Reverend John Towers John Ford Doctor of Physic and Mr William Abington by such Descriptions as therein mentioned and to their Heirs during the normal life of my Son Thomas Hart upon the Trusts and with such Remainder as in my said will are mentioned Now I do hereby give and bequeath unto my Daughter Mercy Hart the sum of fifty five pounds which it is my will shall be raised in the first place by and out of the said Building or Meeting House and I do hereby expressly charge the said Meeting House and its Appurtenances with the payment thereof and also lawful Interest for the same from the time of my decease and except only so far as I have hereby and by another codicil bearing date the eighth day of January one Thousand seven hundred and eighty four altered my said will I do ratify and confirm the same In Witness whereof I have to this codicial which I desire may be considered and taken as and for a part of my said will set my Hand and Seal the twenty seventh Day of January one Thousand seven hundred and ninety Mary Hart (LS) Signed Sealed and Published by the said Testatrix Mary Hart as and for a codicil to her will in the presence of us Frs. Shadd, Edward Falkener, Mary Falkener.

This Will was proved at London with two codicils the eighteenth Day of March in the year of our Lord one Thousand seven hundred and ninety before the worshipful Thomas [B–] Doctor of Laws surrogate of the Right Honourable Sir William Wynne Knight Doctor of Laws Master Keeper or commissary of the prerogative court of Canterbury lawfully constituted by the oath of the Reverend John Towers clerk one of the Executors named in the said will to whom Administration was granted of all singular the Goods Chattels and Credits of the deceased having been first sworn duly to administer power reserved of making the like Grant to John Ford Doctor of Physic William Abington and Benjamin Hart the son of the deceased—the other Executors named in the said will when they or either of them shall apply for the same.—

APPENDIX 6

Joseph Hart's Immediate Family

Hart's parents' names might have been Joseph Hart and Mary Grant. If these were Hart's parents, there is a record of their marriage in *London, England, Clandestine Marriage and Baptism Registers, 1667–1754*, which shows they were married clandestinely in London on April 23, 1718. Their decision to have a clandestine wedding—a wedding not in conformance with the requirements of the Church of England's canon law—was most likely due to their religious nonconformity. If this couple were indeed Hart's parents, one might wonder why they got married in 1718 when Hart was about six years old. A possible reason could be that this was second marriage for his father. Or if they were his birth parents, probably they had already contracted themselves (had the private and solemn exchange of vows), then later decided to have a wedding conducted by a minister. "[I]ndeed," writes Jacob Field, "from the twelfth century all that was theoretically required for a valid marriage was the exchange of vows" (2017, 351). Another possible reason is that the year 1718 in the document is not accurate. As the National Archives warns, "Because of their irregular nature, the registers and notebooks in the Fleet Registers series need to be used with care. The information in them is not always reliable, with some duplicated entries and others that are known to be forged."[1] In fact, there is a record in *England, Marriages, 1538–1973* naming Joseph Hart and Mary Grant as being married in London on December 23, 1715. There is also a record saying the two were married on December 23, 1718. Notice the common element among the three possible wedding dates: December 23, 1715; December 23, 1718; and April 23, 1718.

Given the hazy nature of Hart's parentage, his siblings are difficult to establish. Clearly, he had at least one brother or sister, through which he had two nephews. The title page of the funeral *Sermon* (1768) named John Hughes as

---

1. http://www.nationalarchives.gov.uk/help-with-your-research/research-guides/nonconformists/

his brother-in-law, meaning Hart apparently had at least one sister, or more distantly, one of Hart's wives had a sister who married Hughes.[2]

Joseph Hart (1712–May 24, 1768) and Mary Brown of St Margaret's, Westminster, London were married on September 13, 1749 at St George's Chapel, Hanover Square, Mayfair, London. Hart's first wife must have died sometime before or in 1752.

Joseph Hart and Mary Lamb (*ca.* 1726–1790) were married December 28, 1752 at St Benet Paul's Wharf, London. At the time of their wedding, they were both residents of Saint Dunstan in the West, London. When the widower Hart married Mary Lamb, she was previously unmarried. Mary's will was last revised on January 27, 1790, and she was buried at Bunhill Fields on February 17, 1790.

In the Advertisement in *The Christian Warrior Finishing His Course. A Sermon Occasioned by the Death of the Rev. Mr. Joseph Hart, preached in Jewin-Street, June 5, 1768. By John Hughes*, [...] *And An Oration Delivered at His Interment by Andrew Kinsman* (London, 1768), the following notice was given:

> As the professed design of publishing this sermon, is to inform the benevolent of the state of Mr. HART's family, they are desired to take notice that Mr. HART has left a *widow* and *five* children entirely unprovided for, except the subscription lately made for himself, and *this* for his family. The widow has been for some months in a bad state of health, and is now incapable of doing any thing. Four of the children are unable to get their living, viz. A boy of fourteen, almost stupid by epileptic fits. Two boys, one eight, the other ten years, and an infant of sixteen months.

Joseph Hart had six children:[3]

1) Mary, referred to as the one able to get her living, must have been a teenager when Hart died. She was probably from Joseph Hart's first marriage, born *ca.* 1750–1752, since he and his second wife were married on December 28, 1752 and had Joseph on March 24, 1754 (not enough time for two pregnancies). From Mary Lamb's last will and testament, we know this daughter likely died shortly before January 8, 1787.

---

2. Hughes's wife's name was Mercy.
3. Except for the second child's name, all their names were mentioned in Mary Hart's last will and testament (see appendix 5). The fifth child died in 1763 before her will was written.

Appendix 6

2) Joseph, referred to as "almost stupid by epileptic fits."
   Birth: March 24, 1754
   Baptism: April 19, 1754
   Baptism place: St Dunstan-in-the-West, London

3) Thomas
   Birth: February 14, 1758
   Baptism: March 3, 1758
   Baptism place: St Martin-in-the-Fields, Westminster, London

4) Benjamin
   Birth: September 27, 1759
   Baptism: October 8, 1759
   Baptism place: St Martin-in-the-Fields, Westminster, London
   Marriage: July 6, 1797
   Wife: Ann Eliza Thorold (bap. June 26, 1772)
   Marriage place: St Mary le Strand, Westminster, London
   Death: September 19, 1836

Note: In 1781, Benjamin studied at Homerton Academy, a dissenting college.

5) Daniel
   Birth: c.1760?
   Death: August 18, 1763 (at age three)

6) Mercy
   Birth: January 22, 1767
   Birth place: 1000 St Martin-in-the-Fields, Westminster, London
   Marriage: July 1791
   Marriage Place: Saint Luke Old Street, Finsbury, London
   Husband: Alexander Moor (bap. August 16, 1757–d. 1793)
   Death: 1801
   Burial Date: April 19, 1801

Bibliography

Primary Sources

I. Hart's Hymns (arranged chronologically)

1st Edition

Hymns, &c. Composed on various subjects. With a preface, containing a brief and summary account of the author's experience, and the great things that God hath done for his soul. London: Printed by J. Everingham; and sold by T. Waller, in Fleet-Street; G. Keith in Gracechurch-Street; and D. Wilson and D. Durham, opposite Buckingham-Street in the Strand, 1759.

2nd Edition

Hymns, &c. Composed on various subjects. London: Printed for the author; and sold at his House. [...], 1762.

3rd Edition

Hymns, &c. composed on various subjects. London: printed for the author; and sold at his house; Hart's warehouse (the Lamb); and at the meeting in Jewin Street, 1763.

Hymns, &c. composed on various subjects. London printed. Worcester, [Massachusetts] re-printed by I. Thomas, at his office near the Court-House., MDCCLXXXII [1782].

4th Edition

Hymns composed on various subjects. London: Printed for the Proprietors by W. Day, 1811.

Hymns composed on various subjects. Brunswick [Me.]: Printed and for sale by Griffin & Weld, 1822. [This is a revised and corrected version of the fourth edition.]

5th Edition
Hymns, &c. composed on various subjects. London: printed by M. Lewis. And sold by F. Newbery; and at the author's house; and at the meeting in Jewin-Street, 1767.

6th Edition
Hymns, &c. composed on various subjects. London: Printed by M. Lewis, in Pater-noster-Row; and sold by F. Newbery, at the Crown the corner of St. Paul's Church-Yard, Ludgate-Street; and at the Author's House (the Lamb) near Durham-Yard, in the Strand; and at the meeting in Jewin-Street, 1769.

7th Edition
Hymns, &c. Composed on various subjects. London: Printed by M. Lewis, in Pater-noster-Row; and sold for by F. Newbery, at the Crown, the corner of St. Paul's Church-Yard, Ludgate-Hill; and by the author's widow (the Lamb) near Durham-Yard, in the Strand; and at the Meetings in Jewin-Street, and Bartholomew-Close, [1770?].
Hart's Hymns. Camberwell Grove, London: Sovereign Grace Union, 1900. [This is a verbatim reprint of the seventh edition.]
H.S.N. in *Hart's Hymns.* Choteau, MT: Old Paths Gospel Press, n.d.

8th Edition
Hymns, &c. Composed on various subjects. Dublin: Printed by John Charrurier, 1787.

9th Edition
Hymns, &c. composed on various subjects. London, Printed by H. Trapp, 1777.

10th Edition
Hymns, &c. composed on various subjects. Elizabeth Town [N.J.]: Printed and sold by Shepard Kollock; –likewise sold by R. Hodge, New York., [1787].

11th Edition
Hymns, &c. composed on various subjects. London: Printed by H. Trapp […] and sold by E. Newbery […] and by the author's widow […], 1788.

13th Edition
Hymns, &c. composed on various subjects. Advertisement by John Towers. London: printed by T. Bensley; and sold by the author's daughter; Mrs. Newbury; M. Priestley; and at the meetings in Jewin Street and Barbican, 1796.

14th Edition
Hymns, &c. composed on various subjects. Advertisement by John Towers. London: Printed and sold by V. Griffiths [...] also sold by the author's daughter [...] and by J. Mathews. 1799.

15th Edition
Hymns, &c. composed on various subjects. Elizabeth-Town [N.J.]: Printed and sold by S. Kollock., 1799.

16th Edition
Hymns, &c. composed on various subjects. London: Printed and published by Ruffy and Evans, 1803.

22nd Edition
Hymns on various subjects. London: Printed by Kaygill & Rowe, 1818.

II. Other Editions

Hymns on various subjects. London: Houlston and Sons, [after 1768].

Hymns on various subjects. London: Printed for Hamilton, Adams, & Co., [1771?].

Hymns on various subjects. London, Printed by T. Bensley, for E. Huntington, 1808.

Hymns composed on various subjects. London: Printed for the Proprietors by W. Day, 1811.

Hymns composed on various subjects. London: William Baynes, 1816.

Hymns composed on various subjects. Edited by John Towers. Shacklewell printed, London reprinted, 1819.

Hymns composed on various subjects. London, sold by E. Huntington and Richard Baynes, 1820.

Hymns on various subjects. Royston: J. Warren, 1821.

Hymns on various subjects. London: pr. for R. Baynes, 1824.

Hymns on various subjects. Lewes [England]: Printed for J. Baxter, 1826.

Hymns on various subjects. London: Hamilton, Adams, & Co., [1837].

Hymns composed on various subjects. Brighton [England]: J. Tyler, 1841.

Hymns composed on various subjects. London, Chidley, 1844.

Hymns on various subjects. London: Printed for Hamilton, Adams, & Co., Paternoster Row, 1851.

Hymns Composed on Various Subjects: With the Author's Experience. "Memoir of Joseph Hart" by Henry Fowler. London: Groombridge & Sons, 1851.

Hymns composed on various subjects. London: Groombridge & Sons, 1853.

Hymns Composed on Various Subjects. Includes "An Elegy on the Late Rev. Joseph Hart" by John Towers. London: E. Palmer & Son, 1856.

Hymns composed on various subjects. London: Groombridge, 1857.

Hymns on various subjects. London, Aylott and Jones [1858?].

Hymns composed on various subjects. London: E. Palmer & Son, 1863.

Hart's hymns. London: Collingridge, [1882?].

Hymns, etc. composed on various subjects. [London]: Hawker & Co.: M. Lewis, 1911.

Hymns on various subjects. Sovereign Grace Union: Redhill, [1965].

Hymns, etc. composed on various subjects. Chouteau, MT: Old Paths Gospel Press, 1965.

III. Other Works by Hart

The Unreasonableness of Religion. Being Remarks and Animadversions on Mr. John Wesley's Sermon on Romans viii. 32. Printed for the Author, 1741; revised by George Terry as *Calvinism and Arminianism, Fairly Stated and Fully Explained by a Learned Layman, who Afterwards Became an Eminent Preacher: Published in the Year 1741.* London: E. Justins, 1812.

Poiema Nouthetikon: or, the Preceptive Poem of Phocylides, Translated into English. London: J. Robinson, 1744.

Herodian's History of His Own Time: or, of the Roman Empire After Marcus, Translated into English. London: For the Author, 1749.

A Sermon Preached at Jewin Street Meeting on a Christmas-Day Morning in the Year 1768. London: G. Terry, 1814.

The King of the Jews: A Sermon, Preached at Jewin Street Meeting, on Christmas-day Morning, in the Year MDCCLXVIII. London: Ebenezer Huntington, 1821.

IV. Manuscript Materials

Marriage of Joseph Hart to Mary Lamb, 27 December 1752. Diocese of Winchester, Archdeaconry of Surrey, Marriage Bonds and Allegations. London Metropolitan Archives, England. Accessible via Ancestry.com.

Letter from Joseph Hart to William Shrubsole, 10 June 1766. University of Manchester, John Rylands Library, Thomas Raffles Collection, MS 370, No. 58.

Letter from Joseph Hart to His Nephew, 29 Dec. 1767, reprinted in *Memorial to Mr. Joseph Hart* (1877) and Thomas Wright, *Joseph Hart* (1910).

Will and Testament of Joseph Hart, 17 May 1768 (proved 30 May 1768). Prerogative Court of Canterbury and related Probate Jurisdictions: Will Registers (PROB 11), The National Archives, Kew, England. Accessible via Ancestry.com.

Will and Testament of Mary Hart, 26 Feb. 1784 (codicils 8 Jan. 1787, 27 Jan. 1790, proved 18 Mar. 1790). Prerogative Court of Canterbury and related Probate Jurisdictions: Will Registers (PROB 11), the National Archives, Kew, England. Accessible via Ancestry.com.

Secondary Sources

I. Articles

ANTHONY, MICHAEL J. (2001), Enlightenment, in Evangelical Dictionary of Christian Education, Grand Rapids: Baker Book House, 249.

BEBBINGTON, DAVID W. (2021), Evangelical Conversion, c. 1740–c.1850, in The Evangelical Quadrilateral: Characterizing the British Gospel Movement 1, Waco, TX: Baylor University, 167–91.

BEEKE, JOEL R./MARK JONES (2012), The Puritans on Regeneration, in A Puritan Theology: Doctrine for Life, Grand Rapids: Reformation Heritage Books, 463–80.

BELA, TERESA (2011), Faith, Doubt and Despair in William Cowper's Selected Poetry and Prose, in Anna Niżegorodcew/Maria Jodłowiec (ed.), Beyond Sounds and Words: Volume in Honour of Janina Aniela Ozga, Kraków: Wydawnictwo Uniwersytetu Jagiellońskiego, 77–90.

BILLINGS, J. TODD (Mar. 2011), The Problem with TULIP, or More than TULIPs in this Field, Perspectives: A Journal of Reformed Thought 9, 9–12.

Biography: The Rev. Andrew Kinsman (Aug. 1793), The Evangelical Magazine 1, 45–60.

CARLSON, G. WILLIAM (2011), Pietism, in Glen G. Scorgie (ed.), Dictionary of Christian Spirituality, Grand Rapids: Zondervan, 673.

CLIFFORD, ALLAN (1985), Benjamin Keach and Nonconformist Hymnology, Spiritual Worship, London: Westminster Conference, 69–93.

COX, LEO G. (1969), Prevenient Grace: A Wesleyan View, Journal of the Evangelical Theological Society 12/3, 143–49.

DANIEL, CURT (1997), John Gill and Calvinistic Antinomianism, in Michael A.G. Haykin (ed.), The Life and Thought of John Gill (1697–1771), Leiden: Brill, 171–90.

———. (2004), Andrew Fuller and Antinomianism, in Michael A.G. Haykin (ed.), At the Pure Fountain of Thy Word: Andrew Fuller as an Apologist, Eugene, OR: Wipf & Stock, 74–82.

DIXON, MICHAEL F./HUGH F. STEELE-SMITH (July 1988), Anne Steele's Health: A Modern Diagnosis, Baptist Quarterly 32/7, 351–56.

ENGEN, JOHN VAN (2017), Natural Theology, in Evangelical Dictionary of Theology, Grand Rapids: Baker Book House, 815.

FENNER, CHRIS (Aug. 2015), The Hymns of Anne Steele: Boyce Centennial Library Archives Acquires First Edition, Towers 14/1, 21.

FERGUSON, EVERETT (2004), Congregational Singing in the Early Church, Acta Patristica et Byzantina 15/1, 144–59.

FIELD, JACOB F. (2017), Clandestine Weddings at the Fleet Prison, c. 1710–1750: Who Married There?, Continuity and Change 32, 351.

FRANK, ALBERT H./NOLA REED KNOUSE (2008), Hymnody of the Moravian Church, in Nola Reed Knouse (ed.), The Music of the Moravian Church in America, New York: University of Rochester, 44.

GLADSTONE, WILLIAM (1879), The Evangelical Movement: Its Parentage, Progress, and Issue, in *Gleanings from Past Years* 7, London, 201–41.

GOLDEN AGE OF HYMNS: CHRISTIAN HISTORY, THE (1991), Christian History 31.

GOMES, ALAN W. (1993), 'De Jesu Christo Servatore': Faustus Socinus on the Satisfaction of Christ, Westminster Theological Journal 55/2, 209–10.

HAYKIN, MICHAEL A.G./C. JEFFREY ROBINSON (2011). Particular Baptist Debates about Communion and Hymn-Singing, in Michael A.G. Haykin/Mark Jones (ed.), Drawn into Controversie: Reformed Theological Diversity and Debates Within Seventeenth-century British Puritanism, Göttingen: Vandenhoeck & Ruprecht, 248–308.

HEDLEY, DOUGLAS HEDLEY (2005), Persons of Substance and the Cambridge Connection: Some Roots and Ramifications of the Trinitarian Controversy in Seventeenth-Century England, in Martin Mulsow/ Jan Rohls (ed.), Socinianism and Arminianism: Antitrinitarians, Calvinists, and Cultural Exchange in Seventeenth-century Europe, Boston: Brill, 225–40.

HELM, PAUL (2018). 'The Modern Question': Hyper-Calvinism, in Mark Jones/Michael A.G. Haykin (ed.), A New Divinity: Transatlantic Reformed Evangelical Debates During the Long Eighteenth Century. Göttingen: Vandenhoeck & Ruprecht, 2018.

HINDMARSH, D. BRUCE (1993), 'I Am a Sort of Middle-Man': The Politically Correct Evangelicalism of John Newton, in George A. Rawlyk/Mark A. Noll (ed.), Amazing Grace: Evangelicalism in Australia, Britain, Canada, and the United States, Grand Rapids: Baker, 29–55.

JULIAN, JOHN (1892), Joseph Hart, in A Dictionary of Hymnology, London: J. Murray, 492–93.

KOLODZIEJ, BENJAMIN A. (July 2004), Isaac Watts, the Wesleys, and the Evolution of 18th-Century English Congregational Song, Methodist History 42/4, 236–48.

KUBRIGHT, PAUL (2017), Racovian Catechism (1605), in Evangelical Dictionary of Theology, 979.

LARSEN, TIMOTHY (2007), Defining and Locating Evangelicalism, in Timothy Larsen/Daniel J. Treier (ed.), The Cambridge Companion to Evangelical Theology, Cambridge: University Press, 1–14.

LEAVER, ROBIN A. (1978), Isaac Watts's Hermeneutical Principles and the Decline of English Metrical Psalmody, Churchman 92/1, 56–60.

LEWIS, DONALD M. (2004), Joseph Hart, Dictionary of Evangelical Biography 1730–1860, Peabody, MA: Hendrickson, 1:263.

Marco, Jonathan S. (2017), Deism, in Harry S. Stout/Kenneth P. Minkema/ Adriaan C. Neele, The Jonathan Edwards Encyclopedia, Grand Rapids: Eerdmans, 137.

McClintock, John/James Strong (1896), Antinomians, in Cyclopedia of Biblical, Theological, and Ecclesiastical Literature 1, New York: Harper and Brothers, 264–25.

Messenger, Ruth E. (1942), Christian Hymns of the First Three Centuries, Papers of the Hymn Society 9, 3–27.

Miller, Perry (June 1943), 'Preparation for Salvation' in New England, Journal of the History of Ideas 4/3, 253–86.

Najapfour, Brian G. (2013), A Sketch of Christian Spirituality: From the Patristic to the Evangelical Era, Puritan Reformed Journal 5/1, 47–60.

Noll, Mark A. (2004), The Defining Role of Hymns in Early Evangelicalism, in Wonderful Words of Life: Hymns in American Protestant History & Theology, Grand Rapids: Eerdmans, 3–16.

———. (2016), Whitefield, Hymnody, and Evangelical Spirituality, in Geordan Hammond/David Ceri Jones (ed.), George Whitefield: Life, Context, and Legacy, Oxford: University Press, 241–60.

Oliver, Robert W. (Nov. 18, 2000), The Life and Hymns of Joseph Hart, 1712–1768, Lecture given at Newhouse Baptist Church, Unpublished.

Peuker, Paul (2011), Moravian Spirituality, in Glen G. Scorgie (ed.), Dictionary of Christian Spiritualit, Grand Rapids: Zondervan, 623.

Pratt, Waldo Selden (1935), The Importance of the Early French Psalter, The Musical Quarterly 21/1, 25–32.

Priest, Gerald L. (2004), Andrew Fuller, Hyper-Calvinism, and the 'Modern Question,' in Michael A.G. Haykin (ed.), At the Pure Fountain of Thy Word: Andrew Fuller as an Apologist, Eugene, OR: Wipf & Stock, 43–72.

Principe, Walter H. (1983), Toward Defining Spirituality, Studies in Religion 12/2, 127–41.

Rae, Peter C. (Spring 1988), Joseph Hart and His Hymns, Scottish Bulletin of Evangelical Theology 6, 20–39.

Randall, Ian M. (Oct. 2006), A Missional Spirituality: Moravian Brethren and Eighteenth Century English Evangelicalism, Transformation 23/4, 204–14.

RAZZELL, PETER/CHRISTINE SPENCE (2005), Social Capital and the History of Mortality in Britain, International Journal of Epidemiology 34/2, 477–78.

RIGG, JAMES M. (1891), Joseph Hart (1712?–1768), in Leslie Stephen and Sidney Lee (ed.), Dictionary of National Biography 25, London: Smith, Elder & Co., 62.

ROUTLEY, ERIK (Jan. 1951), Joseph Hart, 1712–68, The Hymn Society of Great Britain and Ireland Bulletin 13, 196–208.

RUFF, ANTHONY (2019), The Early Church and the Middle Ages, in Lutheran Service Book: Companion to the Hymns 2, St. Louis, MO: Concordia, 9–12.

RUHL, DEBORAH A. (2014), 'Feeling Religion': High Calvinism, Experimentalism, and Evangelism in William Gadsby's A Selection of Hymns for Public Worship, The Hymn 65/2, 14–22.

SCHWARZE, W.N. (1944), Early Hymnals of the Bohemian Brethren (A Paper Presented at the John Hus Conference, Watertown, Wisconsin, Aug. 5, 1937), Transactions of the Moravian Historical Society 13/3, 163–73.

SHAW, IAN J. (2013), 'The Only Certain Rule of Faith and Practice': The Interpretation of Scripture Among English High Calvinists, c.1780s–1850, in Scott Mandelbrote/Michael Ledger-Lomas (ed.), Dissent & the Bible in Britain, c.1650–1950, Oxford: University Press, 133–52.

SHELDRAKE, PHILIP (2005), Moravian Spirituality, in The New Westminster Dictionary of Christian Spirituality, Louisville, KY: Westminster John Knox, 447.

———. (2000), What Is Spirituality, in Kenneth J. Collins (ed.), Exploring Christian Spirituality, Grand Rapids: Baker, 21–42.

SPURGEON, CHARLES (1862), Exposition of the Doctrines of Grace, in Metropolitan Tabernacle Pulpit 7, London: Passmore & Alabaster, 297–304.

STACKHOUSE, ROCHELLE A. (2019), Isaac Watts: Composer of Psalms and Hymns, in Mark A. Lamport/Benjamin K. Forrest/Vernon M. Whaley (ed.), Hymns and Hymnody: Historical and Theological Introductions 2, Eugene, OR: Cascade Books, 197–209.

STALCUP, ERIKA K.R. (2019), The Wesleys: Charles and John, in Mark A. Lamport/Benjamin K. Forrest/Vernon M. Whaley (ed.), Hymns and

Hymnody: Historical and Theological Introductions 2, Eugene, OR: Cascade Books, 210–25.

TERRY, RICHARD R. (1930), Calvin's First Psalter, 1539, Proceedings of the Musical Association 57, 1–21.

THOMPSON, DAVID M. (2018), Theology and the Bible, in Andrew C. Thompson (ed.), The Oxford History of Protestant Dissenting Traditions: The Long Eighteenth Century, c.1689–c.1828, Oxford: University Press, 322.

TUCKER, KAREN B. WESTERFIELD (2019). Evangelical Anglican Hymnists, in Mark A. Lamport/Benjamin K. Forrest/Vernon M. Whaley (ed.), Hymns and Hymnody: Historical and Theological Introductions 2, Eugene, OR: Cascade, 240–53.

WESLEY, JOHN (1839), On Working Out Our Own Salvation, Sermons on Several Occasions 2, NY: T. Mason & G. Lane, 233–38.

WILLIAMS, S.N. (1988), Deism, in Sinclair B. Ferguson/David F. Wright/J.I. Packer (ed.), New Dictionary of Theology, Downers Grove, IL: Intervarsity, 190.

WOOD, A. SKEVINGTON (2004), William Romaine, in Donald M. Lewis (ed.), Dictionary of Evangelical Biography 1730–1860, Peabody, MA: Hendrickson, 2:954.

II. Books

AALDERS, CYNTHIA Y. (2009), To Express the Ineffable: The Hymns and Spirituality of Anne Steele, Eugene, OR: Wipf & Stock.

AMES, WILLIAM (1639), Conscience with the Power and Cases Thereof Devided into V. Bookes, London: W. Christiaens, E. Griffin, J. Dawson.

ATWOOD, CRAIG D. (2004), Community of the Cross Moravian Piety in Colonial Bethlehem, University Park, PA: Pennsylvania State University.

BAXTER, A.J. (1874), The Gospel Advocate 6, London: Houlston and Sons.

BAXTER, RICHARD (1692), Mr. Richard Baxter's Paraphrase on the Psalms of David in Metre with Other Hymns, London.

———. (1830), The Practical Works of Richard Baxter 1, London: 1830.

BAYNES, ROBERT HALL (1863), The Canterbury Hymnal, London: Houlston & Wright.

BEBBINGTON, DAVID W. (1989). Evangelicalism in Modern Britain: A History from the 1730s to the 1980s, London: Routledge.

BEEKE, JOEL R./MARTIN I. KLAUBER (2020), The Synod of Dort: Historical, Theological, and Experiential Perspectives, Göttingen: Vandenhoeck & Ruprecht.

BEEKE, JOEL R./PAUL M. SMALLEY (2013), Prepared by Grace, for Grace: The Puritans on God's Ordinary Way of Leading Sinners to Christ, Grand Rapids: Reformation Heritage.

BENSON, LOUIS F. (1915), The English Hymn: Its Development and Use in Worship, London: Hodder and Stoughton.

BIDDLE, JOHN (1647), Twelve Arguments Drawn Out of the Scripture, Wherein the Commonly Received Opinion Touching the Deity of the Holy Spirit, is Clearly and Fully Refuted, [London].

———. (1652), The Recovian Catechisme, Amsterledam: Brooer Janz.

———. (1691), The Apostolical and True Opinion Concerning the Holy Trinity, Revived and Asserted [...] All Reprinted, Anno 1653 [...] Now Again with the Life of the Author Prefixed, [London].

BLACKSTONE, WILLIAM (1915), Commentaries on the Laws of England, William C. Jones (ed.), San Francisco: Bancroft-Whitney Company.

BLISS, PHILIP P. (1874), Gospel Songs, Cincinnati: John Church & Co.

BOETTNER, LORAINE (1932), The Reformed Doctrine of Predestination, Grand Rapids: Eerdmans.

BOURNE, SAMUEL THE YOUNGER (1739), A Dialogue between a Baptist and a Churchman, London.

BOWERS, J.D. (2010), Joseph Priestley and English Unitarianism in America, University Park, PA: Pennsylvania State University.

BRINE, JOHN (1732), A Defence of the Doctrine of Eternal Justification, London.

BROWN, CHRISTOPHER BOYD (2005), Singing the Gospel: Lutheran Hymns and the Success of the Reformation, Cambridge, MA: Harvard University.

BULL, JOSIAH (1870), John Newton [...] An Autobiography and Narrative, Compiled Chiefly from His Diary and Other Unpublished Documents, 2nd ed., London: Religious Tract Society.

BUNYAN, JOHN (1962), Grace Abounding to the Chief of Sinners, Roger Sharrock (ed.), Oxford: Clarendon Press.

BURDER, GEORGE (1784), A Collection of Hymns from Various Authors, Intended as a Supplement to Dr. Watts's Hymns, and Imitation of the Psalms, Coventry: Luckman.

BUTTERWORTH, HEZEKIAH (1875). The Story of the Hymns; or, Hymns that Have a History: An Account of the Origin of Hymns of Personal Religious Experience, New York: American Tract Society.

CALVIN, JOHN (1996), The Bondage and Liberation of the Will: A Defense of the Orthodox Doctrine of Human Choice against Pighius, A.N.S. Lane (ed.), Translated by G.I. Davies, Grand Rapids: Baker.

CARNES, JAMES P. (1984), The Famous Mr. Keach: Benjamin Keach and His Influence on Congregational Singing in Seventeenth Century England, MA thesis, Denton, TX: North Texas State University.

CARTER, GRAYSON (2001), Anglican Evangelicals: Protestant Secessions from the Via Media, c.1800–1850, Eugene, OR: Wipf and Stock.

CARY, EARNEST/HERBERT BALDWIN FOSTER (1914–55), Dio's Roman History, 9 Vols., London: William Heinemann.

CECIL, DAVID (1929), The Stricken Deer, or the Life of Cowper, London: Constable.

COLLIGAN, J. HAY (1915), Eighteenth Century Nonconformity, London: Longmans, Green & Co.

CONYERS, RICHARD (1767), A Collection of Psalms and Hymns, London: T. and J.W. Pasham.

COOK, FAITH (2005), Our Hymn Writers and Their Hymns, Darlington, England: Evangelical Press.

COTTON, JOHN (1647), Singing of Psalmes, a Gospel-Ordinance; or A Treatise, Wherein Are Handled These Foure Particulars. 1. Touching the Duty It Selfe. 2. Touching the Matter to Be Sung. 3. Touching the Singers. 4. Touching the Manner of Singing, London.

COWPER, WILLIAM (1785), The Task, A Poem, in Six Books, London.

DAVIE, DONALD (1993), The Eighteenth Century Hymn in England, Cambridge: University Press.

DICKINSON, HELEN A./CLARENCE DICKINSON (1917), Excursions in Musical History, New York: H. W. Gray.

DODSON, C. LAWRENCE (1997), The Justified Believer, Harrisonburg, VA: Sprinkle.

Dutton, Anne (1740), A Discourse Upon Justification: Shewing the Matter, Manner, Time and Effects of It. By the Author of The Discourse Concerning the New-Birth, London.

———. (1740), A Discourse Concerning the New-birth: To Which are Added Two Poems: the One on Salvation in Christ, by Free-grace, for the Chief of Sinners: the Other on a Believer's Safety and Duty, London.

Echols, Edward C. (1961), Herodian of Antioch's History of the Roman Empire from the Death of Marcus Aurelius to the Accession of Gordian III, Los Angeles: University of California.

Edwards, John (1695), Some Thoughts Concerning the Several Causes and Occasions of Atheism, Especially in the Present Age with Some Brief Reflections on Socinianism, and on a Late Book Entitled, The Reasonableness of Christianity as Delivered in the Scriptures, London: J. Robinson.

Edwards, Jonathan (1992), Sermons and Discourses 1720–1723, Wilson H. Kimnach (ed.), The Works of Jonathan Edwards 10, New Haven: Yale.

———. (1998), Letters and Personal Writings, George S. Claghorn (ed.), The Works of Jonathan Edwards 16, New Haven: Yale.

———. (1999), Sermons and Discourses, 1730–1733, Mark Valeri (ed.), The Works of Jonathan Edwards 17, New Haven: Yale.

Ellis, Mark A. (2005), The Arminian Confession of 1621, Eugene, OR: Pickwick.

Eskew, Harry/Hugh T. McElrath (1980), Sing with Understanding: An Introduction to Christian Hymnology, Nashville, TN: Broadman Press.

Farooq, Jennifer (2013), Preaching in Eighteenth-Century London, Woodbridge: Boydell Press.

Fenner, Chris/Brian G. Najapfour (2020), Amazing Love! How Can It Be: Studies on Hymns by Charles Wesley, Eugene, OR: Wipf & Stock.

Fernandez, Abner F. (2017), The Doctrine of Prevenient Grace in the Theology of Jacobus Arminius, PhD diss., Andrews University.

Fuller, Andrew (1785), The Gospel of Christ Worthy of All Acceptation, London.

FULLER, RICHARD/JOSEPH P. HOLBROOK (1871), The Baptist Praise Book for Congregational Singing, NY: A.S. Barnes.

GADSBY, WILLIAM (1838), A Selection of Hymns for Public Worship, London.

GAMBLE, WHITNEY G. (2018), Christ and the Law: Antinomianism at the Westminster Assembly, Grand Rapids: Reformation Heritage Books.

GILL, JOHN (1752), The Doctrine of Predestination Stated and set in the Scripture-Light; in Opposition to Mr. Wesley's Predestination Calmly Consider'd, 3rd Ed., London.

———. (1773), A Collection of Sermons and Tracts 2, London.

———. (1796), A Complete Body of Doctrinal and Practical Divinity; or A System of Evangelical Truths, Deduced from the Sacred Scriptures 1, London: W. Winterbotham.

GOUDRIAAN, AZA/FRED VAN LIEBURG (2011), Revisiting the Synod of Dordt (1618–1619), Boston: Brill.

GRANT, KEITH S. (2013), Andrew Fuller and the Evangelical Renewal of Pastoral Theology, Eugene, OR: Wipf & Stock.

GREATHEED, SAMUEL (1814), Memoirs of the Life and Writings of William Cowper, Esq. Rev. Ed., London: Whittingham & Arliss.

GREAVES, RICHARD (2002), Glimpses of Glory: John Bunyan and English Dissent, Stanford, CA: Stanford University.

GREGORY, ARTHUR E. (1904), The Hymn-Book of the Modern Church, London: Charles H. Kelly.

HALL, DAVID D. (1990), The Antinomianism Controversy, 1636–1638, 2nd ed., Durham, NC: Duke University.

HAZARD, PAUL (1953), The Crisis of the European Mind 1680–1715, New Haven: Yale.

HEITZENRATER, RICHARD P. (2013), Wesley and the People Called Methodists, 2nd ed., Nashville: Abingdon.

HINDMARSH, D. BRUCE (1996), John Newton and the English Evangelical Tradition, Oxford: Clarendon.

———. (2005), The Evangelical Conversion Narrative: Spiritual Autobiography in Early Modern England, Oxford: University Press.

———. (2018), The Spirit of Early Evangelicalism, Oxford: University Press.

HOLLAND, JOHN/JAMES EVERETT (1854–56), Memoirs of the Life and Writings of James Montgomery, 7 Vols., London: Longman, Brown, Green, and Longmans.

Hughes, John (1768), The Christian Warrior Finishing His Course. A Sermon Occasioned by the Death of the Rev. Mr. Joseph Hart, Preached in Jewin-Street, June 5, 1768 [...] And An Oration Delivered at His Interment by Andrew Kinsman, London.

Jackson, Alverey (1752), The Question Answered, Whether Saving Faith in Christ is a Duty Required by the Moral Law, of All Those Who Live Under the Gospel Revelation, London.

Jenyns, Soame (1761), A Free Inquiry into the Nature and Origin of Evil, 4th Ed., London.

Jocelyn, Marthe (2005), A Home for Foundlings. Toronto: Tundra Books.

Keach, Benjamin (1691), Spiritual Melody, Containing Near Three Hundred Sacred Hymns, London.

———. (1691), The Breach Repaired in God's Worship, or, Singing of Psalms, Hymns, and Spiritual Songs, Proved to Be an Holy Ordinance of Jesus Christ with an Answer to All Objections, London.

Kidd, Thomas S. (2007), The Great Awakening: The Roots of Evangelical Christianity in Colonial America, New Haven, CT: Yale.

———. (2014), George Whitefield: America's Spiritual Founding Father, New Haven: Yale.

Kingham, John A. (2015), A Prodigal Made a Blessing: The Life and Hymns of Joseph Hart, Hertfordshire: Gospel Standard Trust.

Knouse, Nola Reed (2008), The Music of the Moravian Church in America, New York: University of Rochester.

Lalor, Stephen (2006), Matthew Tindal, Freethinker: An Eighteenth-Century Assault on Religion, London: Continuum.

Lamport, Mark A./Benjamin K. Forrest/Vernon M. Whaley (2019), Hymns and Hymnody: Historical and Theological Introductions 1, Eugene, OR: Cascade Books.

Larsen, Timothy (2003), Biographical Dictionary of Evangelicals, Nottingham, England: InterVarsity.

Larsen, Timothy/Daniel J. Treier (2007), The Cambridge Companion to Evangelical Theology, Cambridge: University Press.

Leaver, Robin A. (2017), The Whole Church Sings: Congregational Singing in Luther's Wittenberg, Grand Rapids: Eerdmans.

Lewis, Donald M. (2004), Dictionary of Evangelical Biography 1730–1860, 2 Vols., Peabody, MA: Hendrickson.

Lim, Paul C.H. (2012), Mystery Unveiled: The Crisis of the Trinity in Early Modern England, Oxford: University Press.

Lloyd, Walter (1899), The Story of Protestant Dissent and English Unitarianism, London: Philip Green.

Locke, John (1695), A Vindication of The Reasonableness of Christianity, &c. from Mr. Edwards's Reflections, London: Awnsham and John Churchil.

———. (1777), An Essay Concerning Human Understanding, The Works of John Locke 1, 8th Ed., London: W. Strahan.

Lucci, Diego (2008), Scripture and Deism: The Biblical Criticism of the Eighteenth-century British Deists, NY: Peter Lang.

M'Millan, Samuel (1850), The Whole Works of the Late Reverend Thomas Boston of Ettrick, Aberdeen: George and Robert King.

Maag, Karin (2016), Lifting Hearts to the Lord: Worship with John Calvin in Sixteenth-Century Geneva, Grand Rapids: Eerdmans.

Mackenzie, W.B. (1997), The Justified Believer, Foreword by C. Lawrence Dodson, Harrisonburg, VA: Sprinkle.

Macpherson, John (1875), Revival and Revival-work, a Record of the Labours of D.L. Moody and I.D. Sankey and Other Evangelists, London: Morgan and Scott.

Madan, Martin (1760), A Collection of Psalms and Hymns, Extracted from Various Authors, London.

Marlow, Isaac (1690), A Brief Discourse Concerning Singing, London.

Marsden, George M. (2003), Jonathan Edwards: A Life, New Haven: Yale.

Martin, Hugh (1961), Benjamin Keach, Pioneer of Congregational Hymn Singing, London: Independent Press.

Martin, John (1795), The Advantage of Correct Thoughts on the Sinfulness of Sin. A Sermon, London.

McCart, Thomas K. (1998), The Matter and Manner of Praise: The Controversial Evolution of Hymnody in the Church of England 1760–1820, Lanham, MD: Scarecrow.

McClure, Ruth K. (1981), Coram's Children: The London Foundling Hospital in the Eighteenth Century, New Haven, CT: Yale.

McGrath, Alister E. (1999), Christian Spirituality: An Introduction, Oxford: Blackwell.

McLachlan, H. John (1951), Socinianism in Seventeenth-Century England, Oxford: University Press.

Mills, Simon (2009), Joseph Priestley and the Intellectual Culture of Rational Dissent, 1752–1796, Ph.D. diss., Queen Mary, University of London.

Minkema, Kenneth P. (1988), The Edwardses: A Ministerial Family in Eighteenth-Century New England, PhD diss., University of Connecticut.

Music, David W./Paul A. Richardson (2008), "I Will Sing the Wondrous Story": A History of Baptist Hymnody in North America, Macon, GA: Mercer University.

Newton, John (1790), The Christian Correspondent; or, A Series of Religious Letters, Written by the Rev. John Newton [...] to Captain Alexr. Clunie, from the Year 1761, to the Death of the Latter in 1770, Hull.

Noll, Mark A. (2001), American Evangelical Christianity: An Introduction, Oxford: Blackwell.

———. (2003), The Rise of Evangelicalism: The Age of Edwards, Whitefield and the Wesleys, Downers Grove, IL: Intervarsity.

Nye, Stephen (1687), A Brief History of the Unitarians, Called Also Socinians in Four Letters, Written to a Friend, [London].

Olsen, Kristin (1999), Daily Life in 18th-Century England, Westport, CT: Greenwood Press.

Owen, John (1655), "Vindiciae Evangelicae," Or the Mystery of the Gospell Vindicated and Socinianisme Examined, in the Consideration and Confutation of a Catechisme, Called a Scripture Catechisme, Oxford.

———. (1959), The Death of Death in the Death of Christ, Introduction by J.I. Packer, London: Banner of Truth.

Packer, James I. (1961), Evangelism and the Sovereignty of God, Downers Grove, IL: Intervarsity.

Palmer, Ray (1880), Voices of Hope and Gladness, London: James Nisbet & Co.

Pettit, Norman (1966), The Heart Prepared: Grace and Conversion in Puritan Spiritual Life, New Heaven: Yale.

Pfizenmaier, Thomas C. (1997), The Trinitarian Theology of Dr. Samuel Clarke (1675–1729): Context, Sources, and Controversy, Leiden: Brill.

Pidoux, Pierre (1962), Le psautier huguenot du XVIe siècle 1, Basel: Bärenreiter.

Priestley, Joseph (1794), Institutes of Natural and Revealed Religion, 3rd Ed., 3 Vols., London.

———. (1796), Unitarianism Explained and Defended: in a Discourse Delivered in the Church of the Universalists, at Philadelphia.

Pugh, Gilliam (2007), London's Forgotten Children: Thomas Coram and the Foundling Hospital, Stroud: History Press.

Rees, Thomas (1818), The Racovian Catechism with Notes and Illustrations, Translated from the Latin: To Which is Prefixed A Sketch of the History of Unitarianism in Poland and the Adjacent Countries, London: Longman, Hurst, et al.

Richardson, Paul A./Erik Routley (2005), A Panorama of Christian Hymnody, Chicago: GIA.

Rippon, John (1787), A Selection of Hymns from the Best Authors, Intended to be an Appendix to Dr. Watts's Psalms and Hymns, London: Thomas Wilkins.

Rogers, Timothy (1691), A Discourse Concerning Trouble of Mind and the Disease of Melancholly in Three Parts: Written for the Use of Such As Are, or Have Been Exercised by the Same, London.

Romaine, William (1775), An Essay on Psalmody, London.

———. (1830), Select Letters of the Rev. William Romaine, Glasgow.

———. (1880), An Essay on Psalmody, Chesley: A.S. Elliot. Also included in The Whole Works of the Late Reverend William Romaine, London, 1837, 963–1003.

Roper, Cecil Mizelle (1972), The Strasbourg French psalters, 1539–1553, PhD diss., University of Southern California.

Routley, Erik (1959), Hymns and Human Life, 2nd Ed., Grand Rapids: Eerdmans.

Ruhl, Deborah A. (2013), Engaging the Heart: Orthodoxy and Experimentalism in William Gadsby's A Selection of Hymns for Public Worship, Ph.D. diss., Ohio State University.

Ryden, Ernest E. (1959), The Story of Christian Hymnody, Philadelphia: Fortress Press.

Sallee, James E. (1978), A History of Evangelistic Hymnody, Grand Rapids: Baker.

SAMPSON, GEORGE (1943), The Century of Divine Songs, London: Humphrey Milford.

SCHWANDA, TOM (2016), The Emergence of Evangelical Spirituality, Foreword by Mark Noll, New York: Paulist Press.

SCOUGAL, HENRY (1677), The Life of God in the Soul of Man, or, The Nature and Excellency of the Christian Religion with the Method of Attaining the Happiness It Proposes: and An Account of the Beginnings and Advances of a Spiritual Life: in Two Letters Written to Persons of Honour, London.

SELDERHUIS, HERMAN J. (2017), Calvin's Theology of the Psalms, Grand Rapids: Baker.

———. (2017), Martin Luther: A Spiritual Biography, Wheaton, IL: Crossway.

SELL, ALAN P.F. (2011), Christ and Controversy: The Person of Christ in Nonconformist Thought and Ecclesial Experience, 1600–2000, Eugene, OR: Pickwick.

SHELTON, W. BRIAN (2014), Prevenient Grace: God's Provision for Fallen Humanity, Wilmore, KY: Francis Asbury Press.

SHENTON, TIM (2004), An Iron Pillar: The Life and Times of William Romaine, Darlington: Evangelical Press.

SHRUBSOLE, WILLIAM (1810), Christian Memoirs in the Form of a New Pilgrimage to the Heavenly Jerusalem, 4th Ed., Philadelphia.

SMITH, VALERIE (2021), Rational Dissenters in Late Eighteenth-Century England: 'An Ardent Desire of Truth,' Woodbridge, Suffolk, UK: Boydell & Brewer.

SOCINUS, FAUSTUS (1732), A Demonstration of the Truth of the Christian Religion from the Latin of Socinius, 2nd Ed., London.

SPURGEON, CHARLES H. (1866). Our Own Hymn-Book, London: Passmore & Alabaster.

SPURGEON, SUSANNAH/JOSEPH HARROLD (1898–1900), The Autobiography of Charles H. Spurgeon, 4 Vols., London: Passmore & Alabaster.

STEELE, ANNE [THEODOSIA] (1780), Miscellaneous Pieces in Verse and Prose, Preface by Caleb Evans, Bristol.

STEELE, DAVID N./CURTIS C. THOMAS (1963), The Five Points of Calvinism: Defined, Defended, Documented, Phillipsburg, NJ: P&R.

STEPHENS, WILLIAM (1696), An Account of the Growth of Deism in England, London.

SULLIVAN, ROBERT E. (1982), John Toland and the Deist Controversy, Cambridge, Mass.: University Press.

THIESSEN, HENRY C. (1979), Lectures in Systematic Theology, Rev. Ed., Grand Rapids: Eerdmans.

TIMPSON, THOMAS (1859), Church History of Kent, London.

TOLAND, JOHN (1696), Christianity Not Mysterious: Or a Treatise Shewing that There is Nothing in the Gospel Contrary to Reason, Nor Above It: And that No Christian Doctrine Can Be Properly Call'd a Mystery, London.

TOON, PETER (2011), The Emergence of Hyper-Calvinism in English Nonconformity, 1689–1765, Reprint, Eugene, OR: Wipf & Stock.

TOPLADY, AUGUSTUS (1776), Psalms and Hymns for Public and Private Worship, London: E. and C. Dilly.

———. (1825), The Works of Augustus M. Toplady, 6 Vols., London.

TYERMAN, LUKE (1870), The Life and Times of the Rev. John Wesley, 3 Vols., London: Hodder & Stoughton.

VAUGHAN, EDWARD THOMAS (1816), Some Account of the Reverend Thomas Robinson, London.

W., R. (1768), An Elegy on the Death of the Rev. Mr. Joseph Hart.

WARD, W. REGINALD/RICHARD P. HEITZENRATER (1988), The Works of John Wesley 18, Nashville: Abingdon.

WATSON, J.R. (1997), The English Hymn: A Critical and Historical Study, Oxford: University Press.

WATTS, ISAAC (1707), Hymns and Spiritual Songs, London.

———. (1719), The Psalms of David Imitated in the Language of the New Testament, And Apply'd to the Christian State and Worship, London.

WESLEY, JOHN (1739), Free Grace, Bristol.

———. (1751), Serious Thoughts Upon the Perseverance of the Saints, London.

———. (1755), Predestination Calmly Considered, 3rd Ed., London.

———. (1774), A Short History of Methodism, London.

———. (1827), The Works of the Rev. John Wesley 9, New York: J. & J. Harper.

———. (1829), Sermons on Several Occasions 2, 10th Ed., London: Thomas Tegg.

———. (1830), The Works of the Rev. John Wesley 8, 3rd Ed., London.

———. (1855), The Journal of the Reverend John Wesley, New York: Carlton and Phillips.

———. (1931), The Letters of the Rev. John Wesley 7, Epworth Press.

WHITEFIELD, GEORGE (1741), Free Grace Indeed! A Letter to the Reverend Mr. John Wesley, Relating to His Sermon against Absolute Election; Published under the Title of Free Grace, London.

———. (1965), George Whitefield's Journals, Introduction by Iain Murray, London: Banner of Truth Trust.

The Whole Booke of Psalmes Faithfully Translated into English Metre (1640) [Bay Psalm Book].

WIBBERLEY, BRIAN (1934), Music and Religion: A Historical and Philosophical Survey, London: Epworth.

WILBERFORCE, ROBERT/SAMUEL WILBERFORCE (1838), The Life of William Wilberforce, London: John Murray.

WILLS, THOMAS (1795), The Dying Believer. The Substance of a Sermon, Occasioned by the Much Lamented Death of the Rev. W. Romaine, London.

WILSON, WALTER (1808–14), The History and Antiquities of Dissenting Churches and Meeting Houses, 4 Vols., London: For the Author.

WOOD, ABRAHAM (1800), A Funeral Elegy on the Death of General George Washington. Adapted to the 22d of February, Boston: Thomas & Andrews.

WORCESTER, ELWOOD (1889), The Religious Opinions of John Locke, University of Leipzig.

WRIGHT, THOMAS (1910), Joseph Hart, London: Farncombe & Son.

YEAGER, JONATHAN M. (2013), Early Evangelicalism: A Reader, Oxford: University Press.

YUILLE, J. STEPHEN (2019), The First Book of the Cases of Conscience. The Works of William Perkins 8, Grand Rapids: Reformation Heritage.

III. Electronic Sources

BAIRD, JOHN D. (2013), William Cowper (1731–1800), Poet and Letter-Writer, in Oxford Dictionary of National Biography, https://doi.org/10.1093/ref:odnb/6513

BROWN, ANDREW JAMES (n.d.), Unitarian Hymnody, British, in Canterbury Dictionary of Hymnology, Norwich: Canterbury Press, http://www.hymnology.co.uk/u/unitarian-hymnody,-british

COSNETT, ELIZABETH (n.d.), There Is a Fountain Filled with Blood, in Canterbury Dictionary of Hymnology, Norwich: Canterbury Press, http://www.hymnology.co.uk/t/there-is-a-fountain-filled-with-blood

CROOKSHANK, ESTHER R. (2013), Isaac Watts, in Grove Music Online, Oxford University Press, https://doi.org/10.1093/gmo/9781561592630.article.A2259340

EMSLEY, CLIVE/TIM HITCHCOCK/ROBERT SHOEMAKER (n.d.), London History: A Population History of London, in Old Bailey Proceedings Online, http://www.oldbaileyonline.org

FENNER, CHRIS (2018–2021), Hymnology Archive, https://www.hymnologyarchive.com

GORDON, ALEXANDER/M.J. MERCER (2004), Joseph Towers (1737–1799), in Oxford Dictionary of National Biography, https://doi.org/10.1093/ref:odnb/27588

HAYDEN, ROGER (2004), Caleb Evans (1737–1791), in Oxford Dictionary of National Biography, https://doi.org/10.1093/ref:odnb/40192

HILLAR, MARIAN (10–15 Aug. 1998), The Philosophical Legacy of the 16th and 17th Century Socinians: Their Rationality, Twentieth World Congress of Philosophy, Boston, Massachusetts, http://www.bu.edu/wcp/Papers/Reli/ReliHill.htm

HUGH, HENRY (1908), Congregational Singing, in The Catholic Encyclopedia 4, New York: Robert Appleton Company, http://www.newadvent.org/cathen/04241a.htm

MADDOX, RANDY L. (n.d.), Charles Wesley's Published Verse, Duke Divinity School, The Center for Studies in the Wesleyan Tradition, https://divinity.duke.edu/initiatives/cswt/charles-published-verse

MERCER, M.J. (2004), John Shower (bap.1657, d.1715), Presbyterian Minister, in Oxford Dictionary of National Biography, https://doi.org/10.1093/ref:odnb/25472

MORTIMER, SARAH (2016), Early Modern Socinianism and Unitarianism, in Ulrich L. Lehner/Richard A. Muller/A. G. Roeber (ed.), The Oxford Handbook of Early Modern Theology, 1600–1800, Oxford: University Press, http://dx.doi.org/10.1093/oxfordhb/9780199937943.013.12

OKIE, LAIRD (2004), Daniel Neal (1678–1743), Independent Minister and Historian, Oxford Dictionary of National Biography, https://doi.org/10.1093/ref:odnb/19817

RIGG, J. M./JOHN S. ANDREWS (2004), Joseph Hart, Oxford Dictionary National Biography, https://doi.org/10.1093/ref:odnb/12485

ROUSE, MARYLYNN, *The John Newton Project*, https://www.johnnewton.org

SCHWEIZER, KARL WOLFGANG (2007), Israel Mauduit (1708–1787), Colonial Official and Political Writer, in Oxford Dictionary of National Biography, https://doi.org/10.1093/ref:odnb/18360

WARD, W.R. (2004), John Thomas (1696–1781), Bishop of Winchester, in Oxford Dictionary of National Biography, https://doi.org/10.1093/ref:odnb/27223

WATSON, J.R. (2004), Anne Steele (1717–1778), Hymn Writer and Poet, in Oxford Dictionary of National Biography, https://doi.org/10.1093/ref:odnb/26343

WATSON, J.R. (n.d.), Joseph Hart, Canterbury Dictionary of Hymnology, Norwich: Canterbury Press, https://hymnology.hymnsam.co.uk/j/joseph-hart

WELCH, EDWIN (2004), John Thornton (1720–1790), Merchant and Philanthropist, in Oxford Dictionary of National Biography, https://doi.org/10.1093/ref:odnb/27358

YOUNG, CARLTON (n.d.), John Wesley's Collection of Psalms and Hymns (1737), Canterbury Dictionary of Hymnology, Norwich: Canterbury Press, http://www.hymnology.co.uk/j/john-wesleys-collection-of-psalms-and-hymns-(1737)

IV. Archival Sources

Letter from John Newton to John Thornton, 3 Aug. 1775, Cambridge University, Thornton Papers, Ms Add 7826.

Letter from John Newton to John Thornton, 12 Sept. 1776, Cambridge University, Thornton Papers, Ms Add 7674.

About the Author

Born and reared in the Philippines, Brian G. Najapfour holds a ThM from Puritan Reformed Theological Seminary and a PhD from Theological University of Apeldoorn. He has been a minister of the gospel since 2001 and has served both in the Philippines and in the U.S. He now lives in Canada, pastoring Heritage Reformed Congregation of Jordan, Ontario. He has authored and coedited numerous books and has contributed several articles to journals, periodicals, and encyclopedias. He and his wife Sarah have five children.

www.ingramcontent.com/pod-product-compliance
Lightning Source LLC
Chambersburg PA
CBHW032003060526
44107CB00158B/1339/J